MONEY, WOMEN, and  GUNS

SHAPIRO
USED CLOTH
SHOP
HOT

MONEY, WOMEN, and

GUNS

Crime Movies From *Bonnie and Clyde* to the Present

Douglas Brode

A Citadel Press Book
Published by Carol Publishing Group

A Citadel Press Book
Published by Carol Publishing Group
Citadel Press is a registered trademark of Carol Communications, Inc.
Editorial Offices: 600 Madison Avenue, New York, N.Y. 10022
Sales and Distribution Offices: 120 Enterprise Avenue, Secaucus, N.J. 07094
In Canada: Canadian Manda Group, One Atlantic Avenue, Suite 105, Toronto, Ontario, M6K 3E7
Queries regarding rights and permissions should be addressed to Carol Publishing Group, 600 Madison Avenue, New York, N.Y. 10022

Carol Publishing Group books are available at special discounts for bulk purchases, sales promotion, fund-raising, or educational purposes. Special editions can be created to specifications. For details, contact: Special Sales Department, Carol Publishing Group, 120 Enterprise Avenue, Secaucus, N.J. 07094

Manufactured in the United States of America
10 9 8 7 6 5 4 3 2 1

Designed by Andrew B. Gardner

Library of Congress Cataloging-in-Publication Data
Brode, Douglas, 1943–
Money, women, and guns : crime movies from Bonnie & Clyde to the present / by Douglas Brode.
p. cm.
"A Citadel Press book."
ISBN 0-8065-1608-9 (pbk.)
1. Gangster films—History and criticism. I. Title.
PN1995.9.G3B76 1995
791.43'655—dc20 94-47240
CIP

For
Joseph Brode

who, like Meyer, Bugsy, and Dutch,
escaped the slums of the Lower East Side,
though my father moved up and out
with an artist's brush
instead of a gun

Books by Douglas Brode

The Films of the Fifties
Last Films of the Fifties
The Films of the Sixties
The Films of the Eighties
Woody Allen: His Films and Career
The Films of Robert De Niro
The Films of Dustin Hoffman
The Films of Jack Nicholson
The Films of Steven Spielberg

Contents

Acknowledgments

With appreciation to Mercy Sandberg-Wright, who over and over again proves the old adage that a friend in need is a friend indeed; Michael Varone and Carlo Pastori, for their highly appreciated hours of volunteer research work; John Nucifora and Chimney's Video, for providing screening tapes; in New York, Jerry Ohlinger's Movie Material Store and Photofest; in Los Angeles, Cinema Collectors; and to all my helpful friends at Touchstone Pictures, Warner Brothers, Twentieth Century-Fox, Universal Pictures, Paramount Pictures, TriStar Pictures, Orion Pictures, United Artists, First Artists/National General, Miramax Films, Cinerarma Releasing Corporation, Faces Distribution, Metro-Goldwyn-Mayer, the Ladd Company, Gramercy Pictures, and MGM/UA.

MONEY, WOMEN, and

GUNS

FOR RENT
DRESSMAKING
SEWING · LACE
BUTTONS

INTRODUCTION

Deconstruction, Reflexivity, and Self-Referencing—an Approach to the Modern Crime Movie

The modern American crime movie was invented not in Hollywood but in Paris, France. That should not surprise us too much: after all, the French have always demonstrated a unique appreciation for our film genres. During the 1940s and 1950s, they were the ones who made Americans realize that the westerns of John Ford and Howard Hawks, the comedies of Charlie Chapin and Buster Keaton, the musicals of Busby Berkeley and Gene Kelly, and the horror pictures of James Whale and Karl Freund were major works, in terms of purely cinematic storytelling and lasting value. Americans had naively been praising those talky, self-important "serious" dramas that regularly won all the Oscars, only to quickly date and then be forgotten. So in 1959, when what came to be called the French New Wave began, when such film critics (all adoring fans of gangster movies) turned writer-director/"auteurs" as François Truffaut and Jean-Luc Godard shot their initial wildly paced, freewheeling films, they broke every rule of conventional moviemaking, and mounted these works as homages to the American gangster films.

In 1962, Truffaut's *Shoot the Piano Player* featured Charles Aznavour as the owner/performer of a bohemian cafe, a combination of both Rick and Sam from *Casablanca,* who becomes involved with thugs while trying to placate the woman he loves. Aznavour's character may have been unaware of his resemblance to Bogart, and the roles played by that seminal star, but that was not true of an even more significant incarnation of the modern gangster-hero. Bogart, or the abiding image of him, all but dominated Godard's *Breathless,* the 1959 film with Jean-Paul Belmondo as a Parisian lowlife and petty crook. The opening sequence forever changed motion pictures: Belmondo's character stands in front of an art house where the Bogart cult has taken hold and old Warner Brothers crime epics are continually rerun on double bills. He stares at a larger-than-life poster of the actor, with those famous squinty eyes projecting an ideal of tough-guy behavior.

We watch as Belmondo gazes at the poster; we see his view of it, the camera peering up at the icon from a low angle, emphasizing the mythic quality of this movie image; we see Belmondo from a slightly downward angle, suggesting his idolization of the man and/or the myth, the camera hinting that while this ordinary fellow may spend his entire life attempting to emulate what he sees in those films, he will never quite rise to truly heroic proportions. That's true if only because the Belmondo character lives in "the real world" (or what, in the context of the film, we temporarily accept as the real world), not the magical realm of movies. A film is where things can and do work out the way they ought to, according to an unspoken but implicit agreement between the moviemakers and their audience.

The contrast between real life and reel life dominates *Breathless,* as well as countless other gangster films to follow. In Godard's film, Belmondo will continually attempt to live the kind of life his screen hero enjoys. He takes up with a beautiful American bohemian (Jean

Life on the Streets: Chicago in the late 1920s and early thirties, as here re-created in 1967 by Roger Corman for *The St. Valentine's Day Massacre,* has become the twentieth century's equivalent of the post–Civil War West, a specific period in history transformed into pure myth (courtesy Roger Corman).

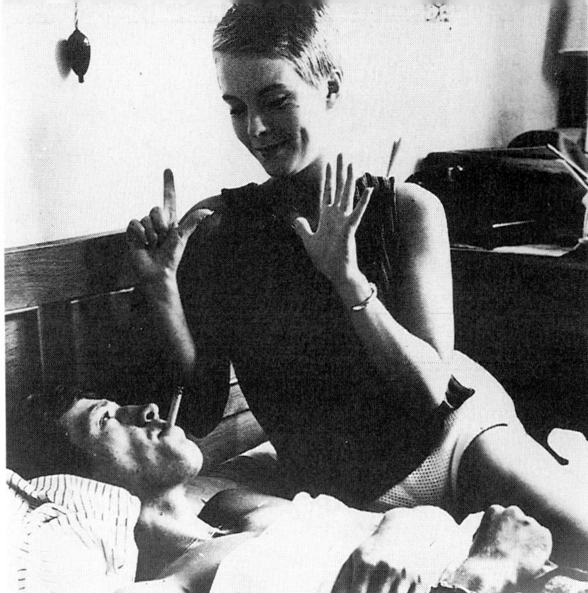

Birth of the Nouveau Crime Film: Jean-Paul Belmondo aspires to be a Bogart-like loner, with Jean Seberg as his gun moll, in *Breathless*; Nick Adams portrayed the title character of *Young Dillinger* less as a 1930s bank robber than as a 1950s juvenile delinquent, here seen seducing Mary Ann Mobley.

Seberg) who strolls the boulevards in a stylishly casual T-shirt, selling the international edition of the *Herald Tribune*. This was the de rigueur occupation of those avant-garde expatriate women who dropped out of college and the conventional lifestyle during the late 1950s. Her hair cut boyishly short she is, in the hero's mind, the perfect mistress for the character he self-consciously wants to be, a Parisian Bogie; like him, she is playacting life, eventually turning out be far less radical than she wants to appear. When the police close in on him with guns ready (he has killed a cop), she quickly decides that while it's been fun pretending to be in an old gangster movie, playtime is over. She betrays him to save herself. Unlike the movies (particularly Hollywood movies), where young lover/criminals embrace and share a final quick kiss before being gunned down in a hail of bullets, reality is in fact an unpleasant place where, when push comes to shove, most people will choose to survive rather than live up to a Romeo-and-Juliet ideal of sweet sorrow.

Dying, he leans forward, desperate to say one last word. She, expecting him to continue his role-playing until the very end, is shocked that, instead of muttering something about how much he has always loved her while insisting she is worth dying for, he spits out not such a final idealization but an all too real condemnation: "Bitch!" She looks stunned; like him, she can't understand why actuality isn't more like the movies. Working from a script by Truffaut, director Godard shot his film with a handheld camera, creating what would come to be called cinema verité: films of truth that, with their revolutionary disregard for classic niceties of filmmaking technique, now depicted everyday life as it was lived in the real world. Yet if the style suggested a new realism, the substance insisted on the impact of movie fantasies on our lives, the indelible myths that have

An Important Predecessor: The filmmakers of today are highly influenced by key directors and seminal films from the fifties; Robert Aldrich's *Kiss Me Deadly* with Ralph Meeker as Mike Hammer set the stage for such unsavory antiheroes as Mickey Rourke in Michael Cimino's *Year of the Dragon*, and Harvey Keitel in Quentin Tarantino's *Reservoir Dogs* (photos courtesy United Artists).

The Last Gangster: In the early 1960s, Warner Brothers cultivated actor Ray Danton as their last classic gangster actor, a throwback to the tradition of Bogart and George Raft; he played the title character in *The Rise and Fall of Legs Diamond* (*right*, courtesy Warner Bros.).

become a part of our everyday existence, shaping the way we perceive the world and, more significant still, impacting on our attempts to deal with it.

No wonder, then, that Godard dedicated *Breathless* to Monogram Pictures, that long-deceased purveyor of lurid B crime flicks and westerns that provided matinee fodder for an entire generation. It was a generation that came of age devouring movies and, all too often, actually believing the fantastical stories depicted in them. That, of course, has always been the power, and danger, of films, be they crime movies or those of other genres. Seeing, we are told, is believing, so mythic visions in films took on a semblance of conviction in the public's mind that stories read in books did not, could not.

At the same time that Godard and Truffaut were creating sophisticated European works of art about the impact of American films in general, crime films in particular, and the way in which our collective perception had

A Change of Image: Aging matinee idols from the 1950s, eager to change their images, opted for tough-guy gangster roles in B-budget period piece crime films; Fabian Forte was cast as rural gangster Floyd in *A Bullet for Pretty Boy* (*below left*, courtesy American International), while Tony Curtis left light comedy behind and turned to killing in *Lepke* (*above left*, courtesy Warner Bros.).

The Many Faces of Crime: Numerous character actors have found their best roles in gangster films; *counterclockwise:* Danny DeVito played the diminutive mafioso in Brian De Palma's *Wise Guys* (courtesy M-G-M), Armand Assante enacted the high-powered mob boss who corrupts the title character in *Hoffa* (courtesy 20th Century–Fox, photo credit François Duhamel), and Chazz Palminteri portrayed the local godfather role he had himself written, originally for the stage, in *A Bronx Tale* (courtesy Savoy Pictures, photo credit Philip Caruso).

forever been altered by such seemingly passing entertainments, Hollywood itself was tentatively moving in just such directions. During the 1950s, once-fresh genre stories had gradually degenerated into cliché.

The last conventional Hollywood gangster film may very well have been Nicholas Ray's *Party Girl,* a 1958 M-G-M programmer turned out mainly to fulfill the long-term contracts of aging stars Robert Taylor and Cyd Charisse before they were put out to pasture. In one key scene, a Capone-like gangster, played by Lee J. Cobb, is comforted by his chief hit man, John Ireland, over the fact that the mob boss's mistress (Charisse) may be fooling around with other men. In a dazzling sequence that revealed director Ray's ability to pump new energy into an old cliché, Cobb draws out his gun and "assassinates" the picture of his show girl/lover, literally putting a bullet through the framed image of the lovely lady's head. We realize that this vulgar, garrulous man is in fact a closet romantic; though not yet convinced he ought to kill the gorgeous woman in question, he's ready to execute the ideal of an image, a dream he believes in, but one she clearly cannot live up to. In another key sequence, he calls for a meeting with various thugs, knowing full well who the traitor in their midst is. Pretending to be an in-control leader, he gradually allows his temper to rise and eventually whacks the man.

While watching that scene, audiences of the time experienced a vague sense of familiarity with what transpired on-screen. Hadn't we seen it all before, or at least some extremely similar act, performed by Edward G.

The Passing of the Torch: Actors from differnt generations often meet like ships passing in the night while working on a gangster film; Roger Corman's *Capone* provided John Cassavetes (*left,* as Frankie Yale) with his final gangster role and Sylvester Stallone (as Frank Nitti) with his first (courtesy 20th Century–Fox).

Robinson or James Cagney in one of those 1930s gangster movies that had recently been playing endlessly on the then-new medium of TV? Though *Party Girl* may not feature an exact replay of any one such sequence, it nonetheless resembled many moments in numerous pictures. One year later, that fact was acknowledged in Billy Wilder's *Some Like It Hot,* a dark comedy set against the aftermath of the infamous St. Valentine's Day Massacre in 1929. In the film, Tony Curtis and Jack Lemmon (playing musicians who inadvertently witness the "seven against the wall" event) hide out from the gangsters chasing them. The two cross-dress, passing themselves off as women traveling with an all-girl band to Florida. When they arrive at the resort hotel at which they are to play a gig, they discover a convention of mobsters—including the very men chasing them—has just assembled.

The lead gangster, who dominates the proceedings, is called Little Bonaparte, clearly a tongue-in-cheek reference to the role played by Edward G. Robinson in his classic 1930 film, *Little Caesar.* Not surprisingly, filmmaker Billy Wilder had approached Robinson about playing this role, in the manner of self-satire, though the aging star declined. However, he did an about-face a mere five years later, appearing in a considerably less memorable film, *Robin and the Seven Hoods.* Apparently, the lure of a self-referential performance was too strong for Robinson to resist, particularly at a time when the public had developed a nostalgic fondness for what were once considered frightening stereotypes of criminal behavior.

Though the actor playing Bonaparte, Nehemiah Persoff, never achieved the big-screen superstardom that Robinson had known a quarter century earlier, he was no stranger to gangster roles. Persoff was just then playing the part of Jake "Greasy Thumb" Guzik, Al Capone's sleazy bookkeeper, on TV's *The Untouchables;* to Wilder's film, he brought his familiarity with such characterizations, playing off the fact that the audience could be trusted to bring their collective viewing experience with them. Context, simply, was everything. Despite the fact that *Some Like It Hot* is, ostensibly, a comedy, Little Bonaparte calls a gangland meeting, which he opens by speaking softly. Beginning in a seemingly friendly manner to an opposing gangster, Bonaparte allows his voice to rise until it's obvious to everyone in the room that his enemy, Spats Columbo, will never leave in one piece.

In *Party Girl,* such a scene had been played straight for the final time; in *Some Like It Hot,* it was parodied for the first time. During the year that passed between the former drama and the latter comedy, the public had entered an era when the traditional gangster film, once the ultimate in contemporary realism, solidified into pure movie mythology, ripe for satire of a loving order. Not surprisingly, the indefatigable police officer pursuing these gangsters in *Some Like It Hot* was played by Pat O'Brien, in an appealing approximation of the similar parts he'd played at Warner Brothers in the good old days. Spats was enacted by (in one of his last roles) George Raft, in the early 1930s Warner Brothers' top gangster star. Raft lost that status after unwisely passing on such top crime-film projects as *The Petrified Forest* and *High Sierra,* allowing

The Gangster Film as Comedy: Many contemporary crime films parody the clichés of classic gangster films. In *Johnny Dangerously* Michael Keaton plays a Cagney-esque gangster dominated by his mother (Maureen Stapleton) (courtesy 20th Century–Fox), while Peter Falk (*right*, with Emily Lloyd) is an old-fashioned gangster with a new-fangled daughter in *Cookie* (courtesy Warner Bros.).

them to go instead to his minor league counterpart, Bogart.

Bogie, of course, turned in such striking performances as Duke Mantee and Roy Earle that the status of the two actors was reversed; Bogie shortly emerged as the ongoing superstar, while Raft was relegated to his B-budget equivalent. Raft played not so much a gangster in *Some Like It Hot* as a self-referential role that relied, for its effectiveness, on the audience's familiarity with his own earlier parts.

At one point Spats notices a young hotel employee flipping a half-dollar into the air, catching it, then repeating the action. "Where'd you learn that cheap trick?" Spats asks the boy. Removed from any kind of pop culture context, the line is meaningless and certainly not very funny. The audience howled, however, because they got the joke: the young man "learned" that cheap trick from the 1931 film *Scarface*. While, filming Raft—cast as one of the gang members who follow Paul Muni's Capone-like mob boss around—responded to director Howard Hawks's admonishment that he ought to "find something interesting to do" and add texture to his character. Raft reached into his pocket and, necessity indeed proving to be the better part of invention, flipped the coin that he happened to find there.

The "bit" became so associated with Raft that it helped propel him to stardom. Supposedly, Raft had been something of a gangster (or at least an associate of gangsters, as well as a noted Broadway hoofer) before breaking into the movies; intriguingly enough, he resisted typecasting as a movie gangster, desiring to play anything but, yet was invariably cast in just such roles. That life experience provided the subject for *The George Raft Story*, a 1961 tribute to Warner's leading gangster star of thirty years earlier. Ray Danton, a darkly slick young actor who was just then being hyped as the new generation's answer to George Raft, was cast in the role. The film, by B-budget expert Joseph M. Newman, set the pace for crime films to follow: in its first half, *The George Raft Story* is about gangsters and, in the second, about the making of gangster movies. Featured prominently is, of course, the abovementioned scene in which Danton as Raft improvises his coin-flipping routine. So is another, more fascinating moment, one that's highly significant in setting the pace for future crime films.

The film's Raft, a whitewashed and simplified portrait of the real man, learns that gangster Al Capone has heard Warner Brothers is preparing a film based on the Chicago gangster's life. Big Al shows up in Hollywood to "check up" on how it's going; Raft is scared stiff that the real gangster may find fault with the reel gangster he's portraying. When Capone strolls onto the set, he turns out to be (at least in this film's context) a regular guy, a kind of lovable (and seemingly harmless) *Guys and Dolls*

The Many Faces of Al Capone: The real-life Chicago gangster has been turned into a character as legendary as Billy the Kid, though no two interpretations agree on his essential personality; he has been played (*clockwise, from top left*) by Neville Brand (with Robert Stack as Eliot Ness), as a snarling tough guy in *The Alcatraz Express* (1963), by Rod Steiger as a psychologically tormented but weak man in *Al Capone* (1959), by Ben Gazzara as a macho playboy in *Capone* (1975), and by Jason Robards as a calculating businessman in *The St. Valentine's Day Massacre* (1967, photos courtesy Desilu and 20th Century–Fox).

The Rural Gangster Film: Following the success of *Bonnie and Clyde* in 1967, Hollywood hurriedly turned out a cycle of rural gangster movies; among the best was Robert Aldrich's *The Grissom Gang*, which combined classic crime film elements of the Ma Barker story with a kidnapped-heiress situation not unlike the then-current Patty Hearst case (courtesy Cinerama Releasing).

The Meanest of the Mean: Henry Silva fashioned a successful career playing retro-heavies in contemporary gangster films; he ruthlessly executed an enticing menage-à-trois at their moment of passion in *Wipeout! (below)*, planned vengeance on Chuck Norris in *Code of Silence* (*bottom;* photo credit James Zenk).

gangster. Capone talks tough but winks at Raft to let the actor know everything appears to be okay. The Capone we see, then, is not a realistic portrait of the actual Al Capone, but a romanticized portrait of Capone as filtered through the Runyonesque approach to mobsters which had, over the years, transformed such creatures into garish charmers.

Adding to the aura of artistic complication is the fact that Capone is here played by Neville Brand, the character actor who had always hoped to become a latter-day Wallace Beery. His big break came when he was cast as Capone in the 1958 *Desilu Playhouse* two-part TV-film drama based on the book *The Untouchables* by Eliot Ness with Oscar Fraley. Though the real Capone had been a pudgy, nondescript (except for the notable scar) man, Brand played him, in an effectively grandstanding manner, as a firebrand tough guy, in a sharp contrast to the psychological portrait that Rod Steiger offered in the acclaimed 1959 film *Al Capone*. The public preferred Brand's myth to Steiger's reality: when *The Untouchables* became a weekly series, Desilu's writers stretched to contrive ways to bring the Capone character back, though he had been sent off to Alcatraz in the pilot.

Once more, a key movie moment was derived from pop culture myth (itself a gross caricature of reality) rather than the actual record. Like George Raft in *Some Like It Hot*, Neville Brand in *The George Raft Story* was not playing a character, in any singular movie-role sense of the term, but an ongoing cinematic legend. Throughout the first half of the 1960s, such an approach would gradually take hold and seal off the old-fashioned notion of the gangster film, firmly setting it into the pantheon of classic films, along with clichéd cowboys and now-beloved monster-movie stereotypes. At the same time, a new, contemporary crime film would gradually emerge to take its place, though this nouveau-gangster genre would necessarily rely heavily on references to the older movies in order to make its point.

One such film was 1965's *Young Dillinger,* actor Nick Adams's final attempt to achieve full-blown movie stardom. The film, released (significantly) at mid-decade, stood halfway between the classic and the contemporary gangster films, intriguingly bridging the gap between the two types. Adams had arrived in Hollywood ten years earlier, wandering in from a coal-mining town in Pennsylvania where he had been so smitten with the 1930s gangster films starring James Cagney and his 1940s counterparts with John Garfield that Adams was inspired to try to become their fifties counterpart. Instead, he

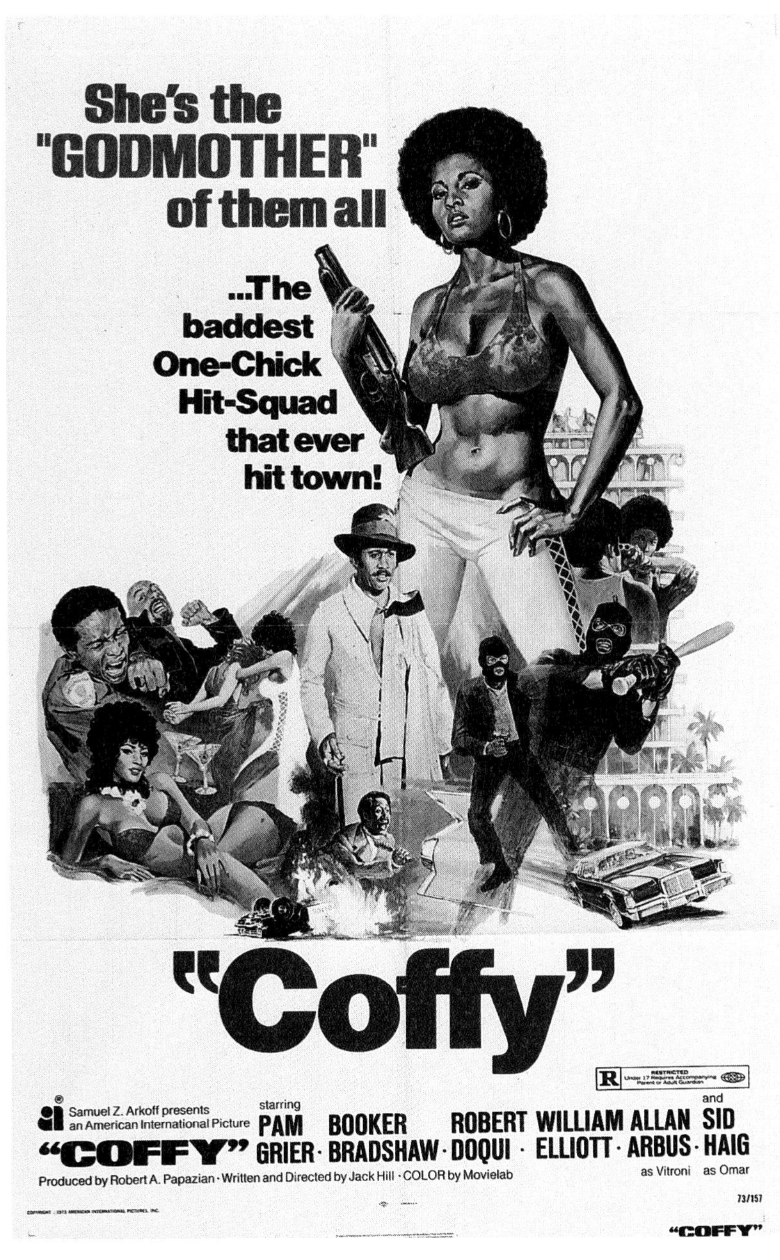

Contemporary crime films acknowledge their post-feminist perspective by allowing macho women to hold their own in the world of men, as the similar advertising artwork for *Coffy* (1973) and, a full two decades later, *Point of No Return* (1993) prove.

found himself cast as troubled teenagers in the then-emerging social epics about troubled youth.

Adams played character roles in various films of the late 1950s, briefly achieving the stardom he so hungered for via an offbeat TV western, *The Rebel* (1959–61), which reset the troubled teenager on the wild frontier. When the show ended and Adams found himself once more relegated to supporting roles, he coproduced *Young Dillinger* as a showcase, presenting himself as he'd always wanted the public to perceive him.

Though the film does follow the general outlines of John Dillinger's life, it's clearly a case of a 1930s character being reinvented for a 1950s actor who idolized the movie stars of Dillinger's era, whom the gangster had himself greatly admired; he was, after all, killed while exiting *Manhattan Melodrama* (a crime film) with the fabled woman in red. The first time we see Adams as Dillinger, it's easy to wrongly believe the film takes place in the fifties: Adams wears a black leather jacket of the type he wore in *Rebel Without a Cause,* a costuming bit already relegated to instant nostalgia by the time *Young Dillinger* was made. He gestures like the Method-mad punk kid he played in *Rebel;* as his girlfriend, Mary Ann Mobley does a Natalie Wood imitation. It appears as if, the film's title be damned, Adams is actually mounting a remake of *Rebel Without a Cause,* with himself in the leading role this time.

The Ethnic Gangster: Contemporary crime films only occasionally deal with the Sicilian mafioso, more often focusing on gangsters from various minority groups: Al Pacino played a Cuban gangster in the Miami of the the mid-eighties in *Scarface* (*left,* courtesy Universal Pictures), while Wesley Snipes enacted an African-American ganglord whom success has gradually gentrified in *Sugar Hill* (*above,* courtesy 2oth Century-Fox).

Then, he and his woman walk to their car, and it's a vintage 1930s auto. Yet there's a halfheartedness to the period trappings; Dillinger's gang members are played by out-of-work actors who, like Adams, portrayed juvenile delinquents a decade earlier. Early rock 'n' rollers enjoyed a combination of costume party and reunion here, in the 1960s re-creating the thirties in the spirit of the fifties. At one point, Adams even gets to live out his ultimate fantasy, suggesting through a key scene that what he really wanted out of life was to have been born James Cagney.

He and his moll, staying at a big-city hotel, decide to catch a movie. Adams/Dillinger insists that it must be a gangster film starring his idol. He then allows himself the ultimate indulgence, doing a take off of Cagney: "You dirty rat...you killed my mutha...I'm gonna kill your fadda...you dirty rat." Of course, Cagney never actually uttered those words, and no one living back in the 1930s ever believed that he did. But over the years, onstage and on TV, impressionists had arrived at an agreed-upon composite Cagney. Adams's delivery is based more on those impressions than reality.

When the film failed at the box office, Adams quickly faded from sight. Two years later, on the very night when that movie was shown on television, he died of a drug overdose variously written off as an accident or a suicide. One reason supporting the latter theory: CBS-TV decided Adams was so completely forgotten that they listed a supporting actor, Robert Conrad, as the "star."

At virtually the same time, however, *Bonnie and Clyde*

was released, immediately becoming a sensation. One of the many reasons why *Bonnie and Clyde* succeeded where *Young Dillinger* had failed was its ability to speak for and about its own time while appearing to be about another era. Young people felt more disenfranchised during the late sixties than at any point since the Great Depression, though the problems were now less economic than social. The killing of young people by the Establishment at the end of *Bonnie and Clyde* left the youthful audience with an strong sense that the film was essentially reflexive: it was about them. Also, the image of the film's youthful dropout hero and heroine learning to love freely was informed, however subtly, by the hippie movement just then emerging. Whereas *Young Dillinger* had been a strange, unconvincing brew, *Bonnie and Clyde* effectively employed the thirties as a metaphor for the sixties.

Its inclusion of graphic bloodshed drew on, while expanding, the violence introduced to commercial films by Alfred Hitchcock in 1960. *Psycho* rates not only as one of the all-time great thrillers (though it certainly is that) but the first truly important American film of the decade. In *Psycho*, Hitchcock depicted, in vivid and specific form, the new American nightmare vision of crime: the boy next door as a closet ax-murderer.

The famed shower sequence caused Hitchcock to be accused of irresponsibly introducing a horrid new aura to films, destroying the polite "code" that had always kept mainstream entertainment clean. To a degree, that was true. Just as undeniable, however, was the fact that Hitchcock early on sensed some major changes blowing in the wind; it's difficult to tell now whether the violence he portrayed in *Psycho* led to ever-greater violence in society or merely reflected the awful truth already evolving.

The sixties may have begun with President Kennedy's bright promise of a New Frontier, though that dream would shortly be shattered by an assassin's bullet. For the better part of the decade, Americans attempted to get their bearings, grasp whether we were moving on with the Kennedy vision though without the man, or retreating to where we had come from. Further assassinations, and an escalating sense of everyday urban violence, clouded our vision. So filmmakers did what they had always done, responding by creating movies that captured the spirit of the times.

The crime films, like other movie genres, can simultaneously communicate the personalities of the filmmakers and the more universalized sensibility of the era during which they were made. When D.W. Griffith directed the first real gangster film in New York's mean streets, his 1912 mini-epic *The Musketeers of Pig Alley* captured the

Working Both Sides of the Law: Like Cagney before him, Clint Eastwood is adept at playing crimebusters (*left*, in *City Heat* courtesy Warner Bros.) and criminals (in *Escape From Alcatraz*, courtesy Paramount Pictures).

The Asian Gangster: Even as the Orient has made itself felt on culture and capital, so has it influenced the contemporary crime film: gangsters face off in John Woo's cult film *The Killer (above),* while California is overrun with Asian gangsters in the compromised film version of Michael Crichton's nightmare-scenario novel, *Rising Sun.*

immigrants' idealistic dream of an American city rubbing up against the harsh reality they found. During the 1920s, at a time when the public tossed old notions of respectability to the wind, breaking the law by openly drinking bootleg whiskey in illegal roadhouses, Hollywood responded by portraying the gangster as the Robin Hood figure that Americans then generally viewed him as. *The Narrow Street, Eternal City,* and *Underworld* all showed criminals as highly appealing characters, helping normal folks get the booze they wanted in defiance of a government that had outlawed our favorite pastime—drinking—and in so doing turned the general population into a nation of outlaws.

Then came the St. Valentine's Day Massacre and, several years thereafter, the repeal of Prohibition. Random, monstrous violence, accompanied by the advent of the Great Depression, truly had (no pun intended) a sobering impact. Gangsters no longer seemed so simple. In the triumvirate of 1930s classics—*Little Caesar, The Public Enemy, Scarface*—and dozens of lesser imitations, urban outlaws were transformed into what Robert Warshow later called "the gangster as tragic hero," little men who take what they want but pay a terrible price at the end. Gangster heroes of thirties films—mostly based on characters from the preceding decade—served as wish fulfillment fantasy figures for the audience. Watching Cagney, Bogart, or Robinson stealing from the banks provided a cathartic release for the newly impoverished.

When Franklin D. Roosevelt was elected, the New Deal began, and a sense of order was restored, movies again changing to reflect the times. Now, Cagney would be cast not as the gangster but the dedicated cop trying to stop crime, in movies like *"G" Men.* The war years allowed Hollywood to revamp the gangster film to suggest that any Americans, even hoodlums, could redeem themselves by taking on the Nazis, as Bogart did in *All Through the Night.* During the postwar years, as the American cinema turned ever more Freudian and movies offered psychologically complex characters, the gangster likewise emerged as a mother-dominated split personality, most notably Cody Jarrett in Raoul Walsh's *White Heat.*

The 1950s continued this trend, as Senator Kefauver's Committee on Crime resulted in *The Phenix City Story* and *On the Waterfront,* with their images of decent American communities invaded by the criminal element. This was the state of the art when a new American cinema was born with *Bonnie and Clyde* in 1967. Suddenly, the old Production Code, with its limitations on what could or could not be portrayed, was scuttled; society was in too much of a flux for outmoded standards to continue. In its place was the new rating system, with a wide-open attitude; in the movies, as in modern life, the approach was suddenly one of "Anything goes!"

And so, as a string of filmmakers—serious minded artists and exploitation-oriented hacks alike—approached the gangster genre, they virtually reinvented it. All those seeds that had been planted during the 1960s were sprouting; gangster movies would reflect society at large and the audience watching the films, while deconstructing the experience of watching a crime film by making us aware of our being involved in that very experience. The result: movies that are as concerned with the impact of crime movies as they are with the reality of crime.

What follows are fifty of the most vivid examples.

THE FILMS

ONE

Bonnie and Clyde

(1967)

A Warner Bros. Release

CAST:

Warren Beatty *(Clyde Barrow)*; Faye Dunaway *(Bonnie Parker)*; Michael J. Pollard *(C. W. Moss)*; Estelle Parsons *(Blanche)*; Gene Hackman *(Buck)*; Denver Pyle *(Frank Hamer)*; Dub Taylor *(Ivan Moss)*; Evans Evans *(Velma)*; Gene Wilder *(Eugene)*.

CREDITS:

Producer, Warren Beatty; director, Arthur Penn; screenplay, David Newman and Robert Benton; special consultant, Robert Towne; cinematography, Burnett Guffey; editor, Dede Allen; art director, Dean Tavoularis; costumes, Theodore van Runkle; music, Charles Strouse; running time, 111 minutes; rating, R.

To claim that *Bonnie and Clyde* forever changed the crime genre is to make a gross understatement. Beyond that, the 1967 release of this rural gangster film, concurrent with the distribution of *The Graduate* and *2001: A Space Odyssey*, permanently altered the shape, form, and substance of popular films, for better or worse. One indicator of the culture shock: Jay Cocks of *Time* magazine casually dismissed *Bonnie and Clyde* as an overly sexual, explicitly violent youth-exploitation film only to do an unheard-of about-face in the following issue, hailing this as the cornerstone of the New American Cinema.

One key theme of modern crime movies introduced here was the notion that the movie we're watching is about movies, a contemporary film dealing with the immense impact of classic films. This is suggested even before the film proper begins. The famed Warner Bros. shield that precedes all their pictures isn't the brightly colored version used throughout the 1960s, but an old black-and-white rendering, the type featured during the period in which *Bonnie and Clyde* is set. This concept is taken further in the first key conversation between Bonnie Parker and Clyde Barrow. They meet in 1931 as she, beautiful and frustrated in her small Texas town, spots him trying to steal her mother's car. The film begins with a richly saturated color close-up of her pretty, pouty mouth, a movie-star mouth redolent with lush bloodred lipstick. Filmmaker Arthur Penn then cuts to Bonnie (Faye Dunaway) admiring her nude body in a mirror, as perfectly proportioned as any of the era's popular stars, unable to understand why she's stuck in this rattrap while they live the good life in Hollywood. Despairing, she plops down on the bed, photographed from such an angle that she appears behind bars.

"We rob banks!": Warren Beatty and Faye Dunaway as Clyde Barrow and Bonnie Parker (courtesy Warner Bros.).

Then, Bonnie hears Clyde outside, throws on some clothes, and rushes out to speak with the intriguing "bad boy." He instinctively understands her problem:

> CLYDE: (flattering) I bet you're a movie star.
> BONNIE: (shaking her head no) What do you really think I am?
> CLYDE: (realistically) A waitress.

She grows sullen; he's hit the nail right on the head. But he makes her feel like a movie star; when she's with him, it's as if Bonnie becomes one of those gun molls Jean Harlow plays in the films Bonnie adores. Which suggests why this "good girl" is willing to join Clyde's robbery of the store down the street, then drive off with him; he makes her feel like a character in a gangster movie.

Unfortunately, they live in the real world or, more correctly, what we accept as the real world while watching. Understandably, then, what they experience will prove considerably less glamorous than the adventures Cagney and Harlow enjoy in *The Public Enemy*. Yet even if *Bonnie and Clyde* is accepted as a modern revisionist portrait of 1930s gangsters, it is, after all, one more

C. W. Moss (Michael J. Pollard, *left*) and Bonnie Parker case out a possible target (courtesy Warner Bros.).

Hollywood movie, and a Warner Bros. movie at that. However much people spoke about Hollywood's "new realism," *Bonnie and Clyde* ultimately satisfied as a work of entertainment. The title characters are played by attractive stars, and their physicalities automatically romanticize what we see, however much the script may strive for "honesty."

One element of that honesty is the portrait of Clyde Barrow as a washout in bed. "I ain't much of a lover boy," he admits when Bonnie grabs him following their first robbery. "Never saw no percentage in it." She's stunned; Bonnie expected a man who acts out robberies like those perpetrated by the fantasy movie gangster to likewise perform as a fantasy lover. Part of the scene's power derives from a key irony of casting: Clyde is played by a star whose reputation as Hollywood's leading stud was well-known. Clearly, Bonnie was turned on by Clyde's dangerousness; the first time he showed her his "gun," Bonnie touched it with erotic fascination, the angle of Penn's camera (emphasizing that Clyde holds it upward, from just below his belt) turning the pistol into a phallic symbol.

When Bonnie and Clyde rush away from another bank robbery, now in the company of their grinning idiot sidekick C. W. Moss (Michael J. Pollard), Clyde shoots a bank manager who hops onto the running board of the car, the bullet smashing through the man's glasses and killing him. The moment is a reference to a classic shot in Sergei Eisenstein's 1925 Russian masterpiece, *Potemkin,* in which a protester on the Odessa steps is killed in precisely that manner. It's worth noting that François Truffaut, leading proponent of the French New Wave, was originally approached to direct *Bonnie and Clyde*; his films are filled wth just such homages to great films of the past, creating a sense of cinematic history encapsulated within the context of the current film. Truffaut—like his contemporary Jean-Luc Godard—held the American crime genre dear; both *Shoot The Piano Player* and *Breathless* represented French attempts to re-create, in modern terms, the beloved American film noir.

Bonnie and Clyde is, then, the American equivalent of those French New Wave movies, emulating their visually poetic lyricism in scenes featuring Bonnie, Clyde, and their gang members slipping away to pastoral country settings, or the self-consciousness of the French directors, as when a wild getaway is speeded up slightly to recall

The gun as phallic symbol: To compensate for his lack of sexual prowess, Clyde proves his machismo by allowing an aroused Bonnie to "fondle" his pistol (courtesy Warner Bros.).

our collective unconscious movie-memories of the Keystone Kops and their silent slapstick antics, even as banjo music creates a comedic tone for what would ordinarily be a thriller scene. It's not surprising, then, that following the foiled bank robbery, the gang rushes off to a movie: a Warner Brothers movie at that, *The Gold Diggers of 1933*. No matter that we've been informed they story takes place in 1931; producer/star Beatty sacrificed literal realism for a more significant symbolic purpose. We watch the characters watching the famed "We're in the Money" segment, in which beautiful blondes—looking a little like this film's incarnation of Bonnie—are draped with chains of coins. Bonnie sits apart from her cohorts (Clyde and C. W. argue about the failed robbery), staring transfixed at the screen; she will, throughout this film, be singled out by the camera as she slips chains of jewels around her neck, in an endless attempt to be at one with the characters briefly glimpsed on-screen.

Even mindless little C. W. is a movie lover. When the trio meet up with Clyde's anarchic brother Buck (Gene Hackman) and his flighty wife, Blanche (Estelle Parsons), C. W. can't resist asking if that's a copy of *Screenland* magazine in their car, asking to read an article about his personal favorite, Myrna Loy. Still-photography represents the business of shooting a film. The opening-credit sequence features a series of still photographs of the real Bonnie and Clyde, notably unpleasant looking. Then, as the movie proper begins, the filmmakers dissolve to black-and-white shots of glamorous Beatty and Dunaway, a relief to viewers, who, after all, came to see movie stars.

The moment Bonnie and Clyde join Buck and Blanche, they begin taking photographs of one another with Blanche's camera. Bonnie, in particular, poses in a provocative manner, wearing her sporty beret, smoking a cigarette in a rebellious manner, casually cradling a gun to make her appear dangerously alluring. The photographing of one another, which began as a serious attempt to document the reality of their existence, transforms into an exercise in mythmaking, true, too, of the filmmakers "shooting" *Bonnie and Clyde*. Later, as Buck reads newspaper reports out loud, detailing the gang's activities—reports that get some of the details right, also exaggerating events—Blanche fondles her camera, pointing it at the others, implying the film we're watching is concerned with the process by which the real Bonnie and Clyde were elevated into the myth of Bonnie and Clyde. Even a policeman who fails to apprehend the gang, and bystanders who witness robberies, are shown being photographed, celebrities because they had a brush with fame, allowing them their own pre-Warholian fifteen minutes.

When, shot to pieces, Bonnie and Clyde stop at an Okie camp, those poor people provide the robbers with what little food and water they can spare, touching the outlaws as if they were religious figures. An entirely different attitude is taken by Frank Hamer (Denver Pyle), the old Texas Ranger who, attempting to apprehend the gang, was captured by them, then forced to pose for degrading photographs. "I figure to have my picture taken with them just one more time," he tells the posse. Hamer can only redeem his reputation by posing with the dead bodies of the criminals.

The film created a craze for retro-clothing from the 1930s among hippie-era youth (courtesy Warner Bros.).

But Bonnie and Clyde are self-mythologizers even when the camera isn't present. "We rob banks," each intones early on, the epigram becoming their motto, a kind of guttural pop poetry. Bonnie eventually writes "The Story of Bonnie and Clyde" in verse and sends it to the papers; in her poem, Bonnie compares their gang to the famous James-Younger gang of the past century, also popularly perceived as contemporary Robin Hoods:

> You've heard the story of Jesse James
> How he lived and died
> Now, if you need more to read,
> Here's the story of Bonnie and Clyde.

The film's bank-robbery sequences are played at a fever pitch, often to the tune of banjo music, evoking the Keystone Kop films of the past and consciously reminding the audience that we are watching a film, not reality (courtesy Warner Bros.).

Her imperfect sense of rhyme and garish sentimentality aside, Bonnie's poem strikes a public nerve: the victims of the Great Depression need a Robin Hood myth as badly as the victims of the post–Civil War South did. When Bonnie sends that poem to the newspapers, it's printed in a place where people expect to find only facts. The transformation of Bonnie and Clyde into mythological characters, aided and abetted by the media that loves a good story more than it respects absolute truth, is a fait accompli.

For one brief, glorious moment, Bonnie and Clyde experience the ideal made real; having achieved full fame, they at last have good sex. "You did just perfect," Bonnie tells Clyde, who has apparently not been able to consummate their relationship previously. Clyde was less in love with Bonnie's body than with a mental image of the great lady he envisioned her as; though a country-bumpkin gangster, Clyde is something of a rube romantic. Their story, at that moment, is essentially over, having reached its inevitable closure; it comes as no great surprise that they are shortly betrayed and killed in the infamous "ballet of blood" that allows us to see their emotionally true, rather than literally real, demise.

The two are demolished owing to C. W.'s betrayal of their trust: like Judas or Jesse James's traitorous gang member Robert Ford, C. W. allows his friends to drive into an ambush. He does that not for twenty pieces of silver, but out of loyalty to his elderly father, Ivan (Dub Taylor), who has cut a deal with Hamer. This notion of family loyalties in conflict—the biological family as opposed to the youth-cult alternative family—was particularly fitting for the counterculture era during which the film was produced; it was also indicative of a key theme that would come to permeate crime films for the next three decades.

Lawman Frank Hamer (Denver Pyle) is forced to pose for pictures with Bonnie, who uses the "seeing is believing" quality of photographs to convince the public that she and Hamer enjoy a sexual relationship. Beginning with this movie, the modern crime film will employ photographing within the film to warn viewers about the mythmaking being achieved by the movie we are watching (courtesy Warner Bros.).

TWO

Point Blank

(1967)

A Metro-Goldwyn-Mayer Release

CAST:

Lee Marvin *(Walker);* Angie Dickinson *(Chris);* Keenan Wynn *("Yost");* Carroll O'Connor *(Brewster);* Lloyd Bochner *(Carter);* Michael Strong *(Stegman);* John Vernon *(Reese);* Sharon Acker *(Lynne);* James Sikking *(Hit Man);* Kathleen Freeman *(Society Matron);* Susan Holloway *(Woman Buying Car).*

CREDITS:

Producers, Judd Bernard, Irwin Winkler, and Robert Chartoff; director, John Boorman; screenplay, Alexander Jacobs and David and Rafe Newhouse, from the novel *The Hunter* by Richard Stark (Donald E. Westlake); cinematography, Philip H. Lathrop; editor, Henry Berman; music, Johnny Mandel; art direction, George W. Davis and Albert Brenner; running time, 92 minutes.

This violent, stylish, thought-provoking motion picture represents the first milestone attempt by Hollywood to bridge the gap between the traditional gangster film, which had fallen from favor, and the contemporary gangster film to evolve during the early 1970s. BBC documentarian John Boorman revived and reinvented a subgenre of the gangster film, the urban tale of a tough older gangster betrayed by his buddies who then takes the notion of rugged individualism to the edge of chaos.

Lee Marvin, a holdover from 1950s underworld flicks, was perfectly cast as The Last Gangster: a throwback to the independent-minded criminal with a code of honor, a lumbering Neanderthal in a slick sharkskin suit. What made the movie's concept arresting was that this man, who looked identical to gangsters in earlier films, now stumbled through a world as alien to him as if he had just landed on another planet. Walker (we never learn his first name) is a throwback, alternately confounded by or oblivious to a world populated with acid-rock music, modern kitchen conveniences, go-go dancing girls in miniskirts, parallel plastic bubble helmets in beauty parlors, and assorted other elements he cannot connect with. But what Walker has the most problem making sense of is the new corporate image of organized crime.

The images of gangland Chicago in the 1930s increasingly became a source of nostalgia, giving way to a new vision of the underworld as having come above ground, insinuating itself into every aspect of American life, including our most revered institutions, now run not by gaudily dressed mobsters with scars across their faces but by button-down executives in three-piece suits. "Murf." of *Variety* hinted at this early on, noting that Carroll O'Connor's Brewster "is a flesh-and-blood accountant who pursues his criminal career with as much businesslike detachment as his counterpart in any corporation." Already the modern gangster was becoming virtually indistinguishable from the corporate executive, a fitting commentary on life in an age that would run the gamut from Watergate to the S&L scandal. As Brendan Gill pointed out in his *New Yorker* review, "the chief crooks bear three of the most distinguished names in American history: Carter, Fairfax, and Brewster," allowing the gangster film to move sharply away from stereotypical portraits of Sicilian mobsters.

Boorman modernized the look, as well as substance, of gangster films by employing the same sort of purposefully disorienting jumps in time and place that had characterized European art-house experimental items of the midsixties. The film opens with a furiously paced recap of the complex events that precipated the good-bad man's relentless quest. By accident, Walker encounters a well-appointed (in today's terms, yuppified) businessman named Reese at some unspecified reunion event. Reese insinuates himself into the relationship of Walker and his wife, Lynne; after manipulating a ménage-à-trois, he talks Walker into helping on a criminal caper, intercepting a gangland helicopter drop of cash on deserted Alcatraz island. But rather than hitting

Walker takes aim at the despised bed of the woman who betrayed him (courtesy Metro-Goldwyn-Mayer).

the gang members over the head and stealing the loot, as agreed upon, Reese brutally kills them. When he realizes there isn't enough money to pay off his debts to the organization (one of the more pronounced oddities of the plot is that Reese robs from the very same mob he will use this money to pay back debts to), Reese shoots Walker to confiscate his share as well, leaving the betrayed man in a prison cell.

After surviving the Alcatraz betrayal, Walker somehow manages to swim away, despite his life-threatening bullet wounds; realist critics scoffed that this was totally unbelievable, dismissing the picture. While they were in a sense correct—no mortal man could survive under such circumstances—they missed the greater point entirely. Walker is no ordinary man; ordinary men, after all, have first names. Walker is the gangster equivalent of Clint Eastwood's Man With No Name in the modern western film, a compendium of every loner-gangster hero who preceded him. In *Films and Filming,* David Austen spoke of Walker's "resurrection"; though he intended the comment sarcastically, it in fact is precisely the right word.

Masochistically circling Alcatraz in a tour boat, Walker is (at some indeterminate time in the future) approached by a stranger who identifies himself only as "Yost" (Keenan Wynn). This cynical man somehow knows who Walker is and what happened; he claims to have his own grudge against the mob, thereby agreeing to supply Walker with any information he needs to seek revenge. First, Yost provides Walker with Lynne's address in L.A., mentioning that Reese lives there, too. Walker crashes into the apartment, gagging the astonished Lynne with his hand, then emptying the pistol into the bed where he assumes Reese will be. In fact, the bed is empty, and Lynne informs him that Reese dumped her months earlier, their only contact being a monthly payment of $1,000 hush money.

The shooting into the bed is the most vivid of the visual Freudian symbols, as *Point Blank*—and modern gangster films to follow—equate acts of murder with acts of sex. Though it is seemingly the middle of the afternoon when he arrives, Walker assumes Reese will be waiting for Lynne, as if their relationship allowed for no other activity. He "kills" her bed but not, importantly, Lynne—nor, for that matter (however surprisingly), anyone else during the entire movie. "Murf." pointed out in passing what is in fact an important element: "[Walker] precipitates [his enemies'] deaths, although he never seems to have actually been the direct cause of death."

Perhaps we can write off Walker's sparing Lynne as dramatic convenience; it would be difficult for audiences to sympathize with the antihero if he murdered such a

Lee Marvin as Walker: cinematographer Philip Lathrop carefully modulates the shadows on Marvin's face to imply dark recesses within his character's personality (courtesy M-G-M).

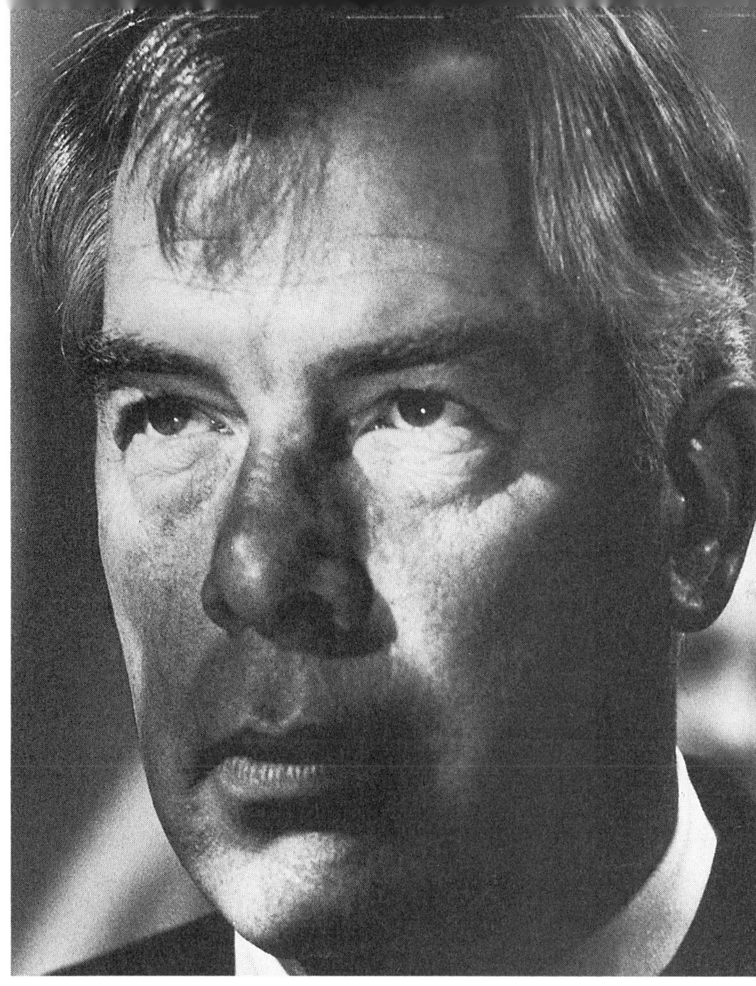

underling conspirators out to get him. Walker gazes on as Yost/Fairfax and his hit man walk away; the feud is over, since Fairfax was wise enough to leave the money.

Everyone assumes the money must be an excuse for Walker's activities, which could be the pursuit of power or revenge. That belief partly explains why the mobsters don't simply pay him off, the $93,000 being nothing more than a drop in the bucket compared to their multimillions. In fact, though, Walker does not have any ulterior motives at all:

> BREWSTER: (disbelieving) You threaten a financial structure like this for ninety-three thousand dollars? Come on, Walker. What do you really want?
>
> WALKER: (surprisingly vulnerable) Nothing. I just want my money.

Another key theme is the ambiguous woman, not easily identifiable as good girl or bad. The character of Chris is so groundbreaking that many critics mistook her ambiguous nature as a flaw. Richard Schickel wrote in *Life* that "Marvin persuades a seemingly nice girl to divert one of [Walker's] enemies with the offer of herself so that he can sneak up behind the punk and murder him. It is the oldest ploy, and the girl registers a mod-

Looking like Eugene O'Neill's "hairy ape," though dressed as a sharkskin-suited Establishment killer from past crime films, Walker senses he's an anachronism in the incomprehensible hippie-era haunts of then-modern psychedelic America (courtesy M-G-M).

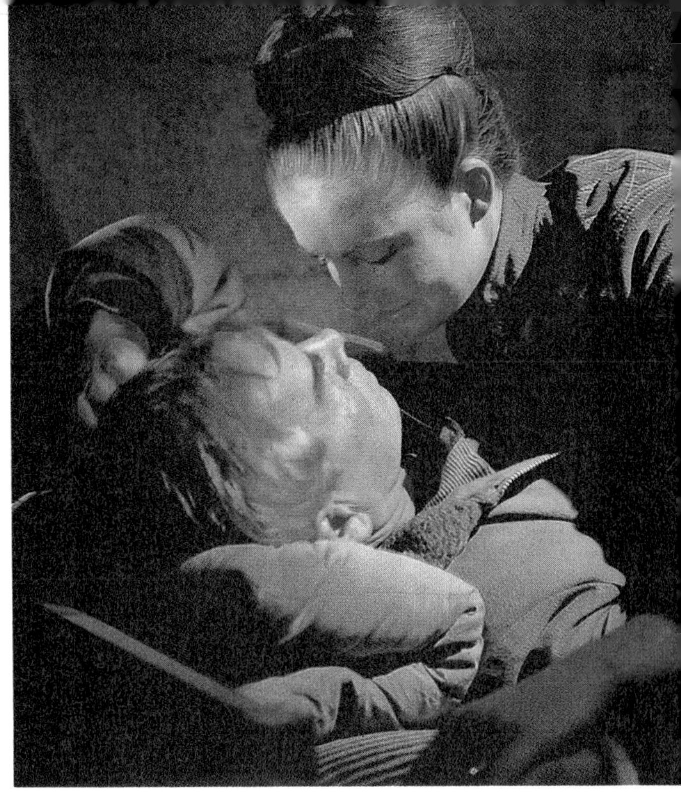

Flashback, dream, or both? Walker recalls his lost love and, however unlikely a candidate he may seem, transforms into the gangster as romantic hero (courtesy Metro-Goldwyn-Mayer).

beautiful woman, however questionable her morality. But Walker does not murder anyone; he traps Reese on the top of a penthouse apartment, and the man's death—falling off the building and spinning down, naked—appears to be an accident. Lynne's sister Chris (Angie Dickinson), used as a Trojan horse to get Walker into Reese's fortified apartment, senses this is not what she expected. "You should have killed him," she comments. "You owed it to yourself."

Importantly, what seemed to be shaping up as a revenge play, à la *Out of the Past,* turns out to be anything but. Early in the story, both betrayers are dead. In fact, though, the story has just begun. While we may have assumed Walker was out for revenge, he never actually said that to anyone. He said only that he wanted his share of the money, and this turns out, remarkably enough, to be true. Insisting on the $93,000 Reese owed him, Walker (with the silent-partner help of Yost) works his way up the mob hierarchy, insisting to each man that if he turns over the money, the feud will end.

Brewster, the most gregarious and agreeable of the mobsters, would happily turn the money over. "We deal in millions," he honestly explains, "but I don't have more than eleven dollars in my pocket." However, when Brewster devises a way to pay off Walker, revisiting Alcatraz for the weekly mob run (like all good myths, this one ends where it began), Brewster is shot by the hit man who works for "Yost"—actually Fairfax, the top man in the mob, who has been using Walker to kill off

The new violence: Following Arthur Penn's *Bonnie and Clyde,* the gangster film—rural or urban—would ever more graphically violent, and *Point Blank* was no exception to that rule (courtesy Metro-Goldwyn-Mayer).

icum of disgust at it. Then, with that aimless amorality that characterizes all present, she carries it through. Now Mr. Boorman's camera abandons its previous discreet mood and plunges forward to make a detailed record of the squirmings and shudderings of loveless sex, including the convulsive separation of the pair when Marvin yanks them apart for the kill." But Schickel's phrase "aimless amorality" is less effective as intended criticism than as apt description of the sensibility of the modern gangster film, a cinematic response to the emerging lifestyle that these movies reflected.

Chris goes along with Walker's plan because, if she did not, he would leave her; cooperating on a conspiracy that disgusts her is the only way to keep Walker around and, perhaps, make him her own, which is why she follows through with his plan, then is disgusted to realize he thinks she did it for money. "You really did die on Alcatraz," she sighs.

Now the lover of Chris, Walker patiently awaits her return, unable to guess that they exist on two separate planes of life. The audience grasps this, however, as it is implied in the carefully designed placement of people and objects within the frame (courtesy M-G-M).

In a memorable sequence, Chris beats Walker with her fists, but is unable to make a dent on him. While Walker sits, watching inane TV commercials, Chris turns on every modern "convenience" in the house: blenders, tape recorders, and other electronic gadgets together create a bizarre contemporary cacophony of mindless noise. When Walker—looking as lost and confused as the ancient beast King Kong loose in 1930s New York—chases after Chris, the delicate-looking lady whacks him with a pool cue, sending the beast of a man flying down to the floor. Momentarily, violence transforms into sex; they make love, Walker unable to ascertain whether this is Chris or Lynne. To a degree, he doesn't really care.

But she cares very much when, the morning after, he prepares to go through with his kidnapping of Brewster. Like any modern woman who wants a man to acknowledge her identity, she confronts him, hoping this was not merely anonymous sex.

CHRIS: What's my last name?
WALKER: (after a pause) What's my first name?

Their give-and-take sets the stage for confrontations between countless other throwback men and enlightened women in modern gangster films to follow.

THREE

The Last Run

(1971)

A Metro-Goldwyn-Mayer Release

CAST:

George C. Scott *(Harry Garmes);* Tony Musante *(Paul Rickard);* Trish Van Devere *(Claudie Scherrer);* Colleen Dewhurst *(Monique);* also featuring Aldo Sanbrell, Antonio Tarruella, Robert Coleby, Robert J. Zurica, Rocky Taylor.

CREDITS:

Producer, Carter De Haven; director, Richard Fleischer (and, uncredited, John Huston); screenplay, Alan Sharp; cinematography, Sven Nykvist; editor, Russell Lloyd; music, Jerry Goldsmith; art direction, Roy Walker and Jose Maria Tapiador; running time, 92 minutes; rating, PG.

A significant attempt to simultaneously revive and revise the gangster film was *The Last Run,* starring George C. Scott, then riding the crest of his Oscar win (and legendary no-show at the ceremonies) for *Patton* a year earlier. The film is a fascinating if less than entirely successful attempt to update the old *High Sierra/Key Largo* type of lone, anachronistic, noble gangster-on-the-run tale. No great surprise, then, that John Huston himself began directing the film, though he hastily departed, for reasons variously stated as dissatisfaction with the script and an inability to come to a comfortable working relationship with Scott on the order of the one he had, decades earlier, enjoyed with Bogart. This, despite the fact that Scott's role was a virtual replay of the old Bogart gangsters.

Scott plays a gangster closely connected to his car. In the opening sequence, onetime Chicago-mob driver Harry Garmes, known for his incredibly fast getaways, tinkers with the fine-tuning on a sports car souped up so as to be capable of incredibly fast speeds while taking a beating no normal car could withstand. Then, just to make sure it's as smooth-running a machine as ever, Garmes slips behind the wheel and, as in the days of yore, drives the customized 1957 BMW 503 cabriolet down a winding Mediterranean mountain road at dazzling speeds, burning rubber every inch of the way. Clearly, he still has it: Garmes is a professional, a perfectionist at what he does. By the time he reaches the bottom of that mountain, there is no doubt in his mind that he and his car can still function under the most intense time pressures.

In the film, the character Harry Garmes has a fascinating parallel with the actor playing him, as Scott romances Colleen Dewhurst, the woman he was married to as well as Trish Van Devere (right), the woman he would shortly divorce Dewhurst in order to marry (courtesy M-G-M).

That is the setup for the story that follows. We need to know (having seen rather than heard secondhand) what Garmes and his car are capable of. Garmes will soon set out on the ride of his life, the last run of the title. His no-longer-young face makes clear that he is a world-weary man. Nine years before, his only child died; since that time, Garmes has retired from his driving career as well as from life itself. He lives an isolated Hemingwayesque life in a Portuguese fishing village, apparently never having heard the adage that no man is an island. He tools and retools his car, but has no plans to use it.

But even Harry Garmes can only live in existential isolation for so long. A young international triggerman, Paul Rickard (Tony Musante), has been tried and condemned in Spain; he will be taken, by bus, to a prison and there incarcerated. Garmes's assignment is to waylay that bus, pull Rickard from it, and spirit him away as quickly as possible, across the border to France, delivering Rickard into the waiting arms of his cohorts.

From the moment Garmes picks up Rickard at the escape site and they travel together across the Iberian Peninsula, down a twisting and threatening stretch of

George C. Scott as Harry Garmes, yet another anachronistic gangster hero, now adrift in a world without noticeable values (courtesy M-G-M).

road from Seville to the Costa del Sol, the movie transforms into an extended, complicated, oftentimes absorbing chase. But the pyrotechnics do not overwhelm the movie. There is an immediate conflict between the noble, anachronistic "old" gangster and the cocky, vulgar, even kinky "young" gangster. Rickard likes to tie women to a bedframe with their own stockings before making love to them. Rickard is an early example of the yuppie gangster in modern mob films, his superficiality and self-interest making him a predecessor of many to follow. Which helps explain why it's so easy for an audience to forgive Garmes his crimes, past and present, accepting him as a true man's man, a person of substance in deeds and thought.

Complicating matters between Garmes and Rickard is the presence of Rickard's girlfriend, Claudie (Trish Van Devere), picked up along the way. The old Hollywood notion of a romantic triangle is revived, as Claudie—initially not appearing to question her "love" for the superficially attractive Garmes—is gradually moved deeply by the sincere older man, perceiving him as an appealing father figure as well as possible lover. Making this tension all the more fascinating is that Van Devere and Scott were even then becoming lovers (later husband and wife, for a time) in real life; more fascinating still, Scott's then-current wife, Colleen Dewhurst, also appears in a supporting role.

Eventually, Scott must face the same sort of moral choice the Hemingway heroes, especially Harry (can the same first name be coincidental?) Morgan in *To Have and Have Not,* ultimately faced. Garmes comes to realize that the mobsters who employed him are anything but criminals with their own code of honor. They wanted Rickard removed from the Spanish authorities because he knew too much and plan to quickly kill him. Garmes must therefore decide whether he'll turn Rickard (whom he never learns to like) over, thereby getting the girl for himself, or do the noble thing, face the mobsters (and inevitably die) while allowing the young couple to escape, which he senses in his gut is the right thing to do. Anyone who has ever seen *Casablanca* knows how the hard-boiled hero will resolve such a situation.

Some critics claimed the pathos of the ending was

The generation gap: wiseguy Paul Rickard represents the future of crime, in which all codes of conduct have been abandoned, while Harry Garmes continues to keep his own lonely counsel (courtesy M-G-M).

The young, hippie-ish gangster couple (Van Devere and Tony Musante) flaunt "the new sexuality" of the swinging sixties and early seventies, causing traditionalist Harry Garmes, out of touch with this new lifestyle, to take the Hemingwayesque approach, reaching for a stiff drink (courtesy M-G-M).

played by Van Devere—a feminist in real life—served as an effective precursor of the more liberated women who would occupy key roles in so many gang films to come: "Bright and independent, Miss Van Devere displays an ambiguity that is as psychologically valid as it is ultimately crucial: is she genuinely attracted to the gracefully weathered Scott? Or is it strictly a ploy in Musante's behalf? Or is it a little bit of both?"

Indeed, dealing with the modern woman would prove to be a devastating experience for many movie gangsters to follow. In *The Last Run,* Garmes admits that he never really got over the wife who, years ago, left him for another man. The old dinosaur tells his young companions that she went to Switzerland to have her breasts lifted. "I thought she meant surgically," he sighs, an extremely modern line of dialogue from a notably old-fashioned gangster.

taken further than necessary. "Scott's death scene is fascinating," John Goff noted in *The Hollywood Reporter,* "as a man, larger than life, pumped with three shots stands like 'the old dinosaur' Musante has likened him to earlier in the film, and then crumples. It is a chilling moment [but] it is marred with the insertion of a scene of his car, established earlier as a respected and loved extension of himself, having been as battered as himself and left running, is turned off; Scott then expunges his last breath and dies. It's a bit too much." The symbol may indeed suffer from visual overkill, but it does work, if in an overly obvious way. The "old dinosaur," a relic not only of earlier gangster days but also earlier gangster films, is not unlike the old cowboy finishing off his wounded horse so the two can expire together. But since this is a gangster film, not a western, the car is his preferred "mount." Like Lee Marvin's Walker in *Point Blank,* Scott's Garmes is not only an anachronism but an anomaly, the last of a dying breed of dangerous rugged individualists who must step aside to make way for slick, superficial young corporate types.

"Despite an often labored script," S.K. Oberbeck noted in *Newsweek,* "Scott offers a splendid portrayal of the still tender tough guy coming carefully out of mothballs, giving Garmes...grittiness and tension...[the film] is really a vehicle for Scott, his dented chin sinking and rising and his prow-brows wrinkling. He can be tough, then suddenly funny—a Bogart of the sixties with fewer wisecracks and more defensive footwork." Yet another critic, Kevin Thomas of the *Los Angeles Times* noticed that the woman

A man and his car: Garmes, the noble dinosaur among crime figures, prepares for "the last run" of the title (courtesy M-G-M).

FOUR

The French Connection

1971

A 20th Century–Fox Film

CAST:

Gene Hackman *(Jimmy "Popeye" Doyle);* Fernando Rey *(Alain Charnier/"Frog I");* Roy Scheider *(Buddy Russo);* Tony LoBianco *(Sal Boca);* Marcel Bozzuffi *(Pierre Nicoli);* Frederic De Pasquale *(Devereaux);* Arnold Gary *(Weinstock);* Eddie Egan *(Simonson);* Sonny Grosso *(Klein).*

CREDITS:

Producer, Phil D'Antoni; director, William Friedkin; screenplay, Ernest Tidyman, based on the book by Robin Moore; cinematography, Owen Roizman; editor, Jerry Greenberg; music, Don Ellis; running time, 104 minutes; rating, R.

The French Connection won five Academy Awards, including Best Picture of the Year. Statuettes also went to Gene Hackman (Best Actor), William Friedkin (director), Ernest Tidyman (screenplay adaptation from another medium), and Jerry Greenberg (editor). That's quite a coup for a cop film, since this genre has been neglected at Oscar time as shamefully as the western or the horror movie. This was the movie that, owing to outstanding reviews, box-office popularity, and ultimately the Oscar sweep, made resoundingly clear once and for all that the American cinema had forever changed.

The French Connection proved that a new 1970s sensibility could be combined with old-fashioned craftsmanship, as well as the gripping narrative drive Hollywood had always been famous for. As critic Stephen Farber noted, this was "a stylish and exciting melodrama but, beyond that, a hellishly precise vision of the disintegration of modern urban life and the ambiguous role of the police in an increasingly polarized and corrupt society. The film's disorienting network of impersonations (characters and institutions continually turn out to be something other than what they first appear as) suggests the erosion of any clear sense of identity, the blurring of traditional moral distinctions, the rootlessness and anomie

Bang, you're dead: William Friedkin directly involved his audience by having tough cop "Popeye" Doyle (Gene Hackman) appear to fire directly into the camera.

A new kind of cop film for a new era in popular culture: The legendary advertisement for *The French Connection* (courtesy 20th Century–Fox).

Sonny Grosso and Eddie Egan as Detective Phil Klein and Lieutenant Simonson. The characters played in the film by Roy Scheider and Hackman were based on real-life cops Grosso and Egan (courtesy 20th Century–Fox).

that contribute to the peculiar desperation of the modern nightmare city." That is the very same city Martin Scorsese focused on in the nongenre film *Taxi Driver* five years later, the 1970s urban hell in which any and all hippie-era dreams of peace and love had long since degenerated into a horrid phantasmagoria of rampant drugs.

Though in fact based on a 1962 incident, an attempted $32 million heroin exchange meticulously chronicled in Robin Moore's book, the movie as filmed was very much of the moment, for and about the emerging seventies sensibility. *The French Connection* proceeded in a journalistic manner resembling the best European-made crime films, rejecting the once classic, now clunky dramaturgy of previous American motion pictures. The opening scene, depicting suave gangster Alain Charnier (Fernando Rey) initiating the complex deal in Marseilles, was shot with a shaky handheld camera, immediately conveying the sense that we are not so much watching characters from a cool distance but walking alongside them. The early scenes in Brooklyn, in which cops Jimmy "Popeye" Doyle (Gene Hackman) and Buddy Russo (Roy Scheider) shake down drug dealers, is unflinchingly honest in a way no previous American police movie had ever been. It's Christmastime, and Popeye stands on a street corner in a Santa Claus suit, ringing his bell, making small talk with black children until his partner (disguised as a hot dog vendor) spots their mark; they pursue. The image of Popeye, ripping away his false beard and relentlessly chasing the man while still garbed in his red costume, immediately entered the emerging iconography of the nouveaux American crime film.

Nothing in *The French Connection* is as "realistic" as Popeye's characterization. Sporting a jauntily cocked porkpie hat, Popeye is a bigot, shooting off horrible racial slurs even though he ought to know better, since his best and brightest undercover agent is a black man. Popeye takes a notable pleasure (again, never explained in dialogue but utterly clear from the gleam in his eyes) whenever he and Buddy walk into an all-black bar and hassle the clientele. He's a foot fetishist, attracted to women not as human beings but only if they sport and shake the then-popular plastic booties.

Previously, this type of gross, vulgar characterization might have been possible if the filmmakers were depicting a bad cop, one who would pay the price at movie's end. Here, though, Popeye is the good cop, or as near to a good cop as the film has to offer. He is the film's hero, despite endless offensive details, for one simple reason: Popeye is truly dedicated to his job. He wants to bust the heroin shipment other cops insist isn't even happening. And, by the end, he wins our admiration. As Roger Greenspun noted in the *New York Times*, "he exists neither to rise nor to fall, to excite neither pity nor terror—but to function. To function in New York City is its own heroism, and the film recognizes that, but it is not the heroism of conventional gesture."

How effective, then, that the film's gangster/drug dealer is the exact opposite of Doyle. From the moment we first catch a glimpse of Charnier, the Frenchman (hence his code name, Frog) is the shimmering symbol of European elegance. Wearing finely tailored suits, speaking in a soft-spoken voice, living in a seaside mansion with a beautiful young mistress, Charnier epitomizes sophistication. We cannot even take offense, considering him an upscale snob, for there's a down-to-earth, utterly ironic quality to Charnier. He notes, at one point, that he began life as a longshoreman, so he's clearly a variation on that recurring character in the modern gangster film, the self-made man. Charnier is as appealing as Popeye is crass, yet he is the bad guy because he's the drug dealer, whereas Popeye is the good guy because he's the cop.

It's as simple as that, though in fact the source of this film's brilliance is that nothing in it is truly simple. When Charnier dines on a gourmet meal in a posh Manhattan eatery while Popeye stands outside in the drizzle, wolfing down a bedraggled piece of pizza, we can't help but root for this man of the people. Yet we would (given the choice) much prefer to be in that haute-cuisine palace, would probably prefer the quiet conversation of Charnier to Popeye's prejudiced rantings. In

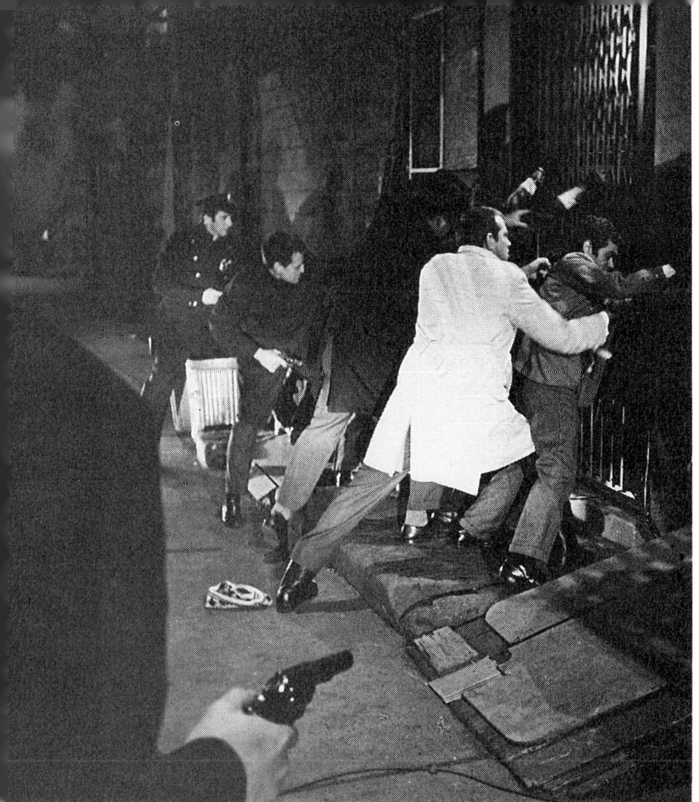

The arrest sequences, as directed by William Friedkin, borrow from France's cinema-verité style, which had developed a decade earlier. What was considered an innovation at the time, at least for American moviemaking, would gradually become an accepted approach, culminating in TV's *N.Y.P.D. Blue* (courtesy 20th Century–Fox).

one of the film's dazzlingly edited sequences, Doyle pursues Charnier down into the New York subway, tailing his mark, hoping he will not be spotted. Charnier, aware he's being followed, deftly steps out of the subway car, causing Doyle to follow suit. Charnier then uses the exquisite designer umbrella he's carrying to stop the subway door from closing, slipping back inside while Popeye is left standing at the station. When Charnier waves a neat little bye-bye to Doyle, we share the hero's frustration, but cannot help but be charmed by Charnier's unflappable poise.

The film's great chase, however, involves Popeye in pursuit of Frog's paid assassin, who attempts to shoot the policeman from high atop an apartment house, instead killing an innocent bystander. This was the cinema's first full recognition of the modern city, where death can strike anyone at any moment and nobody is ever safe. Popeye pursues the man on foot, then hops into a car and follows below the elevated railroad car that the sniper has commandeered, driving like a maniac, screaming at cars and people who get in his way. He is even more dangerous to the public at large than the villain he's pursuing, whom he eventually shoots—in the back, once more in a manner we do not associate with police "heroes."

Even the ending was something of a shocker. Doyle, accused by another police officer of being an out-of-control cowboy who inadvertently got a good cop killed, fires at a man he believes to be Frog, quickly realizing he has killed that very accusatory policeman. Then, Popeye shows not the slightest remorse for his mistake. Audiences waiting for the expected sense of closure, in which Doyle captures or kills Frog, were shocked when Charnier instead slipped away, the first time the villain went scot-free in an American crime movie. Despite the fact that the heroin shipment was nabbed by the police, closing credits include information about what happened to each of the criminals, the results casting a cynical cloud on Popeye's "victory." Each and every one of the principal perpetrators managed to plea-bargain his or her way into a light sentence; rather than being rewarded, Popeye and his partner were assigned to a less sensitive area of police work.

In actuality, Frog (real name, Urbain Giaume) was sentenced to prison in France in 1978, after being convicted of heading a drug-smuggling ring that shipped a ton of pure heroin, valued at $4 million, into the United States between 1969 and 1974. He was released in 1981 after it was discovered that he was dying of cancer. Like his earlier American counterpart, Al Capone, who died slowly of syphilis, he and the other gangsters in crime movies (even modern crime movies) invariably meet more exciting and explosive ends than their real-life counterparts.

Foreigners Pierre Nicoli (Marcel Bozzuffi, *left*) and Frog wait for an accomplice near a Brooklyn pier. Though the actual French Connection had taken place during the 1960s, filmmaker Friedkin transformed it into a metaphor for the drug culture that was encompassing America and the world during the early seventies (courtesy 20th Century–Fox).

The poster that turned a film into a phenomenon; the film that transformed star Clint Eastwood into a superstar (courtesy Warner Bros.).

FIVE

Dirty Harry

(1971)

A Warner Bros. Film

CAST:

Clint Eastwood *(Harry Callahan);* Reni Santoni *(Chico Gonzalas);* Andy Robinson *(Killer);* John Vernon *(Mayor);* Harry Guardino *(Bressler);* John Larch *(Chief);* John Mitchum *(DeGeorgio);* Lyn Edington *(Norma);* JoDe Winter *(Miss Willis).*

CREDITS:

Producer and director, Don Siegel; screenplay, Harry Julian Fink, R. M. Fink, and Dean Reisner; cinematography, Bruce Surtees; editor, Carl Pingitore; music, Lalo Schifrin; executive producer, Robert Daley; art director, Dale Hennessey; running time, 102 minutes; rating, R.

If *The French Connection* was the first of the new breed of realistic/neoconservative police films to appear during the posthippie period of the early 1970s, then *Dirty Harry* was its mythic companion piece. Once again, an individualistic and blatantly bigoted police office stood against the forces of darkness, throwing away the book and operating as a loose cannon. The film implied this was absolutely necessary if anything was to be done about a criminal situation spiraling out of control. But whereas Gene Hackman's unshaven New York street detective appeared to have stepped out of the evening news, Clint Eastwood's laconic, unruffled cop—who calmly walked to each confrontation as if he were the legendary Wyatt Earp heading for the O.K. Corral—clearly represented a modern myth in the making.

A perfect example of director Don Siegel's willingness to make the audience conscious of the fact that they were watching a movie occurs early on. Harry Callahan, wolfing down a hot dog in a shabby diner following a particularly grueling day's work, notices a robbery occurring across the street. Whereas Popeye Doyle would have rushed out wildly, Callahan calmly draws his .45 magnum, then marches down the street while still chewing his frankfurter. Cool-eyed, he casually fires at the fleeing robbers, sending their car into a tailspin. As he does, we note that a theater marquee behind him announces that *Play Misty for Me* is the current feature. Eastwood had starred in and directed that movie (making his behind-the-camera debut) less than a year earlier. Director Siegel appeared briefly in it as a bartender, apparently hanging around the set long enough to ensure that his protégé handled the directorial chores effectively. The theater marquee at once makes us aware of the ultimate artificiality of the film we are watching.

Which is precisely what happens in *Dirty Harry,* brilliantly designed to exploit the hunger of the American public in general, and moviegoers in particular, for a mythic hero, the kind of character John Wayne had played for decades. In *Dirty Harry,* Eastwood made the jump to full-fledged superstar by taking on Wayne's longtime mantle as the singular-minded tough guy who attempts to work within the system but must finally move beyond such group activities to get the job done. In this case, the villain is not the suave international drug trafficker Popeye took on in New York, but a different kind of menace: the deranged serial killer, a baby-faced criminal who looks like the boy next door but subjects the city to a rampage of random murder and clever extortion.

Significantly, *Dirty Harry* was set in San Francisco, the city in which the peace-and-love movement had started. A popular song, which in the late sixties spread word via commercial radio stations of the coming counterculture, insisted:

> If you're going to San Francisco,
> be sure to wear some flowers in your hair...
> You're bound to meet some gentle people there.

In the opening sequence of *Dirty Harry,* we meet a

The post–1970 problem of ever-escalating urban violence is essential to the impact of such contemporary crime films as *Dirty Harry* (courtesy Warner Bros.).

> Being this is a .45 magnum—the most powerful handgun in the world—you've got to ask yourself one question: Do I feel lucky?

The robber does not reach for the gun, and Harry does not shoot him. This is a movie about rugged individualism: the robber makes his choice and, choosing not to grab for his gun, is spared. Important, too, is that in the next scene, Harry is attended in the hospital by a bright young doctor, who also happens to be black. Harry speaks as respectfully to this (black) man as he did coldly and authoritatively to the earlier (black) robber; he is, simply, color-blind, judging every person he meets as an individual.

Or, as Harry's only friend on the force, DeGeorgio (John Mitchum), says, "Harry hates everybody the same." When a young Hispanic (Reni Santoni) is assigned as his new partner, Harry is outraged. But Harry could care less about the youth's ethnicity. He doesn't want a green kid getting killed, which can easily happen to anyone who partners with him. At the very end of the film, Harry will repeat his diner/robbery line about the magnum to the killer, then blow him away, but only after the killer—having been given his choice—reaches for his gun.

Siegel and Eastwood did not intend the virtual exe-

character who at first appears to be one of the "gentle people" that song spoke of. A long-haired young man, wearing a huge peace symbol for a belt buckle, stands atop a San Francisco building, spying on a beautiful young woman across the way as she swims in a pool. He has murder, not love, in mind. The killer (Andy Robinson) seizes a high-powered rifle and shoots the woman, whose beautiful body then floats in the pool like a wilted flower. Calling himself Scorpio (a thinly disguised reference to the real-life Zodiac Killer), the killer then insists that the city pay him $100,000 or he will kill again.

In 1971, that was interpreted by liberal members of the press as a direct attack on hippies. Though no one could deny the artistry of Siegel's action-oriented filmmaking, many were offended by the substance. Pauline Kael had just then referred to Sam Peckinpah's *Straw Dogs* (in which Dustin Hoffman, as a mild-mannered intellectual, seizes a gun and wipes out a gang attacking his home, afterward realizing he enjoyed the experience immensely) as a "fascist masterpiece"; that phrase expressed how many perceived *Dirty Harry*.

For instance, in that robbery sequence, Harry holds his pistol to the head of a black man, who considers reaching for a gun, and speaks his now-famous line:

More than just an expertly mounted cop film, *Dirty Harry* was perceived by many viewers as a political statement, with the ultimate symbol of right-wing Establishment sentiments taking whatever steps necessary to eliminate a youthful long-hair wearing a peace medallion (courtesy Warner Brothers).

Don Siegel directed the spectacular action sequence with which *Dirty Harry* opens. The movie marquee, featuring Eastwood's previous screen outing, deconstructs the experience of watching by clueing the audience that this movie addresses the very idea of movies, and what they mean to us (courtesy Warner Bros.).

Harry and his new partner, Chico Gonzalas (Reni Santoni), lie in wait for the killer. Though Harry's language is politically incorrect, he nonethelesss harbors no prejudice against minorities, judging each man as an individual in the old John Wayne tradition (courtesy Warner Bros.).

cution of a long-haired young man wearing a peace medallion as their statement that everyone in the country ought to grab guns and shoot hippies, in the manner that Peter Boyle had done in 1970's *Joe.* What they were suggesting was that appearances can be deceiving, that unpleasant people can hide behind the mantle of a hippie-ish appearance, and that any sort of *Greening of America* attitude suggesting all people of any one particular "look" were truly gentle was ridiculous. The signs and symbols of the hippie movement had been coopted, even by criminals; back in 1967, the wearing of a peace medallion or long hair might actually have meant something, suggesting that the person in question devoutly believed in a set of values. By the early 1970s, people had affected such symbols and styles as mere fashion, without the once-potent meaning.

The concept of a sniper had another type of impact: the notion of random violence, crazies who shoot at innocent people for no specific reason. The ever-escalating climate of violence began back in the sixties, perhaps with the assassination of Jack Kennedy. *Dirty Harry* was the first film to frighten Americans with a vivid cinematic portrait of the way things were, while also providing a mythic-level hero who appeared to offer the only answer to a growing problem. Many people who only a few years before had decried police violence directed at antiwar demonstrators now began to acknowledge a need for vigilantism if it was focused on the emerging breed of street criminals that had come into being during the early seventies.

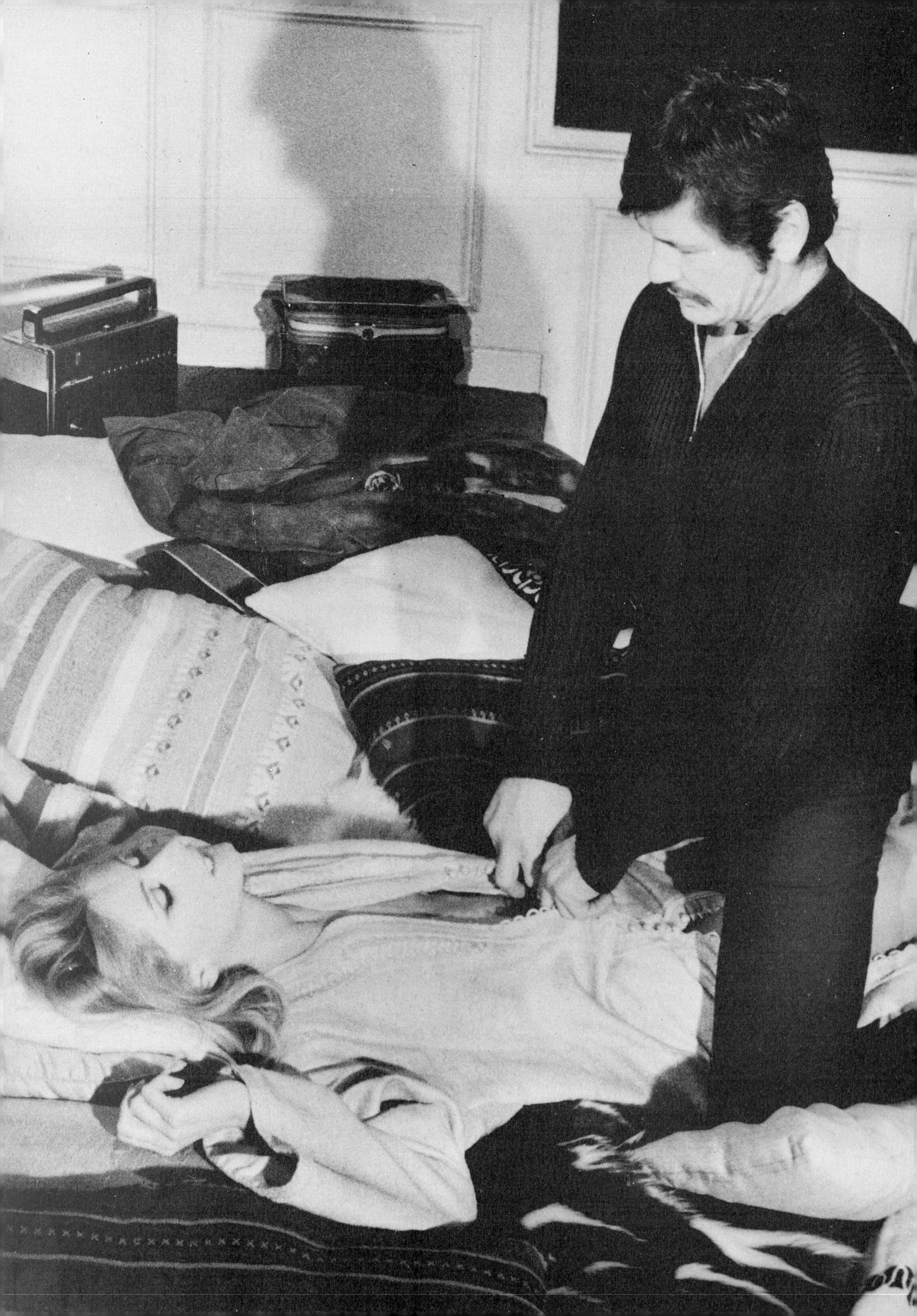

SIX

The Family (aka *Violent City, The Final Shot*)

(1972)

A Universal Release

CAST:

Charles Bronson *(Jeff)*; Jill Ireland *(Vanessa)*; Telly Savalas *(Weber)*; Umberto Orsini *(Steve)*; Michel Constantin *(Killain)*; Ray Sanders *(Prisoner)*; Benjamin Lev *(Young Prisoner)*; George Savalas *(Mobster)*.

CREDITS:

Producers, Giorgio Papi and Arrigo Colombo; director, Sergio Sollima; screenplay; Sauro Scavolini, Gianfranco Calligarish, Lina Wertmuller, and Sergio Sollima; camera, Aldo Tonti; editor, Nino Baragli; music, Ennio Morricone; art director, Francesco Bronzi; running time, 109 minutes.

The Family was one of those international coproduction B-budget junk movies that flourished during the early 1970s, establishing Charles Bronson as a major box-office star. In fact, though, much of this European-financed film was shot in Louisiana. The script had originally been called *Violent City* (the film was released in Italy under that title) but was changed for the American release in a calculated attempt to lure in audiences hoping to see another *Godfather*-like crime saga about a "family" that works for "The Family." However, this is a "family" film in another sense of the term: of all the movies starring Bronson and his wife, Jill Ireland, *The Family* seems the most personal for this pair of movieland gypsies who traveled the world with their attendant entourage and numerous children, making third-rate films whenever someone would put up the money.

It's worth recalling that Bronson met Ireland while shooting 1963's *The Great Escape*. She was then married to his costar, British actor David McCallum (later of *Man from U.N.C.L.E.* TV fame). According to legend, Bronson took one look at the lady, turned to McCallum, and whispered, "Watch out—I'm going to steal her away from you." Bronson then proceeded to do precisely that. Though Ireland became his wife and constant companion until her death from cancer years later, there remained between them a fascinating tension, a sense that she was a mystery woman who had to be watched closely so she would not run off with someone else. *The Family* is about this very sort of relationship; replace moviemaking with organized crime, and you have a story that expresses just such emotions.

The retro-male vs. the woman of tomorrow. Throughout the film, Jeff seems to dominate Vanessa, yet we always have the impression that it is she who controls him (courtesy Universal Pictures/Target Associates).

In the film's opening sequence, Jeff (Bronson) is seen (without explanation) piloting a yacht; Vanessa (Ireland) is the bikini-clad beauty who stands at the helm, staring out at the sea enigmatically as this man—clearly enamored of her—watches in silent admiration. Shortly thereafter, they drive together somewhere in Europe as a menacing car pursues them. A long chase ensues, ending as Jeff drops Vanessa off to save her life. Jeff appears happy to see Coogan, a man he knows, seemingly arriving to help. Jeff is stunned when Coogan shoots him, leaving him for dead, then driving off with Vanessa, whose expression is ambiguous. She appears to be Coogan's willing companion, yet there's a hint that she feels sorrow and regret.

Jeff survives, however, showing up first in a hospital, then a prison. The movie finally features some dialogue, at which point we learn Jeff is a professional hit man who was contracted to kill Coogan's rich old uncle in the Virgin Islands. Vanessa was a glamorous model, and Coogan's mistress; she lured Jeff away to a beach vacation, setting him up so that Coogan could eliminate him now that the hit has been completed. Jeff, eventually released, travels to America where he tracks the cou-

Charles Bronson as Jeff: one more anachronistic Neanderthal, attempting to survive in the slick, superficial world of contemporary crime (courtesy Universal Pictures/Target Associates).

ple to New Orleans, with the help of his old friend and mentor Killain (Michel Constantin). There, he learns millionaire Coogan is a racing fanatic, driving sports cars for pleasure and profit. Jeff hides in the woods near a road and fires at one of Coogan's tires as he whizzes by during a competition, causing Coogan to crash and die.

Jeff than tracks Vanessa to a beautiful plantation where she serves as a southern-belle hostess, giving elegant parties to raise money for deprived children. She willingly slips away, though, joining Jeff in his car so that he can take this self-styled "classy" society matron to the dregs of New Orleans, the dirty docks, where he has rough sex with her repeatedly. He is her weak spot, the dark side of this double-life "lady" that cannot be denied no matter how beautifully she plays the role of the ultra-respectable matron. They are about to fly away together when Jeff receives photographs of himself "hitting" Coogan; someone knows and can blackmail him. He must stay and discover who it is.

He eventually learns the negatives are held by Weber (Telly Savalas), a ganglord who wants to blackmail Jeff into doing hits. Jeff has no option but to agree, despite the warnings that Steve (Umberto Orsini), a lawyer who works for the mob, constantly offers. Vanessa, meanwhile, lures Jeff away to a secluded home in the bayou country, where someone tries to kill them. After Jeff shoots the man, he realizes it is Killain, his old friend who swore that he would never work for the mob. Killain still has the blood money in his pocket.

Jeff finally realizes Vanessa is married to Weber, who has allowed her to slip off and have her little "adventures" whenever she wants. Vanessa betrayed Coogan for Weber, much as she betrayed Jeff for Coogan. She insists, though, that she really does love Jeff, and he desperately wants to believe this. Together, they sneak into Weber's home, recover the incriminating negatives, and burn them, allowing Jeff to get away from the mob once and for all. Then, after Vanessa (who is too "tasteful" to watch the ensuing violence) politely excuses herself, Jeff kills Weber, who dies with one last warning: Vanessa will betray Jeff once again.

In fact, that's precisely what she does. When Jeff arrives at the hotel where he was to meet Vanessa, the police are there instead. She has set him up in order to take over her former husband's crime empire, aided and abetted by Steve. Jeff manages to get away, though. And in the film's memorable finale, he has his revenge. As Vanessa and Steve—the ultimate upscale corporate couple, their dirty dealings swept under the carpet—ride up the side of their company's skyscraper in an outdoor elevator, Jeff, on the rooftop across the way, fires several well-placed shots, killing Steve slowly and painfully. Then, as Vanessa—totally helpless—continues her slow

Jeff and Vanessa in one of their many love/hate bouts. Adding to the film's sexual tension was the audience's knowledge that Bronson and Jill Ireland were a couple in real life (courtesy Universal Pictures/Target Associates).

The gangster as romantic hero: Jeff, who has casually wasted many men, cannot pull the trigger on the gorgeous Vanessa, though he knows she has betrayed him once more (courtesy Universal Pictures/Target Associates).

ride up toward the top floor where a corporate board meeting is about to begin, Jeff takes careful aim at the panicked woman and finally fires.

Vanessa, who has never been able to stand physical pain, desperately intones, "Don't make me suffer, Jeff." We cannot hear her words, since the entire sequence is played in stunning silence. Jeff, viewing her through the telescopic lens of his rifle, takes pity on her, killing her with a single shot to the head.

Obviously, this was not the type of film to be reviewed in places like *The New Yorker;* upscale magazines ignored it, while most daily newspapers dismissed *The Family* with a short, obligatory trashing, owing to the chintzy production values and excessive violence. However, "Werb." of *Variety* did see something here, so far as gangster movies were concerned, noting the film's effective "pitting [of] a hired gun against the modern crime machine," characterizing Jeff as "a solitary killer from another age and fabricating organized crime with such potency that the biggest skyscraper in New Orleans symbolically becomes the possession of the mob." *The Family* is effective in large part because it assumes that all business—including seemingly "respectable" everyday white-collar business—is controlled by organized crime.

Weber is as much an anachronism as is Jeff. "I miss the old days," he sighs at one point, noting a bank. "The first time I ever went in there, I had an automatic [pistol]. Now, I own it." Both are men of the past, recalling an earlier age of rugged individualism in crime, their confrontation working well since Bronson and Savalas were among the few contemporary actors who could suggest the proper world-weariness. *The Family* is, by implication, about the way in which their anachronistic vulgarity takes on a strange nobility as it gives way to the new white-collar criminal class: the elegantly attired lady and the yuppie lawyer.

The impact of screenwriter Lina Wertmuller (who would shortly achieve fame as the writer-director of *Swept Away* and *Seven Beauties*) in helping to create the character of Vanessa cannot be underrated. Vanessa remains a postfeminist enigma throughout, partly a throwback to the double-dealing femmes fatales—Lizabeth Scott, Veronica Lake—of the film noir era, partly the modern career woman assuming her rightful place in a business world that just happens to be mob owned. Is she coldly betraying Jeff, along with everyone else, lying when she insists he's the only man she ever really loved? Or is there a certain truth to that state-

Telly Savalas as Weber. Though Jeff's mortal enemy, Weber is, like the film's antihero, one more example of the old-time gangster, completely out of place in the international corporate structure of modern crime (courtesy Universal Pictures/Target Associates).

Jeff in action; throughout the film, director Sergio Sollima framed Charles Bronson so as to suggest the character's sense of emotional as well as physical entrapment (courtesy Universal Pictures/Target Associates).

ment, making her vulnerable to him and him alone? Does she herself even know for sure how she feels?

The intense bouts of sex and violence between them suggest a Wertmulleresque sadomasochistic relationship that frightens and satisfies each of them. There is a sense of resignation at the end, when Vanessa responds to Jeff's bullets as she had previously responded to his sex. As Kevin Thomas wrote in the *Los Angeles Times*: "what holds the picture together and gives it its crackling tension is the relationship. Their passionate mutual attraction is utterly convincing and is heightened by the fact that both are thoroughly unpredictable. That he may kill her or she betray him at any moment clearly adds fuel to their fire and ignites the film as well.... *The Family* has a tight, logical structure and has been directed...with a great deal of style, an acute sense of pace, and above all, an extraordinary degree of expressiveness."

The contrast between Jeff and Weber is made clear by Weber's statement: "You can't go it alone anymore. You have to belong to an organization." Any nobility that Jeff has—despite his cold-blooded assassinations—derives from the fact that he ignores this, remaining a true individual at all costs and, as such, an anachronism. This, coupled with his appealingly romantic obsession for Vanessa, sets him apart in an age when, as Weber says, "the organization is changing...getting cleaner." It is a cleanliness where amoral yuppie gangsters feel right at home, though older tough guys are all but lost; it's a superficially clean and fundamentally corrupt world where elegant, empowered women bring postfeminist thinking to every heretofore male-dominated endeavor, including organized crime.

In one marvelous flashback scene, Vanessa is glimpsed in hippie dress of that era, her falsely innocent eyes suggesting a love/peace antimaterialism that is nothing but a guise, an outward show that hides rather than communicates her reality, a trendy performance from a woman whom we already know is consumed by a ruthless desire for power and money. Her flower-child costume—a style of dress that would all but disappear within a year or two of the film's release—is merely fashion. In the bayou country, she wears the retro-clothing of a belle, but in the urban center, she chameleonlike picks precisely the right outfit to impress. We witness her assumption of power (Vanessa, previously working for Steve, has reduced him to working for her, a combination lawyer-gigolo at her beck and call); she would ascend to full power were it not for the vengeance of the last "real" man, Jeff, who nihilistically ends Vanessa's reign. For he knows that, like the fated lovers of the Liebestod legend, they depend on one another for sustenance and sense the final fulfillment of their too-intense passion must be death.

SEVEN

Superfly
(1972)

A Warner Bros. Film

CAST:

Ron O'Neal *(Priest);* Carl Lee *(Eddie);* Sheila Frazier *(Georgia);* Julius W. Harris *(Scatter);* Charles MacGregor *(Fat Freddie);* Nate Adams *(Dealer);* Polly Niles *(Cynthia);* "K.C." *(Pimp);* Mike Richards *(Deputy Commissioner);* The Curtis Mayfield Experience *(Musical Group).*

CREDITS:

Producer, Sig Shore; director, Gordon Parks Jr.; screenplay, Philip Feny; cinematography, James Signorelli; editor, Bob Brady; music, Curtis Mayfield; running time, 97 minutes (initial theatrical release), 93 minutes (video version); rating, R.

In the early 1930s, Warner Bros. made a remarkable leap from minor-league film company to a major supplier of commercial motion pictures, thanks to their savvy understanding that in the emerging era of sound, audiences wanted streetwise films that rang with authentic dialogue of the common people. Their most popular items were the gangster epics, which, however inadvertently, glorified the then-contemporary tough guys enacted by Cagney, Bogart, and Robinson, if only because the fact-based characters were played by the most charismatic stars available. Such films proved highly successful at the newly built moving-picture palaces that dominated the downtown of practically every American city during the Great Depression. But by the early 1970s, the inner cities were decaying, as middle-class residents fled to suburbs. The theaters, swiftly reduced to a shabby semblance of their onetime splendor, now instead attracted an ethnic audience. Warner Bros. responded by turning out a new kind of crime film featuring rough language, graphic sex, and intense violence, resulting in films that were, at least on the surface, a far cry from the studio's work in the thirties.

In fact, the essence remained essentially unchanged. Like their half-forgotten predecessors from Hollywood's golden age, the "black exploitation flicks" offered a fascinating combination of street realism and cinematic romanticism in portraying urban criminals. The jive-talking drug dealers who crowded onto inner city streets and their corresponding images on movie screens were, like the bootleggers of some forty years earlier, rugged individualists who seized the capitalistic American dream and, through rough, illegal behavior, transformed it into a nightmare. The audience that flocked to such films responded in much the same manner that the earlier audience had to their own crime films, likewise turned out by Warner Bros. Once again, the gangster emerged as an antihero who takes what he wants while other, lesser men stand around and accept what little the system has to offer.

Other companies made black exploitation flicks, too, just as other companies had in the 1930s tried their hand at gangster films. But in the present as in the past, Warner Bros. turned out the most searingly vivid and, oftentimes, the most controversial. Certainly, no urban crime drama ever created quite as huge a stir as *Superfly,* the debut film of Gordon Parks Jr. His father was a highly respected director best known for a sensitive African-American coming-of-age film, *The Learning Tree,* and an action-adventure flick featuring a black hero, *Shaft. Superfly,* however, glorified not the Shaft-like hero, out to catch the drug dealers, but one of those very dealers, the "public enemy" or "Little Caesar" of his day.

Ron O'Neal plays Priest, a Harlem drug dealer who sports a flashy car, a white mistress, and all the cocaine he can snort. True to his name, at least ironically, Priest employs the cross he wears around his neck to lift the white powder up to his nose and insert it, which he does with regularity. Sometimes he snorts alone, occasionally with Georgia (Sheila Frazer), the black woman he loves. Though a relatively young man, Priest

Ron O'Neal as Priest, the first authentic screen portrait of the new inner-city gangster who had come to power during the early 1970s via drug dealing (courtesy Paramount Pictures).

is already old beyond his years and wants out of the drug trade. He's concocted a scheme whereby he and his partner, Eddie (Carl Lee), can take the $300,000 they've saved and use it to buy thirty kilos of pure coke, if only their old friend and onetime mentor Scatter (Julius W. Harris), now a respectable restaurateur, will get back into the business long enough to score them the drugs from his contacts. To make a cool million before retiring, they need the best they can buy, superior stuff that will have users flying high, the "superfly" of the title.

Various themes of the contemporary crime film are present here, beginning with the hero who wants to make one last run before going straight, only to realize that the underworld does not quietly allow its minions to wander away. Priest and Eddie refer to the fifty people currently dealing for them on the street (most notable among them Fat Freddie, played by Charles MacGregor) as their "family," the gang having become a substitute for the biological families that none of these young men appear to be part of, as well as an imitation of Mafia-style "families" that these African-American gangsters emulate.

Emulation, however, does not imply accommodation; Priest sends Fat Freddie and other cohorts into New Jersey to rob from the old mob, another recurring theme in modern crime dramas. The old gangsters have become a part of the very Establishment that, in the 1930s, they fought against. The movie also conveys a cynical sense of that Establishment as totally corrupt. The white policemen assigned to stop drug trafficking in Harlem in fact run it, planning to kill Scatter for attempting to go straight, then reconcile with Priest by allowing him to take Scatter's place.

The film projects cynicism not only toward such whites, but also the supposedly more "idealistic" element of the black inner-city community. At the end, Priest tricks all his enemies and walks away scot-free, without paying for his past crimes. Such a conclusion would not have been possible a few years earlier, when the old MPPA "code" was still in effect. Now, though, a new amoral cinema was accepted as a reaction to the different world out there; this was, recall, the era of *Taxi Driver.* Many newspaper editorials loudly denounced the film owing to its glorification of Priest. The audience is clearly meant to root for him, and though filmmaker Parks Jr. and writer Philip Feny may have intended to emphasize that Priest did indeed want to get out of the drug trade, ultimately finding it demeaning, most young black male moviegoers took the film in a different light entirely, coveting all that Priest possesses, wanting to emulate his early success.

Fat Freddie (Charles MacGregor) is interrogated by cops, who turn out to be far more vicious than the supposed criminals they pursue. The film was one of the first, and by far the best, of the era's "black exploitation flicks" (courtesy Paramount Pictures).

Sheila Frazier as Georgia, the good "sister" who wants Priest to leave crime behind and join her in trying to make a decent life somewhere else. Whereas Priest's white woman represents corruption, his black lady symbolizes possible salvation (courtesy Paramount Pictures).

In the *New York Times,* Roger Greenspun hailed the film as "a very good movie" and Vincent Canby concurred, calling it "the one recent black movie that has any original distinction as a film." *Superfly* benefited from the vivid score by Curtis Mayfield (who also appeared briefly as a club performer) and was directed with a gritty sense of style and authentic flavor that won Parks Jr. raves for his technical prowess, whatever people may have felt about the film's unsettling implications. When young Parks died suddenly in a plane crash, the general consensus was that a major talent, one that had never enjoyed the opportunity to mature and develop, had been lost. His behind-the-scenes presence was notably absent from the sequel: *Superfly T.N.T.,* directed by actor Ron O'Neal in 1973, truly was an exploitation flick in the worst sense of the term. Concerning Priest's involvement with an emissary from Africa, after the antihero grows bored with the good life in Europe, the film made no sense whatsoever, narratively or morally.

(Left) Like Fat Freddie, Priest is beaten by the white cops. Inner-city audiences left the theater in an angry mood, their abiding sense that the Establishment was out to get them having been intensified by the film (courtesy Paramount Pictures).

Black teenagers flocked to see the film for many reasons, one of them being the chance to get a look at Priest's custom-built Eldorado. Many adult African Americans bitterly complained that the movie, intended to honestly show the life of a pusher, unintentionally glorified it for the targeted inner-city kids who envied Priest's possessions (courtesy Paramount Pictures).

EIGHT

The Getaway

(1972)

A First Artists Film/National General Release

CAST:

Steve McQueen *(Doc McCoy);* Ali MacGraw *(Carol McCoy);* Ben Johnson *(Jack Benyen);* Sally Struthers *(Fran Clinton);* Al Lettieri *(Rudy Butler);* Slim Pickens *(Cowboy);* Richard Bright *(Grifter);* Jack Dodson *(Harold Clinton);* Dub Taylor *(Laughlin);* Bo Hopkins *(Frank Jackson);* Roy Jenson *(Cully);* Dick Crockett *(Bank Guard).*

CREDITS:

Producers, David Foster and Mitchell Brower; director, Sam Peckinpah; screenplay, Walter Hill, from the novel by Jim Thompson; cinematography, Lucien Ballard; editor, Robert Wolfe; music, Quincy Jones; art direction, Ted Haworth and Angelo Graham; running time, 122 minutes; rating, PG.

On its release as a holiday entry during the 1972 Christmas season, the film was written off as a star vehicle for Steve McQueen and Ali MacGraw. They were then the hottest offscreen couple in Hollywood, their respective marriages having broken up during the shooting, their affair reverberating in tabloid headlines. Critics scoffed that what passed between the two in real life was far more interesting that anything that showed up on-screen. "They don't even look right together," Pauline Kael complained; "her head is bigger than his." In fact, the public did not turn out for the film; though not an absolute failure, *The Getaway* enjoyed only mild business.

For its controversial director, the film seemed an uncharacteristically commercial venture, less artistic than his previous work: less lyrical than *Ride the High Country* or *The Ballad of Cable Hogue,* less elegiac than *The Wild Bunch,* less complicated than *Straw Dogs,* less intriguing than such later semicoherent ventures as *Bring Me the Head of Alfredo Garcia.* But this is a film that lingers in the memory; in retrospect, *The Getaway* stands as one of the finest modern gangster films. To enjoy the movie, one must accept the film's flaw, which is the grating Ms. MacGraw; one can only imagine how marvelous either of McQueen's *Cincinnati Kid* costars, Ann-Margret and Tuesday Weld, might have been in the part of Carol McCoy.

That said, everything else about the film works like clockwork. Sam Peckinpah and screenwriter Walter Hill (shortly to direct such films as *The Driver* himself, eventually writing and directing the 1994 *Getaway* remake) combined two previously divergent subgenres of the crime film. In its first half, *The Getaway* is *The Asphalt Jungle* modernized and given a southwestern twang, as a group of sleazy crooks plot a robbery that can't miss but manages to go disastrously wrong; in the second, it transforms into a rural Romeo and Juliet on the run.

The film opens in prison, where Doc (McQueen) leaves the machinery he slaves away at to appear before the parole board. But as he faces the stern-faced judges—with a leering old cowboy named Jack Benyen (Ben Johnson) gazing on knowingly—he hears his request denied, then wanders back to his cell where he gazes at photos of his beautiful wife. When Carol (Ali MacGraw) visits him, Doc simply, desperately instructs her, "Get to Benyen...tell him I'm for sale...his price." By implication, we gather that successful San Antonio businessman Benyen plans to mastermind a bank robbery and needs Doc for the job. Benyen's "respectable" image allows him enough clout to get Doc paroled in order to commit crimes again, the film cynically insisting on that key theme of modern gangster films, the interweaving of the respectable and the criminal.

Carol dutifully does as she's told; we next see her in Benyen's private office, where—before discussing the deal—he lustfully encourages her, "Come on over!" As Carol approaches Benyen, Peckinpah effectively cuts away; we do not know what Carol actually does to secure her husband's release, and perhaps we don't want to know. If this is tough on us, it's worse on Doc. Exiting

Carol and Doc attempt the getaway of the title. The emotional distance between them is visually suggested by the physical distance at which filmmaker Peckinpah sets them (courtesy First Artists/ National General).

prison, he waits for Carol to pick him up; she smiles as she pulls alongside him and is perceptive enough to notice he doesn't smile back. Why not? She's done just what he told her to do, secured his release at any price—apparently, at the price of turning herself into a whore.

But as the couple strolls through a park—peopled by happy families and, this being a film of the early 1970s, groups of hippies—Doc watches as little boys swing on ropes over the water and drop in. We then see Doc's mental images of himself and Carol doing much the same thing, at some time in the past. The photography is so lyric and lovely (contrasting with the film's otherwise starker images) that we can't believe it was ever really this good. We are not seeing flashbacks to real incidents, rather Doc's mental re-creation of those events, impossibly perfect images of the past as it should have been rather than as it was. What Doc wants to reclaim is not what he and Carol once had, but the impossible ideal he has mentally created.

Doc is, like so many of his modern gangster-film cohorts, a romantic, made clear by what happens next: he takes Carol's hand and leads her to the water. Again, Peckinpah does not show us what happens, cutting instead to the event that follows, as Doc (looking less than satisfied) and Carol enter their home, wringing wet. Doc has tried to live out the dream and has been disappointed; reality never lives up to one's dream. Doc and Carol sit on the bed, but it's clear he is momentarily unable to make love; Doc broods over something that's eating away at him. Eventually they do have sex. Doc seems relieved and adjusted the morning after.

Benyen (Ben Johnson) bites the dust. Benyen is one more key example of the modern gangster as a supposedly "respectable" citizen who runs the Establishment (courtesy First Artists/National General).

DOC: Thank you for getting me out.
CAROL: It was a pleasure.

Carol doesn't realize she's just said the wrong thing. It was a pleasure doing something for him because she loves him so much? Or was it a pleasure dealing with Benyen? Doc isn't sure; shortly, he meets Benyen at the Riverwalk, then takes a boat ride on a floating restaurant as Benyen spells out the heist Doc is expected to arrange. As they talk, the boat slips under a bridge and into total darkness, neatly suggesting the moral darkness Doc is about to enter.

Doc is then introduced to hardened-criminal Rudy (Al Lettieri) and baby-faced Jack (Bo Hopkins), who will work with him. They plan the intricate robbery, which involves various explosions and perfect timing, but when they attempt to realize that plan, everything goes wrong. Jack kills a bank guard, and during the getaway, Rudy kills Jack for having bungled it. Though the crooks do have the money, they fight among themselves, Doc shooting (and believing he's killed) Rudy (who is very much alive), then heading for the Benyen ranch. As he and Carol drive, the unpleasant look returns to Doc's face.

DOC: Tell me about Benyen's ranch.

CAROL: I've never been there.

He doesn't appear to believe her; she impulsively suggests they take all the money and run for the border. Doc considers her carefully, insisting that a deal is a deal; Benyen would have his men follow them if they lit out, so he drives to the ranch, where he leaves Carol in the car and finds Benyen alone, waiting. Doc offers to split the money, as planned, despite the botched job.

BENYEN: You still don't get the picture, do you?

Doc realizes Carol has followed him inside; turning, he sees that she holds a gun, pointed at him. Then, she begins to visibly shake; Carol aims the gun back and forth, from Doc to Benyen, suddenly—as if surprising herself—shooting and killing Benyen. Doc pulls out his pistol, and for a moment he and Carol aim at each other. Again, Peckinpah effectively pulls the rug out from under us, not showing what happens next; we see the two speeding away, Doc driving like crazy, Carol barely suppressing screams.

Finally, he pulls over to the side of the road and they get out, then stand silently for a while. He slaps her.

DOC: Why didn't you tell me?
CAROL: There wasn't any way to explain it...you sent me to him, you know....What the hell do you want, anyway?

What Doc wants—and what he can't have—is for Carol to be his romanticized dream girl. What Carol wants is for him to accept her for what she is. She is the female realist, he the male romantic. What stands between them is their diametrically opposed ways of looking at life.

Doc and Carol head for the border, Benyen's henchmen attempting to head them off. There's also Rudy to contend with. He has, in his company, the veterinarian he forced to fix his wounds, as well as the man's wife (Sally Struthers), a seemingly respectable woman who becomes erotically excited at the first sight of Rudy's large gun. Fran will help tie up her husband and make love to her abductor in front of the helpless man, offering a striking foil for Carol.

For if Fran betrays her husband (a certified "doc") for a gangster, Carol—who apparently (offscreen) agreed to do just that—proves unable to. When Doc leaves her alone at a train station to pursue a grifter who made off with the money, Doc is gone for hours; when he returns, Carol is there, waiting. They embrace, and Carol momentarily believes the worst is behind them. But the conversation he initiates proves it's just beginning.

DOC: If you're trying to get me back in prison, you're going about it right.
CAROL: Well, I can always get you out—I can screw every prison official in the state.
DOC: It's a big state.
CAROL: I can handle it.
DOC: I bet you can.
CAROL: You'd do it for me...wouldn't you, Doc?

The modern gangster as abusive male: Sam Peckinpah's film, which psychologically expands on Walter Hill's skeletal action-flick script, vividly dramatizes the basis for domestic violence, the male's frustration that a woman can never live up to his mental ideal of what she ought to be (courtesy First Artists/National General).

A tale of two relationships: Doc finally considers the money, and its ultimate lack of value, as he tenderly cradles Carol...

Tossing his fears in his face, Carol means what she says. As far as she's concerned, Carol has made a sacrifice for Doc that she'd like to believe he would make for her. But he can't believe the girl of his dreams is tarnished, even at his request. So he suggests they split up at the border, though she doesn't want to. Later, as they drive, we see beautifully tended fields outside the car window just behind Doc, as he continues spewing forth his obsessive anger. Now, Carol turns, insisting that if he doesn't stop, there will be nothing left for them, even if they do make it. Doc finally shuts up and listens; as he does, the landscape glimpsed behind him suddenly changes to ugly, unattended scrub oak. What we see is not so much a window on his world as a mirror of his mind.

In sharp contrast to Carol, Fran (Sally Struthers), the supposedly respectable wife of a veterinarian (Jack Dodson, *far right*) slips into a torrid affair with the gangster (Al Lettieri) who kidnaps them (courtesy First Artists/National General).

There are several gory shoot-outs and high-tech chases, including one in which Doc employs a shotgun to fight their way past encroaching policemen. Always, in the grand old Peckinpah manner, children gaze on, fascinated by the guns and killing. Doc and Carol escape in cars and even, at one point, on a passing bus. To escape their pursuers, Doc and Carol hide in a garbage bin and are picked up by a truck, then dropped at the local dump. This is one of those flamboyantly shot and edited sequences for which Peckinpah is famous. Beyond the technical virtuosity, the sequence works on the level of metaphor: owing to Doc's insensitivity, they have reach the point where they are no better than garbage. On some level sensing this, he listens to her for the first time.

CAROL: I chose *you*, not him [Benyen].

Doc has been torturing Carol because he has been unable to deal with the thought that she even considered betraying him. What he has not been dealing with is that, when push came to shove, she couldn't do it, on instinct acting to protect them as a couple. He has been punishing her for not being the perfect person he wanted her to be, while she has been trying to make him see that she, however imperfect, will always stand by him when the chips are down.

Carol does just that when they are ambushed at a border hotel. Grabbing a gun, she proves herself a total equal as well as a supportive wife, fighting alongside Doc as Benyen's henchmen close in. Peckinpah's perfect touch: Fran is there, screaming hysterically, solidifying the contrast to Carol. The final time we see Doc and Carol making love, they are covered with all the money, as good rural gangsters ought to be. The very last time we see them, they are hiking over into Mexico, this being one of the rare Romeo-and-Juliet crime tales to feature a happy ending. That's something more than mere commercialism: it is Peckinpah's vision of a couple who, despite all the barriers and blockades, have managed to make a modern relationship work. None of this substance exists in Hill's script, or in his disappointing 1994 remake, which features only the barest of plots, tying together action sequences. Peckinpah's *The Getaway* proves his merits as an auteur, as he improvises from the skeletal screenplay, creating a flesh-and-blood work of art.

(Opposite) Steve McQueen as Doc: A man of the mind who will shortly rush into violent action.

NINE

Walking Tall

(1973)

A Cinerama Release

CAST:

Joe Don Baker *(Buford Pusser);* Elizabeth Hartman *(Pauline);* Gene Evans *(Sheriff Al Thurman);* Noah Beery Jr. *(Grandpa);* Lurene Tutell *(Grandma);* Brenda Benet *(Luan Paxton);* Rosemary Murphy *(Callie);* John Brascia *(Prentiss);* Bruce Glover *(Grady Coker);* Arch Johnson *(Buell);* Felton Perry *(Obra Eaker);* Douglas Fowley *(Judge).*

CREDITS:

Producer and screenwriter, Mort Briskin; director, Phil Karlson; cinematography, Jack A. Marta; editor, Harry Gerstad; music, Walter Scharf; running time, 125 minutes; rating, R.

The twin successes of the ultrarealistic *French Connection* and mythic-fantasy *Dirty Harry* together proved that urban audiences had been surfeited with escalating crime. They were ready to embrace as a contemporary hero any rugged individualist, however legally questionable his methods might be, who had the gumption to stand up for old-fashioned decency. But there was rural America to be dealt with, too, since the crime rate was likewise mushrooming in once sacrosanct small towns of the deep South and sprawling Midwest. However much the residents of such places might admire Clint Eastwood's big-city cop, they needed a grassroots version all their own. Producer-writer Mort Briskin discovered just such a character one evening when he turned on CBS and heard newsmen singing the praises of one Buford Pusser, comparing the Tennessee sheriff to legendary lawman Wyatt Earp.

Pusser might have enjoyed a Warholian fifteen minutes of fame via his segment on *60 Minutes* except that Briskin smelled the possibility for Hollywood exploitation and developed a film script. The option was picked up by Bing Crosby Productions, at which point Phil Karlson signed to direct a film on location in rural Tennessee, with Pusser himself serving as adviser. A veteran director of high-quality B-budget crime films from the 1950s, Karlson had helmed such minor classics as *The Brothers Rico* and *The Phenix City Story,* the latter a Kefauver-crime-committee-inspired portrait of a medium-size city that stands up to intruding mob elements.

In its time, *The Phenix City Story* had been hailed as a liberal treatise, celebrating the democratic bonding of common people as they strike out against corruption. Not so *Walking Tall,* generally dismissed by big-city critics as being (in the words of the *Village Voice*'s Andrew Sarris) "a fundamentalist fantasy of good and evil," good being the simple, conservative Pusser, who stands alone against evil elements when the townspeople prove too craven to help him. As played by relative newcomer Joe Don Baker (whose only previous film role was as a gangster in Don Siegel's *Charley Varrick*), Pusser appeared to be a new generation's John Wayne, actually living out Teddy Roosevelt's famous dictum about speaking softly and carrying a big stick. Holding his thick hickory club with both hands, Pusser broke into roadhouses (warrants be damned) where moonshine liquor and prostitution were available, smashing the places up with the enthusiasm of Carry Nation. Still, the film was more complex, politically speaking, than many believed.

At the end, when Pusser's wife (Elizabeth Hartman) has been killed by powerful corrupt forces who oppose his cleanup campaign, the sheriff pays his last respects at the cemetery, then drives his car into the roadhouse owned by a blowsy madam (Rosemary Murphy) where local gangsters hide out. In the film, the now embarrassed townspeople—at last realizing the folly of their "don't get involved" approach—follow him to the site

Joe Don Baker as Buford Pusser, the real-life countrified equivalent of Clint Eastwood's fictitious Dirty Harry (courtesy Cinerama Releasing).

A rare tranquil moment: Whereas the backwoods violence had already made *Walking Tall* a huge hit in rural areas of the country, the rare quiet moments involving Pusser and his wife, Pauline (Elizabeth Hartman), were emphasized in advertising and promotion for the eventual New York release (courtesy Cinerama Releasing).

and help destroy the property, vigilante style. The movie, in the tradition of John Ford's *My Darling Clementine* and Howard Hawks's *Rio Bravo,* opts for an all-encompassing balance between those extreme poles of American politics, Republican rugged individualism and the Democratic collective ideal: the singular hero, able to stand on his own for only so long, must eventually be reinforced by the group.

Critic Martin Mitchell spoke for many of New York's Upper West Siders when he admonished the film thusly: "*Walking Tall* goes beyond the usual pandering to audience bloodlust by attempting to justify violence with a dangerous dictum dressed up from frontier days." Indeed, in the film Pusser informs his little boy that "there's nothing wrong with a gun in the hands of the right person," a virtual echo of a line spoken by Alan Ladd to Brandon de Wilde in the 1952 western classic *Shane:* "A gun is merely a tool, Joey, no better or worse than the man using it." But such critical brickbats had little effect on the film's box office. Whereas most movies open in Manhattan and then, after the reviews are in, "go wide," *Walking Tall* did not play New York City until 1974, a full year after doing record-breaking business in the Bible Belt. Residents of Staten Island had seen and applauded the film long before city dwellers did, *Walking Tall* having already earned a then-lofty $35 million before big-city reviews even broke.

A civil rights hero as well as an anticrime activist, Pusser was the first sheriff in his area to appoint an African American (Felton Perry) as chief deputy. His critics carped that this was merely a political ploy to win the black vote (courtesy Cinerama Releasing).

Which helps explain why Vincent Canby began his belated *New York Times* review with the disclaimer that *Walking Tall* arrived "as much a phenomenon to be analyzed as a film to be review-ed." Likewise, Sarris was impressed enough to admit that "*Walking Tall* is saying something very important to many people, and it is saying it with accomplished artistry." Karlson's film was saying precisely what *Dirty Harry* had broken box-office records by saying: crime had been allowed to run out of control owing to legal restrictions that, however decently intended, were now being used by

Sheriff Buford Pusser in action; the film's anti-gambling, anti-prostitution message, while none too subtle, tapped a nerve in the American public during the early 1970s (courtesy Cinerama Releasing).

society's worst element to protect their sleazy operations. Something had to be done about it, and an ever-growing portion of the public was not offended by the concept of a strong retro-man shoving aside the rule book, then whacking the daylights out of every criminal in sight.

That may sound like incipient fascism, yet it's worth nothing that Pusser (in real life and in the film) displays other attitudes toward civil rights that, at least according to a 1950s definition of the term, could only be called liberal. He won the election for sheriff in McNairy County only because he had the full support of the black community, which regarded him as much their hero as did the decent white farm folks. Pusser's number one deputy was a black man: the new sheriff quickly proved himself to be color-blind by being the first elected official to appoint a black man (Felton Perry in the film) to that post based strictly on merit. The previous sheriff, who had allowed white crime to run rampant (was, in fact, part of the criminal establishment), had regularly misused his position to torment law-abiding blacks.

Like so many other contemporary crime films, *Walking Tall* emphasized the intrusion of organized crime into supposedly respectable middle-class institutions. In addition to the former sheriff (Gene Evans, veteran of so many classic Samuel Fuller B pictures in the 1950s), the corrupt officials include a dishonest judge (Douglas Fowley, another fine character actor from that era, perhaps best remembered as Doc Holliday on TV's *Wyatt Earp*). Indeed, with the inclusion of Noah Beery Jr. as Pusser's father, it seems fair to say that director Phil Karlson was lured out of retirement by the chance to make a movie in the 1970s that served as a virtual homage to films he and others made during the fifties. The interesting element is that what had generally been accepted as upstanding social melodrama at that time (the plot of *Walking Tall* is essentially a modernization of *High Noon*) was now attacked, at least by those critics already moving toward what would later come to be called political correctness, as catering to the rednecks, urban or rural.

Like President Johnson, Pusser liked to show off his scars. Here, he makes clear in court that he's been the victim of violence by the Southland's criminal element (courtesy Cinerama Releasing).

MEAN
STREETS

TEN

Mean Streets

(1973)

A Warner Bros. Release

CAST:

Harvey Keitel *(Charlie)*; Amy Robinson *(Theresa)*; Robert De Niro *(Johnny Boy)*; David Proval *(Tony)*; Richard Romanus *(Michael)*; Cesare Danova *(Giovanni)*; Victor Argo *(Mario)*; George Memmoli *(Joey)*; David Carradine *(Drunk)*; Robert Carradine *(Assassin)*; Jeannie Bell *(The Stripper)*.

CREDITS:

Producer, Jonathan T. Taplin; director, Martin Scorsese; screenplay, Scorsese and Mardik Martin; cinematography, Kent Wakeford; editor, Sid Levin; running time, 112 minutes; rating, R.

If Arthur Penn reinvented the rural Romeo-and-Juliet crime drama with 1967's *Bonnie and Clyde,* then Martin Scorsese likewise revised the rules for the urban youth-crime drama with *Mean Streets.* Scorsese demonstrated that old formulas could effectively be adapted to the new rules of post-ratings-system Hollywood, with its tolerance for rough language, graphic sex, and vivid violence. While those lurid possibilities were being exploited by hack filmmakers, the then thirty-year-old editor *(Woodstock)* turned auteur proved that in the hands of an emerging master, such stuff could be transformed into garish, gritty art. Scorsese had already made a serious-minded experimental/independent film, *Who's That Knocking at My Door?* as well as florid Cormanesque drive-in fare, *Boxcar Bertha,* the latter one of many Bonnie-and-Clyde rip-offs. Thus *Mean Streets* was, officially speaking, his third film as director. Yet it had the immediate impact of a first film in terms of confronting the audience with an emerging vision: a singular style perfectly suited to the substance that the artist had chosen or, more correctly, had chosen him.

Scorsese's filmmaking approach would alter not only the shape and content of the crime genre, but of the American motion picture during the final quarter of the twentieth century. Set in New York's Little Italy and derived from his boyhood experiences, *Mean Streets* established an American equivalent to Federico's Fellini's 1953 memory movie of his youth in prewar Italy, *I Vitelloni.* Scorsese created an anecdotal ensemble piece about four men and a woman coming of age during the early sixties, in some cases adapting to and in others reacting against a self-contained world in which organized crime stood as the hard center of everyone's existence.

Martin Scorsese's breakthrough film changed not only the shape of the crime movie, but the entire Hollywood system as it entered a new era. Here, the quintet of young actors take a casually nihilistic attitude to a dead body they discover (courtesy Warner Bros.).

Scorsese revolutionized movie music, employing popular songs of the period not for obvious sentimental reasons (the case with George Lucas's much loved but overrated *American Graffiti* of the same year) but for more complex purposes. As Pauline Kael noted in her *New Yorker* review, "the score is the background music of the characters' lives—and not only the background, because it enters in. It's as if these characters were just naturally part of an opera with pop themes. The music is the electricity in the air of this movie; the music is like an engine that the characters move to.... The music here isn't our music, meant to put us in the mood of the movie, but the characters' music...the music is [an] active participant."

Scorsese later admitted that every time he ever heard a song playing on the radio or jukebox, it would lock into his mind, stored away for the purposes of future filmmaking. Eventually, he would place it in a film at precisely the proper emotional point. This elevated *Mean Streets* above the level of self-indulgence or instant nostalgia. Important, too, was Scorsese's understanding of the revisionist approach so necessary to make gangster sto-

Heir to the throne: In a gangland hangout, the most popular 'godfather' in Little Italy introduces his favorite newphew to the position of power he will someday wield if only the youth does not screw up (courtesy Warner Brothers).

ries accessible for contemporary audiences. Though the film was seemingly brimming with street realism, Scorsese actually shot most of his movie (particularly the interiors) on a soundstage in Hollywood. This allowed for a slightly stylized quality that does not draw attention to itself, but heightens all the on-screen action with an aura of edginess. We see varied past events not as they actually occurred, but as they are recalled later, perhaps during a dream—a nightmare, even—about those events, when the ordinary, everyday occurrences that dominate every person's life are forgotten even as the high and low points come crashing back to consciousness. The lighting, especially in the seedy nightclub owned by one of the boys, is awash in garish shades of red, suggesting this all takes place in some private hell on earth.

Inevitably, the confrontations turn violent; Charlie gradually succumbs to the lifestyle of his demimonde (courtesy Warner Bros.).

Tony (David Proval), owner of the bar, is the quietest and least impulsive of the lot, possessing a pair of dark, brooding eyes that gaze on detached, from a distance, at all that happens. Michael (Richard Romanus), who appears closest of the youths to achieving full status as a local gangster, wears slick, expensive, neatly pressed suits to convey his growing power, though he inwardly fears he's only a shadow of the true tough guys. They would never allow worthless goods to be unloaded on them, as too often happens to the hapless Michael. At the opposite pole in this self-contained universe is Johnny Boy (Robert De Niro), a mindless anarchist who gets his kicks throwing homemade bombs into mailboxes. Then there is numbers runner Charlie (Harvey Keitel), the only member of the group who appears to think about what happens around him. Charlie is with them and, from all outward appearances, of them; indeed, Charlie's uncle is Giovanni, the local capo, a suave old Mafia lieutenant who has no son of his own and would like to see Charlie inherit his little kingdom of crime.

But there's another side to Charlie, a hidden self we hear expressed via voice-over, the confused inner identity Charlie shares with us but not with those around him. While Charlie is indeed motivated by ambitions to please his uncle Giovanni, he's pulled in other directions by conscience and consciousness. Though Johnny Boy was named for Uncle Giovanni, the mafioso strictly forbids Charlie to continue his relationship with such an out-of-control character; the modern mob, run business-style, desires peace and quiet. Theresa (Amy Robinson) may be an Italian Catholic girl from a nice local family, yet she suffers from epilepsy, which in Giovanni's view makes her an unfit candidate for Charlie if he's going to rise in the ranks of the Family. Still, Charlie has been having an affair with Theresa and, worse, has fallen deeply in love with her. Also, he's secretly maintained his relationship with Johnny Boy, unable to break their bond of friendship owing to a sense of loyalty.

Like so many other modern crime films, *Mean Streets* focuses on the concept of loyalty. Charlie is split down the middle, torn between two conflicting loyalties: his loyalty to the youth cult he has walked the mean streets with since childhood; his loyalty to the criminal establishment he hopes to inherit. Charlie, simply and sadly, is in a no-win situation.

The film that follows chronicles his desperate search for something to believe in until, near the end, he gazes upward and, apparently with total conviction, acknowledges the presence of the Lord; significantly, it is his last line of dialogue. Throughout the film, Scorsese calls our attention to ancient relics of traditional Christian thinking, all but ignored by the population as

The anti-heroes of Martin Scorsese films are most often low-life characters who, during the course of the story, transform into Christ figures; in the famed final shot of *Mean Streets,* Harvey Keitel's wiseguy wannabe proves to be no exception to that rule (courtesy Warner Brothers).

Charlie would rather be a lover than a fighter; his sincere romance with Theresa is doomed because his godfather uncle will not accept an epileptic as his heir's wife (courtesy Warner Bros.).

they go about their daily business. A huge statue of Christ, arms outstretched, rises far above the city streets, though these days no one but Charlie ever actually takes the time to consider it. Lighted crosses are everywhere in the giddy street fair taking place throughout the film, but the crowds ignore them, having forgotten the feast's religious origin, heading instead for games of chance. Charlie tries to rise above his milieu, only to be sucked back in again; he attempts to treat black and Jewish women with a respect his friends do not show, then grows fearful of his nonconformity, retreating into the calculated cruelty of the other wiseguys.

Scorsese's vision of gangster life is far from optimistic. When Charlie attempts to abandon the demimonde of Little Italy, borrowing a car and driving over the Brooklyn Bridge with Theresa and Johnny Boy, they are fired on by Michael and crash into a fire hydrant. This is a hermetically sealed existence, Scorsese insists, from which few ever escape.

In that final sequence, when a bloodied Charlie staggers about the streets and a wounded Theresa is pulled from the car, Scorsese purposefully jars his audience by cutting away to a shot from *The Big Heat,* Fritz Lang's classic 1953 crime film, which Scorsese saw and loved as

Johnny Boy is shot and killed as he, along with Theresa and Charlie, attempts to flee by breaking out of their hermetically sealed demi-monde. They might have escaped had they not run off to see one last movie (courtesy Warmer Bros.).

a child. He picks that precise scene in which Glenn Ford yanks a wounded woman from a car, her body appearing identical to Theresa's. In so doing, Scorsese makes us aware he has carried that image with him most of his life and is now dealing with the indelible icon by making it a part of his own work. Additionally, Scorsese deconstructs our experience of watching by making us aware that this is, in fact, only a movie. The final sequence is a bookend companion to the opening, featuring an image of the projector screening the movie we are watching. Scorsese's camera films that projector, moves in toward its magical illumination, then shares with us some "home movies," which give way to the film proper.

Throughout *Mean Streets,* there are reminders that this is a movie about movies. When the young gangsters rip off money from Long Island teens eager to buy illegal fireworks, they rush off to a Forty-second Street grind house and blow the cash on a film, preferring reel life to real life. When asked by Theresa what he most likes in life, Charlie does not hesitate in telling her that John Wayne makes everything worthwhile. Later, when a friend returns from Vietnam, Charlie cannot acknowledge the man's heroism as an act in the real world, but has to transform it into a reference to one of the movies that provide him with his window (however unrealistic) on the world: "In the immortal words of John Garfield, 'Get him in the eyes—get him right in the eyes.'" Charlie, Theresa, and Johnny Boy might actually escape at the end, except that they can't resist stopping to see a Roger Corman/Vincent Price adaptation of an Edgar Allan Poe story. Even the cameo role Scorsese chose to play solidifies this connection between the world of crime and the world of moviemaking: he appears as Michael's hired hit man who shoots Johnny Boy, a perfect part for the person who "shot" the movie we are watching.

"Honorable men go with honorable men," Uncle Giovanni tells Charlie in a classic generation-gap confrontation. Midway through *Mean Streets,* Giovanni watches TV in his favorite restaurant and comments on the politicians, ironically complaining about their dishonesty, insisting, "They know where to come, when they need us." But this power broker will fall by the wayside; at film's end, he's once again watching TV, though now doing so at home, looking less the quietly fierce mafioso observed earlier, reduced to a tired old man. In addition to being a well-wrought character in a memorable movie, Giovanni stands for all the old, anachronistic gangsters who must, during the next two decades, make way for a new kind of gangster youth, then already taking over America's real-life mean streets and, necessarily, their reel-life counterparts as well.

ELEVEN

The Friends of Eddie Coyle

(1973)

A Paramount Picture

CAST:

Robert Mitchum *(Eddie Coyle);* Peter Boyle *(Dillon);* Richard Jordan *(Dave Foley);* Steve Keats *(Jackie Brown);* Alex Rocco *(Scalise);* Joe Santos *(Artie Van);* Mitch Ryan *(Waters);* Peter Maclean *(Partridge);* Margaret Ladd *(Andrea);* Jack Kehoe *("The Beard");* Helena Carroll *(Sheila Coyle).*

CREDITS:

Producer/writer, Paul Monash, from the novel by George V. Higgins; director, Peter Yates; cinematography, Victor J. Kemper; editor, Patricia Lewis Jaffe; music, Dave Grushin; production design, Gene Callahan; running time, 102 minutes; rating, R.

A unique subgenre of the crime film concerns a group of lowlifes, floundering around on the edges of gangsterism, struggling to survive as a community of crooks but inevitably betraying one another as individuals at the drop of a hat. These loser crooks desperately hope for the big win and inevitably end up in the gutter. In the 1950s, classics of the form included John Huston's *The Asphalt Jungle* and Stanley Kubrick's *The Killing.* In 1973, when audiences expected fast-paced car chases from crime films, so *The Friends of Eddie Coyle* seemed inordinately low-key and depressing, and it fared poorly at the box office. Yet, aficionados of this special type of picture considered it a minimasterpiece, and it dates far better than many of the decade's more hyped crime movies.

Friends is based on a novel by George V. Higgins, who (as a state's attorney) combines his insider's street knowledge of cops and robbers with a terse writing style. Like the tight-lipped mobsters in Hemingway's "The Killers," Higgins's characters speak in a punchy, idiomatic city-wise prose. There's not a touch of floridness to his writing, no sentimentality in the drama that might betray the grim gutter realism. Director Peter Yates respectfully acknowledged that in his no-nonsense, straightforward approach. A remarkable group of actors deliver characters who seem less fictional creations than real-life losers, drifting in from the mean streets.

Robert Mitchum plays the title character, who has much in common with criminal characters he's played ever since the film-noir classic *Out of the Past* in 1947. Indeed, his character here might be considered the antihero of that earlier story, now fallen on hard times. Former bank robber Eddie Coyle lives in Quincy, Massachusetts, where he tries to support his wife and two kids in a working-class neighborhood. But he's coming up for a hearing in New Hampshire, having been caught driving a truck containing contraband, and is nervously looking at another long stretch in jail. Still, he makes a living by servicing unsavory underworld characters: buying guns from a dealer and then reselling them to out-of-work construction guys who rob banks during lean periods.

Colin L. Westerbeck Jr. noted in *Commonweal* that "critic Robert Warshow once generalized about the character of all movie hoods, however vestigial, in an article entitled 'The Gangster as Tragic Hero,' Warshow meant *Scarface, The Public Enemy,* and *Little Caesar.* But if these superannuated mythic heroes are our cinematic versions of Oedipus, Macbeth, and big Caesar, then Eddie Coyle is our new Willie Loman—a protagonist from much nearer home, a protagonist of pathetic realism." Noting that Eddie deals with bank robbers but isn't exactly one of them, Westerbeck wrote: "His life has a certain insularity from what we usually think of as crime. It is in the very routine and ordinariness of his activities that his character is seen."

Stanley Kauffmann of *The New Republic* picked up on the notion of Eddie Coyle as Willie Loman–like, suggesting that just as Arthur Miller had attempted to make a new kind of tragic hero out of the common man, so,

Robert Mitchum as one more anachronistic gangster: Eddie Coyle, the small-time, old-fashioned Boston hood who finds himself embroiled in a very modern crime caper (courtesy Paramount Pictures).

too, did Higgins: "There is nothing especially original or twisty in this tale of 'perfect' bank robberies and gun-selling and police-informing. The special flavor is in the sense of sociology; the apparently accurate picture of some interweaving lifestyles in the underworld and its relation with detectives, of status and ethics in that world. And Robert Mitchum as Eddie [is] a lumpen figure trying to get along, trying to beat raps in his life just as Willie Loman did in the surface world above him. *Death of a Salesman of Death* might be another title for the picture."

As far as Eddie is concerned, his only friend is the bartender Dillon (Peter Boyle), who listens to his problems and offers advice. We soon grasp a key fact that Eddie is totally unaware of: Dillon is a paid police informant. He meets with Treasury agent Dave Foley (Richard Jordan), who knows something is coming down; word on the street has it the three characters who have been robbing Boston banks are about to strike again. To save his own skin (like Eddie, Dillon is an ex-con who could easily be sent to jail) Dillon implicates Eddie. Dillon refers to Coyle by his nickname, Eddie Fingers. Doyle plays Iago to Eddie's underworld Othello.

What Dillon does not know—at least, not yet—is that Eddie also meets regularly with Foley, providing information, hoping that in exchange Foley will put in a good word with the New Hampshire DA. Eddie knows the police are out to get anyone using automatic weapons. Eddie is, at heart, an old-fashioned criminal; "I never understood a man wanting a machine gun," he tells the dealer. In one of the film's most telling moments, the gun dealer arranges to sell machine guns to a pair of innocent-looking teenagers—a boy and a girl—who appear to be a hippie-era peace-and-love couple. Even the police, spying on the scene, fail to grasp there's anything dangerous about these kids, who want to buy high-power weapons for their own bank job. The contrast between the now-aged criminals hailing from the film-noir era and the youthful gun-crazy kids is at the heart of *Friends.*

The film shows various bank robberies, including one that goes all wrong during which a teller is shot and killed. It also depicts the good suburban families of the bank presidents, held hostage in their homes by masked gunmen

Old-timer Eddie Coyle attempts to negotiate an underworld deal while watched by Jane House as a hippie-era free-love type who threatens his traditionalist view of man-woman relationships (courtesy Paramount Pictures).

With friends like these, you don't need any enemies: Robert Mitchum and Peter Boyle in the film's penultimate scene (courtesey Paramount Pictures).

as their husbands/fathers are forced to allow the three gunmen in back bank doors, after which they wait for the computerized locks to open the bank safes. There are also scenes in which the gun supplier finds himself at odds with various clients, who would like to lead him into traps and rip him off, perhaps even kill him. Each and every one of the low-life characters rushes about, attempting to make his money, willingly ratting on "friends" to the police. *Friends* is a revisionist gangster film, belying the old myth of "honor among thieves." According to Higgins, there is none.

Certainly, Eddie is something less than a honorable man, though he does project a dignity the others lack. When he picks up guns during a transaction in a supermarket parking lot (the film is set against just such everyday backdrops, rather than the atmospherically sleazy places we expect for a genre film), he notices machine guns in the trunk and immediately calls Foley. In the previous sequence, in which the dealer was ambushed by several punks lurking in the woods, the audience was momentarily seduced into rooting for him. He had, for the time being, become the "hero" of the film. Yet there is no remorse whatsoever when he's subsequently picked up by Foley. Like Higgins's book, the film effectively transfers our emotions from one character to another in turn.

Coyle is positive that Foley will help him. The cop, however, turns out to be another oily, manipulative character, no better or worse than the criminals. Foley informs Eddie at their next meeting that this is a good start, but he needs something more if he's to help: "The man up there said he'd like it better if you were working for Uncle," meaning Uncle Sam. What Foley wants, simply, is for Eddie to tell him who the bank robbers are, and which suburban bank president's home they will hit next. "I should have known better than to trust a cop," Eddie groans.

The next day, Eddie goes to a bar and meets Foley; "I'm ready to deal with you," Eddie says. He has swallowed his pride, given up on any idea of honor among thieves, agrees to betray the bank robbers. Foley looks at him, surprised, and hands Eddie a newspaper; the robbers have been apprehended. Eddie is unable to speak, knowing his last trump card has just been taken away. Someone else informed on the robbers before he could; Foley, realizing this was all Eddie had to offer, walks away without another word; Eddie Coyle is now useless to him, and he will not lift a finger to help his "friend." Friendship, in this harsh little world, is based on mutual accommodation only.

Then, the nearly forgotten Dillon meets with a representative of The Man in a parking lot; they want

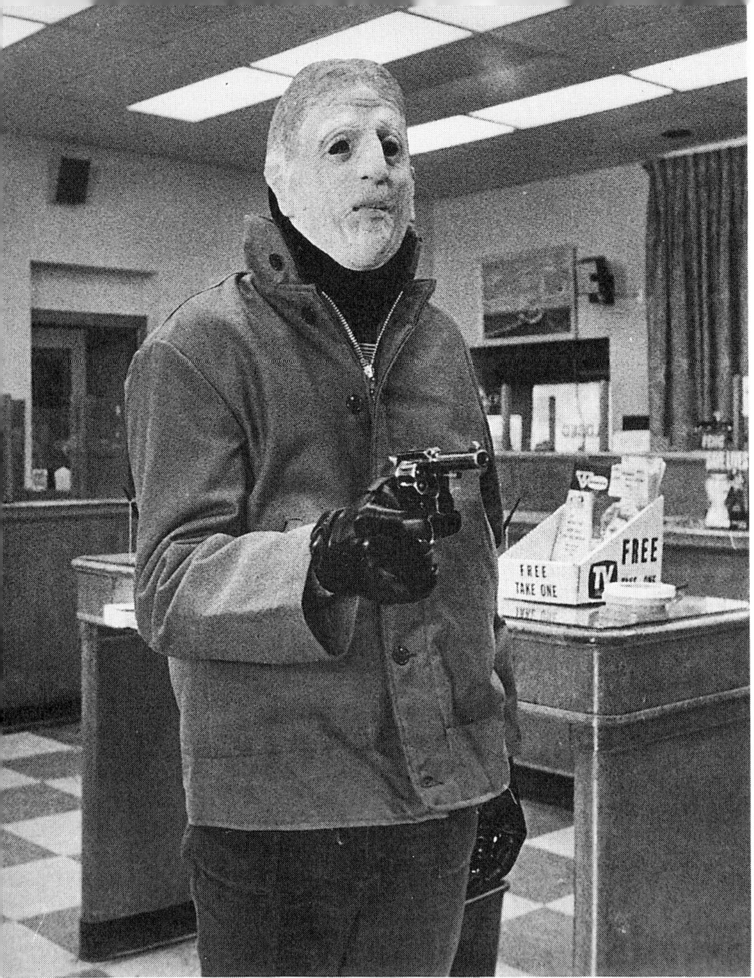

One more bank robbery, one more face mask: Eddie supplies the guns for a caper that, in the tradition of *The Killing*, does not go according to plan (courtesy Paramount Pictures).

Dillon to hit his friend Eddie for turning in the robbers. Dillon agrees and Eddie unsuspectingly shows up in Dillon's bar. Eddie is now a total wreck; he can't even claim to have his integrity intact, yet he does not reap the benefits of informing. While Eddie's there, the phone rings, and Dillon takes the call, from the same agent of The Man he spoke with earlier. Dillon pretends sorrow about what happened to the robbers and pretends to be so offended by stool-pigeon Eddie's "pretense" that he'll do the hit that night. He takes Eddie out to dinner, then to a hockey game, and shoots the drunken Eddie in the head on the way home.

In the film's last scene, Dillon meets with Foley, and it becomes obvious it was Dillon who informed, then set his best friend up as the patsy, also making a profit by committing the execution himself. Dillon walks away a free man, in a world without values where only such a manipulative character can survive. Eddie Coyle's moment of hesitation cost him not only his shot for freedom, but also his life. Yet he seems a better man for that hesitation; he alone among the characters observed here was not cold and clammy, but had a quality that makes his death seem abhorrent.

Eddie's stature derives not only from the quality of the writing and Mitchum's vivid portrayal, but also the happy baggage that Mitchum carried with him to this part. Eddie Coyle was one of his last great roles; his past tough-guy parts, in particular his roots in film noir, were up there on the screen with him as he played in a film that effectively encapsulated a long and significant career. As Richard Schickel wrote in *Time*, "the slope of the belly has grown more acute with the passage of years; the face is puffy and well-worn; even the complexion looks gray, with just a hint of green around the gills...." The weariness, the hooded cynicism, the underlying toughness that seems to consist more of an ability to survive beatings rather than administer them—all have always been there, unspoken factors in a career that has consisted largely of trying to transcend roles that did not fully engage one of the most active and original intelligences in the star business. Now, at last, Mitchum

Director Peter Yates continues the tradition established in *Point Blank*, *The Last Run*, and *The Family* by visually framing his old con from angles that suggest entrapment, suggesting the film's tragic ending early on (courtesy Paramount Pictures).

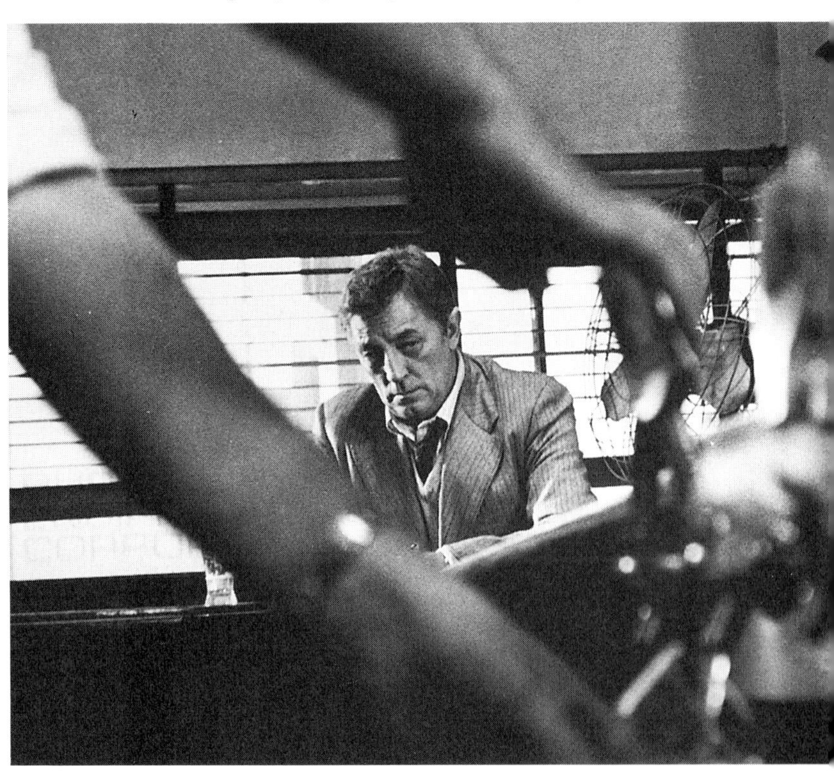

Lost and lonely, Eddie stumbles through a world that has changed drastically from the one he knew how to survive in (courtesy Paramount Pictures).

achieves a kind of apotheosis [of all his previous gangster roles]....Self-consciously, with an old pro's quiet skills, Mitchum explores all of Coyle's contradictory facets. At fifty-six, when many of his contemporaries are hiding out behind the remnants of their youthful images, he has summoned up the skill and the courage to demonstrate a remarkable range of talents."

GORDON'S
DISTILLED
LONDON DRY
GIN

TWELVE

The Sting

(1973)

A Universal Release of a Zanuck-Brown Presentation

CAST:

Paul Newman *(Henry Gondoroff)*; Robert Redford *(Johnny Hooker)*; Robert Shaw *(Doyle Lonnegan)*; Charles Durning *(Lt. William Snyder)*; Ray Walston *(J.J.)*; Eileen Brennan *(Billie)*; Harold Gould *(Kid Twist)*; John Heffernan *(Eddie Niles)*; Dana Elcar *(FBI Agent Polk)*; Robert Earl Jones *(Luther Coleman)*; Jack Kehoe *(Grifter)*; Dimitra Arliss *(Waitress/Assassin)*.

CREDITS:

Producers, Tony Bill and Michael and Julia Phillips; director, George Roy Hill; screenplay, David S. Ward; cinematography, Robert Surtees; editor, William Reynolds; music, Marvin Hamlisch adaptations of Scott Joplin originals; art direction, Henry Bumstead; running time, 129 minutes; rating, R.

Few people recall *The Sting* as a genre film; the Best Picture Oscar winner of 1973 was accepted by the public as a mainstream entertainment, with no rough language or graphic sex and only the slightest hint of violence. In comparison to the previous year's winner, *The Godfather, The Sting* certainly seemed to be a family film, with the charming stars of *Butch Cassidy and the Sundance Kid* reunited, playing similar roles in a different historical situation. Despite that, *The Sting* was and is a crime film; its heroes are grifters who set out to put The Big Con on a despicable mark. He—Doyle Lonnegan (Robert Shaw)—remains one of the key portraits of a gangster to appear the 1970s. Meanwhile, the style of *The Sting* would, following the film's critical and commercial success, set the tone for period-picture gangster films to follow.

Having survived the cultural revolution of the late sixties, the public suddenly sensed a great loss, as the pop culture that had for decades been taken for granted was suddenly gone. As Stanley Kauffmann noted in *The New Republic,* "audiences aren't as nostalgic for the decade itself—most of them are too young to have known it—as they are for films of the decade. [*The Sting*] isn't about the thirties as much as it's an attempt to make a thirties film. It's the Antiques Made to Order business." And, as *The New Yorker* added, an antique made by people who were less than careful about getting their eras right: "The setting is ragtime thirties—a synthetic period compounded of Scott Joplin's rags (Joplin died in 1917) and thirties gangster films...the script by David S. Ward is a collection of Damon Runyon hand-me-downs."

In the early 1970s, Hollywood movies were glutted with buddy-buddy teams of male heroes, who had scant time for women and focused on their male-bonding; there was no better-loved team than Robert Redford *(left)* and Paul Newman (courtesy Universal Pictures).

Simply, the public wasn't nostalgic for a specific time in the past so much as "the past" as a kind of idea and ideal. In the early seventies—the Vietnam War still lingering on, the Watergate scandal creating a sense of mistrust—any old days were suddenly good old days, no matter how bad they had actually been. It made sense, then, that Newman and Redford were made up to look, as Vincent Canby noted in the *New York Times,* "like a couple of guys in old Arrow shirt ads," while "separating sequences (of this chapter play) are title cards that recall Normal Rockwell's *Saturday Evening Post* covers."

There were also "wipes" to change scenes, and other devices that hadn't been used for ages. In their time, such storytelling conventions were accepted without conscious attention by audiences. Now, they were very much noticed; calling attention to themselves, they kicked off the trend for deconstructionist movies that purposefully remind the audience it is indeed watching a film, not peeking in on reality. In the past, Hollywood films had always been somewhat artificial, though they usually attempted to convince the audience of their reality; the modern film either rubs an audience's nose in harsh reality (the street films of Martin Scorsese) or else makes the audience constantly aware this is all in good

Master con artist Henry Gondoroff takes small-time crook Kid Hooker as his assistant to set up Doyle Lonnegan as their mark. The Oscar-winning film was by far the best of the buddy-buddy films so popular in the early 1970s (courtesy Universal Pictures).

fun (as in the *Indiana Jones* movies of Steven Spielberg).

If *Mean Streets* kicked off the former subgenre of modern gangster movies, *The Sting* initiated the latter. Though the gangster does not appear until twenty minutes into the movie, the mob milieu is there from the opening as ragtime music plays on the sound track. But while the songs are Scott Joplin standards, the arrangements are revisionist; Marvin Hamlisch won an Academy Award for revamping the famed rags for a contemporary audience.

Director George Roy Hill's opening shot is an effectively self-conscious pan across a Depression-era street in Joliet, Illinois. By moving his camera from right to left, the opposite of the ordinary and expected movement, he visually suggests the numerous reversals of plot and characterization to follow. The sad, wasted men sitting about, out of work, are the emotional brothers of those in so many gangland films about this era. The camera then moves indoors, to the local branch of a gambling network ranging from New York to the Midwest, owned by Doyle Lonnegan. The branch manager is on the phone to his superiors in Chicago, while putting the day's take into an envelope for a minor mobster to "run" downtown. This mobster is, significantly, seen flipping a coin, a quick homage to George Raft in *Scarface;* it's the mythology, rather than the reality, of 1930s gangsterism that's being played with here.

The Big Con: J.J. (Ray Walston) and Billie (Eileen Brennan) help set up an elaborate though phony gambling den to suck in the greedy Lonnegan (courtesy Universal Pictures).

As the runner makes his move out onto the street, the incident that will trigger the film's crisis takes place. An old black man (Robert Earl Jones) is seemingly being robbed; a blond youth (Robert Redford) tries to chase the "thief" (Jack Kehoe) but can't overtake him. The runner, intrigued by this, is persuaded by the old man to take his wallet full of money, keep $100, and deliver the rest to some rough characters. The blond young man even shows the mob runner how to keep the wallet undercover. But when the mob runner slips into a cab, gloating over the money he plans to keep for himself, he realizes he's been the target of a sting; the "money" he's taken is mere padding, while his own envelope full of the day's take is gone.

The grifters have no idea that they've stolen from the vast Lonnegan operation, until told so by a sleazy cop, Snyder (Charles Durning). By that time, Hooker has dropped a bundle at a gambling table, while word has circulated he's the one who arranged the sting, and the black man has been killed at the express orders of Lonnegan himself. We first see Lonnegan when his Joliet people call him in New York about the missing $11,000; though this is a fortune to the grifters, the amount is

Looking like an extra right out of the gangster flicks of the 1930s, Charles Dierkop plays a movie-inspired bodyguard to Doyle Lonnegan, here putting the muscle on Kid Hooker (courtesy Universal Pictures).

peanuts to "The Big Mick." The image of his place is striking, a wonderland of posh exclusivity: an elegant gambling hall, where Tiffany shades exude subtle light and men stroll about in tuxedos. Lonnegan, unpleasant about being interrupted, acknowledges that for him it is a minor sum, but insists his branch manager have "the local people take care of it; we have to discourage this type of thing."

That is the vague order that results in the all-too-specific death of Luther. Shortly before his murder, Hooker visits Luther's simple apartment, where one of the children listens to reports of Machine Gun Kelly's capture on the radio. The public perception of gangsters as figures who inhabit some separate world, where as special entities they live out splendidly sordid adventures, is basic to what happens next. The little child—and everyone else—realizes gangsters are in fact real, inhabiting the same world as the rest of us, and their orders can impact even on those of us who do not believe we are in any way connected to them. Hooker goes on the run to Chicago, where he looks up Henry Gondoroff (Paul Newman), the greatest living con man, known for being able to execute The Big Con, an elaborate scheme in which some powerful person is conned out of a great deal of money, without knowing—even afterward—that the con ever took place.

The original screenplay by David S. Ward won an Oscar in large part for the intricacies of that scheme, the details of which are fascinatingly complex. Far more important in this context, however, is the nature of Lonnegan's operation and the implications for crime films to follow. While Hooker and Gondoroff plan their strategies, enlisting various experts at the con like

Kid Hooker (Robert Redford) picks up an attractive waitress (Dimitra Arliss), little suspecting she's actually a mob assassin. Though the film's era is the 1930s, Arliss serves as period-piece precursor to the modern liberated and multifaceted woman so prevalent in the early seventies, when the film was made (courtesy Universal Pictures).

Robert Shaw as the film's great gangster character, a ruthless climber who likes to wear sophisticated suits but still runs his crime empire as if it were the jungle (courtesy Universal Pictures).

"Twist" and "J.J." (beautifully played by veteran character actors Harold Gould and Ray Walston), Doyle continues his upscale, seemingly respectable, ultra-expensive lifestyle. We next see him playing croquet at a country club, where he sports the perfect casual wardrobe of the day. Surrounding him are equally fine-looking fellows. It would be easy to assume the scene is precisely what it appears to be: high-class people enjoying an upscale afternoon. In fact, this is anything but. When a runner from the ugly, outside world hurries over and whispers into Lonnegan's ear that one grifter is dead and another being pursued, Lonnegan confides to his underling while pointing at a smiling man some twenty feet away: "Take a look at him.... I've known him since we were six.... If he ever found out that I can be beat by a low-life grifter, I'd have to kill him and every other hood" who might believe Lonnegan was vulnerable and that his illegal empire could be taken away from him.

"Lonnegan gets most of his money from the numbers," Gondoroff says to Kid Hooker and their confederates after doing some research on The Big Mick, "even though he's putting more of his money into savings and loans." That line gets a bigger laugh today than it did back in 1973, owing to the savings-and-loan scandal of the 1980s. Lonnegan can't help but remind us of the old adage that behind every great fortune there is a crime; it is the bulwarks of society who are the most ruthless and dangerous when they believe no one—at least, no one of the class they want to join—is watching. "He wants to be respectable," one of the grifters tells Gondoroff. "He's been telling everyone he's from Forest Hills. [But] he learns a racket, moves in on it, and is vindictive—he kills for pride." To beat Lonnegan as Kid Hooker obsessively wants to do, they will have to play upon the man's pride (his tragic hubris) as well as his image (respectability). He has no other, obvious weaknesses, as Lonnegan is a man who "doesn't drink, smoke, or go out with dames; he's a Grand Knight in the Knights of Columbus." In fact, it is Lonnegan's desperation to keep his respectability intact that will allow the grifters to sting him for a fortune and get away with it at the film's end.

Meanwhile, though, Lonnegan's desire for respecta-bility is next seen as he travels by train from New York to Chicago, on the legendary Twentieth Century Limited, the aptly named ultimate in luxurious travel. Lonnegan is part of a big-time poker game at which, as a witness confides, "he cheats." With him are varied businessmen and bankers who seem proper types; though none are developed beyond the level of cameo, we can assume each, like Lonnegan, made his fortune in some unsavory way. Here, the film's value system is made abundantly clear. Newman's Gondoroff, pretending to be a sleazy, drunken businessman with a big wad of money, blusters his way into the game, and the very elements that most irritate Lonnegan are those very qulities that most endear Gondoroff to the audience. He is playing at being the lovable slob, belching loudly whenever Lonnegan tries to make polite conversation, much to the delight of mainstream moviegoers, who always enjoy cheering on a man of honest vulgarity as he opposes one of phony sophistication.

Lonnegan will be done in by the lovable lowlifes, but not before he tries to have Kid Hooker killed off by Solina (Dimitra Arliss), a hit lady masquerading as a likable hash-slinger at the local diner, who beds Hooker and would then shoot him down if it weren't for a bodyguard assigned by Gondoroff, who shows up in the nick of time and puts a bullet between her pretty eyes. However briefly glimpsed, she is the film's ambiguous woman, a postfeminist image of a female far more complex than the men initially realize. Her death is one of the few graphic acts of violence in a film that delighted critics and audiences alike, but which—despite its mainstream appeal—was in many respects the harbinger of crime movies to come.

THIRTEEN

Thieves Like Us

(1974)

A United Artists Release

CAST:

Keith Carradine *(Bowie);* Shelley Duvall *(Keechie);* John Schuck *(Chicamaw);* Bert Remsen *(T-Dub);* Louise Fletcher *(Mattie);* Ann Latham *(Lula);* Tom Skerritt *(Dee Mobley).*

CREDITS:

Producer, Jerry Bick; executive producer, George Litte; director, Robert Altman; screenplay, Calder Willingham, Joan Tewkesbury, and Altman, from the novel by Edward Anderson; cinematography, Jean Bouffety; editor, Lou Lombardo; running time, 123 minutes; rating, R.

Essentially, Robert Altman's film *Thieves Like Us* can be viewed as the film that *Bonnie and Clyde* would have been (and perhaps should have been) had it been played as a serious work of art rather than as mass entertainment. Not surprisingly, *Thieves* was a critical smash and a box-office disaster; to date, it has not been released on home video or shown on pay cable, though it remains one of the few great gangster films of the 1970s. Like *B&C, Thieves* is about the mythologizing of a couple of rural outlaws. The film is based on Edward Anderson's 1937 novel, which was also the source for debuting director Nicholas Ray's 1948 film noir, *They Live by Night.* Anderson was purportedly inspired to write the book by the real-life Parker and Barrow crime wave.

What fascinated Anderson in his time, and Altman some thirty-five years later, was what he knew must be the contrast between the public perception of such people and their considerably humbler reality. Rather than a pair of impossibly gorgeous actors (Beatty and Dunaway looked glamorous even when being riddled by bullets), Altman chose two ugly ducklings: Keith Carradine as Bowie, the smiling sad rube who would like to be a ballplayer though circumstances lead him into a life of crime, and Shelley Duvall as Keechie, scrawny, sweetly sad, small-town virgin who runs off with him partly because she's convinced that she is madly in love (though she's never been out on a date before), partly to escape the ennui (a word she would not be familiar with) of her oppressing, vacuumlike existence.

When Bowie and Keechie make love, they overhear a popularized version of Shakespeare's *Romeo and Juliet* on the radio. Though they are indeed doomed lovers themselves, the contrast between the elevated poetry being spoken and their own simple gropings establishes Altman's aesthetic. As Bowie and cohorts Chicamaw (John Schuck), a decidedly unpleasant one-quarter Indian, and T-Dub (Bert Remsen), a lame and laconic old thief, rob a bank, we hear the exciting old radio show *Gangbusters* playing. Again, Altman emphasizes the contrast between the excitement of such an event as it is glorified for public conception and the actual event itself, partly a grim matter of casual killing, partly a pathetically comical case of semicompetent thieves nearly managing to botch what should have been an easy job.

Most of the time, though, Altman doesn't even bother to show us the robberies, though these are the incidents that the viewer comes expecting to see. This was in keeping with the consistent approach of Hollywood's great modern iconoclastic, and revisionist director. In each successive film, Altman self-consciously approached yet another genre and purposefully undermined it. In *M*A*S*H,* he had taken the innocuous old fluff-film service-comedy formula *(Don't Go Near the Water)* and turned it inside out, employing the genre as a vehicle for black humor and antiwar sentiments. He moved on to the western *(McCabe and Mrs. Miller),* the detective tale *(The Long Goodbye),* the buddy-buddy film *(California Split),* and the ensemble soap opera *(Nashville).*

Thieves Like Us is a rural gangster film as it had

The Keystone Kops–style, speeded-up actions accompanied by engaging banjo music, which made the robberies so much fun to watch in *Bonnie and Clyde*, are not present in this grim, low-key alternative to Arthur Penn's earlier, flashier film (courtesy United Artists).

never been done before. As Jay Cocks wrote in *Time,* "Altman's basic concept is to use all the conventions of the genre at hand, then play directly against them. Altman omits what is expectable in movies of this sort and includes the scenes other filmmakers have left out.…He is not concerned with the mechanics of the heist but the social subcurrents beneath it. Almost anyone else would have included a lot of hairbreadth getaway sequences, but Altman concentrates on portraying the glowering emptiness that daily confronts the robbers. He is especially good at rendering the sort of foggy existential desperation that surrounds his characters.…Shot in muted autumnal tones, the film seems overcast, sad, and dense with a kind of elemental menace."

At one point, Chicamaw listens to the radio and hears himself described in lofty terms as "Machine Gun Mobley"; "I only held a machine gun once in my life," he mutters, admitting that he never even fired it. "This was supposedly a simpler era," Paul D. Zimmerman wrote of the 1930s in *Newsweek,* "but in Altman's view it was simply an America that saw things simplistically. Other filmmakers have tried to show the thirties' gangsters as human beings, but only Altman succeeds." In time, the gang members will move beyond their amazement and gradually begin to relish their newfound notoriety. In one of the film's most telling sequences, T-Dub reads an overenthusiastic piece of pop journalism about the gang's crimes while his family sits around, eating

Bowie and Keechie (Shelley Duvall) in a rare tender moment. In comparison to *Bonnie and Clyde*'s glamorous Beatty-Dunaway coupling, this film offered a harsh but honest portrait of similar characters, which may account for its box-office failure (courtesy United Artists).

dinner. T-Dub is both delighted and astounded to discover that their sordid exploits are being elevated, through some writer's imaginative prose, into an exciting myth. At first, everyone at the table is intrigued. But as the scene progresses, everyday events take precedence: "Use your bread as a pusher," Mattie (Louise Fletcher) tells the kids, who stick their fingers in the food.

Later, Chicamaw takes the kids out back to play gangsters, actually directing them (and becoming a substitute for the film director) in a romanticized re-creation of the robbery. But when the children (actors) eventually lose interest, Chicamaw turns into a tyrant not unlike such Hollywood directors as Otto Preminger and Michael Curtiz. Altman's movie is by implication as much about him, his audience, and the business of directing movies as it is about crime.

Originally, the popular screenwriter Calder Willingham prepared a script, though Altman rejected it almost entirely, fearing it provided a blueprint for yet another *Bonnie and Clyde*–type film, whereas he was going for an alternative to that movie. Though Willingham (owing to his contract) received collaborative billing in

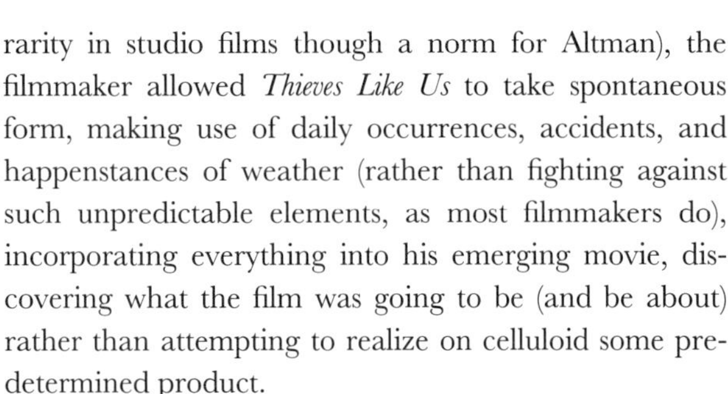

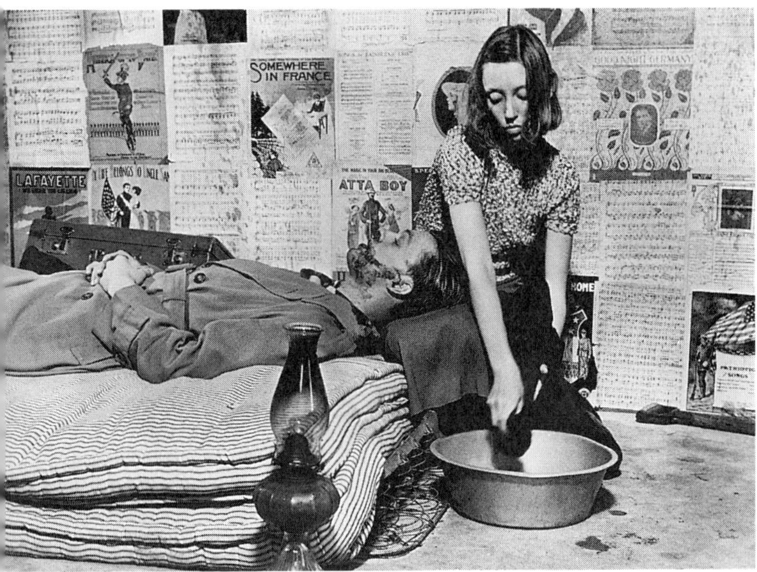

A wounded Bowie is attended to by the drab Keechie. Posters for romantic songs about glamorous getaways to charming places serve as an ironic environment for the decidedly homely but utterly believable team of robbers viewed in Altman's film (courtesy United Artists).

the credits, the film was derived from a script that Altman and his former script girl Joan Tewkesbury devised, from which Altman was able to shape an organic work on location in Mississippi (the book had taken place in Oklahoma and Texas). Shooting in sequence (a rarity in studio films though a norm for Altman), the filmmaker allowed *Thieves Like Us* to take spontaneous form, making use of daily occurrences, accidents, and happenstances of weather (rather than fighting against such unpredictable elements, as most filmmakers do), incorporating everything into his emerging movie, discovering what the film was going to be (and be about) rather than attempting to realize on celluloid some predetermined product.

Altman worked for the first time with French cinematographer Jean Bouffety, so despite the strong element of Americana in the tale and setting, *Thieves* had the look of a classic French art film. Several critics compared it to the early work of Jean Renoir, including *A Day in the Country*, with its lyrical visuals and overriding sense of happy improvisation. Altman's material, of course, is far darker, his southern-gothic sensibility likewise eliciting comparisons to the work of William Faulkner, especially that author's poor-white-trash chronicles of the Snopes clan such as *The Hamlet*. The authenticity was due to the fact that, for the first time, Altman chose not to work with a production designer. Rather, Altman traveled extensively throughout Mississippi until he found areas that had somehow remained unchanged over the intervening forty years, then shot his film there.

A Depression-era social treatise such as Fritz Lang's *You Only Live Once* viewed such a Bonnie-and-Clyde couple as victims of a failed capitalistic system; a postwar noir, such as Ray's *They Live by Night*, took a decidedly Freudian view of young people shunned by adult society. Altman instead depicts his Bowie and Keechie as working-class misfits who are done in partly by circumstances, partly by their own inability to adapt to the realities around them. "As an ambiguity in the film's title is meant to suggest," Colin Westerbeck wrote, "Altman's thieves really *are* like us. It is not the Law or some special Fate that overwhelms them, but the sheer picayunishness of living that afflicts us all."

FOURTEEN

Badlands

(1974)

A Warner Bros. Film

CAST:

Martin Sheen *(Kit Carruthers);* Sissy Spacek *(Holly Sargis);* Warren Oates *(Holly's Father);* Ramon Bieri *(Cato);* Alan Vint *(Deputy Tom);* Gary Littlejohn *(Sheriff);* John Carter *(Rich Man);* Bryan Montgomery *(Boy Victim);* Gail Threlkeld *(Girl Victim);* Howard Ragsdale *(Boss).*

CREDITS

Producer, director, writer, Terrence Malick; executive producer, Edward R. Pressman; cinematography, Brian Probyn, Tak Fujimoto, and Stevan Larner; editor, Robert Estrin; original music, George Tipton; art director, Jack Fisk; running time, 97 minutes; rating, PG.

In the 1950s, another real-life team of rural criminals briefly caught the nation's attention. While Charles Starkweather and Caril Fugate have never become household names like Bonnie and Clyde, their story of youth on the lam, bonded together by a strange passion, is regularly revived, most significantly in Terrence Malick's *Badlands.*

Writer-director-producer Malick (then twenty-nine, making his filmmaking debut after having been a Rhodes Scholar and Harvard philosophy student, then writing the screenplay for *Pocket Money*) changed the names and fictionalized the story to free himself from the bondage of hard, cold facts, allowing him to deal artistically with the essence of the incident—what it meant to us, what it means to him. Once regarded as a young director with the promise of Scorsese and Coppola, Malick has been all but forgotten. Though Malick's films are not easily accessible—too emotionally cold and calculatedly intellectual for mainstream moviegoers—both *Badlands* and *Days of Heaven* (1978) possess striking pictorial composition, as well as validity of theme.

Malick's approach, borrowed from quality literature, is to tell the tale through a narrator who fails to comprehend what is going on, forcing an interpretation that's at once conventional and romantic on complicated, grim events beyond her comprehension. In *Badlands,* this woman is Holly Sargis (Sissy Spacek), a teenager from Texas who, in the late 1950s, has moved with her sign-painting redneck father (Warren Oates) to South Dakota following the death of Holly's mother. "Little did I realize that what would begin in the alleys and back roads of this little town would end in the badlands of Montana," Holly sighs during the film's opening, making clear she is relating imperfect memories of earlier events.

We first see Holly practicing her baton-twirling skills. She appears no different from any other ordinary girl whose greatest ambition at age fifteen is to make the cheerleading team. By chance, she runs into Kit Carruthers (Martin Sheen), a recently fired garbageman who attracts her for one reason, and one reason only: he resembles the late actor and teen idol James Dean. Like so many other modern gangster movies, *Badlands* is about the relationship of life to movies, the way in which people—seemingly normal people—suddenly behave in abnormal ways when they feel the ultimate fantasy is about to come true.

To a degree, Kit happens to look like James Dean; to a degree, Kit nurtures that resemblance. When he smokes a cigarette, he leans back and inhales deeply, posturing to appear like Dean in *Rebel Without a Cause.* When he finds himself in a difficult situation, he wrinkles his brow to appear vulnerable, like Dean in *East of Eden.* When he slings a rifle over his shoulder, he hangs his head and looks crucified, like Dean in *Giant.* His affectations of Dean mannerisms have their intended impact on the childlike Holly, who has lived all her life in stultifying small towns and knows nothing about adventure on the road other than what she's seen in the movies. Previously well-behaved Holly immediately adapts to his

Martin Sheen as Kit Carruthers, the rural gangster as James Dean imitator (courtesy Warner Bros.).

suggested scenario, improvising her role as the bad boy's good-girl-gone-wrong.

Shortly, the nice girl who studied hard at school and diligently worked at her music lessons will lose her virginity to Kit, then calmly stand by as he shoots and kills her own father. Likewise, she will display no obvious emotions as he in turn murders a whole string of people, most of them completely innocent. In one of the most bizarre sequences, Kit—after murdering Holly's father—insists she stop by the school to pick up her books, since they'll shortly be on the road and he doesn't want her to fall behind. The moment is typical of the everyday approach Kit takes toward extraordinary events. Meanwhile, Holly—after dashing to her locker for the texts—tells us "I could have sneaked out the back, but I felt my destiny was now with Kit." Holly sees this not as a lurid criminal act but as the grand adventure she's always secretly hoped would someday happen for her.

We see the story as it occurred, as two of life's losers dart about, shooting people without rhyme or reason. But what we hear is something else entirely, a romanticization in retrospect that transforms common criminality into contemporary myth. Like Bonnie and Clyde before them, Kit and Holly are elevated, by the media of their time, into notorious rural gangsters. During their crime spree, they gradually reconcile themselves, and their sad little existence, to the created reality in the popular imagination of people who know their exploits secondhand, through TV, radio, and newspapers.

There are other resemblances to *Bonnie and Clyde.* The hero kills in large part because he is incapable of successful sex. Like Clyde, Kit initially tells his girl that he doesn't want her just for sex. When, early in the film, they do make love, it's clear he's unable to satisfy her; shortly, he's reaching for his gun as an alternative way to prove his manhood.

Vincent Canby of the *New York Times* called *Badlands* a "cool, sometimes brilliant, always ferociously American film," citing the striking cinematography, which introduced Holly's small town as a place where oak- and maple-lined lawns were so neatly trimmed that they appeared to have been given crew cuts of the type popular back in the Eisenhower era. Malick's film offers an image of the repressed demons always lurking just beneath the surface of even the most seemingly bland and benign society, making ready to explode at unexpected moments. Canby saw *Badlands* as a 1970s comment on the fifties: "Mr. Malick spends no great amount of time invoking Freud to explain the behavior of Kit and Holly, nor is there any Depression to be held ultimately responsible. This is the truth of *Badlands,* something that places it very much in the seventies in spite of its carefully re-created period detail. Kit and Holly are directionless creatures, technically literate but uneducated in any real sense, so desensitized that Kit (in Malick's words at a news conference) can regard the gun with which he shoots people as a kind of magic wand that eliminates small nuisances. Kit and Holly are members of the television generation run amok…if they are at all

The first survivalist: Kit creates an alternative world in the woods where he maintains an elevated vigil (courtesy Warner Brothers).

Sissy Spacek as Holly Sargis, small-town teenager who runs away with Kit because he makes her daily routine "feel a little more like life looks in the movies!" (courtesy Warner Bros.).

aware of their anger (and I'm not sure they are, since they see only boredom), it's because of the difference between the way life is and the way it is presented on the small screen, with commercial breaks instead of lasting consequences."

One sequence powerfully drives home this point. At an isolated prairie house, Kit has just killed an old friend and coworker, Cato (Ramon Bieri). The young couple sits down to watch him die, not in any sadistic way (they actually make pleasant conversation with the man as he slowly expires), but with the same dull entrancement they would exhibit while watching a television show. Then, a nice young couple driving by (Bryan Montgomery and Gail Threlkeld) spot what's happened and have to be killed. Kit leads the young man out into the field to shoot him, the two girls following along. There is no sense of fear or panic as Holly makes small talk with the well-dressed young woman walking alongside her, asking about where she bought her clothes and how far the relationship has progressed with the boy she's dating. They speak as if they were two normal teenagers who had just met, casually chatting on their way to the schoolhouse. Yet Holly knows Kit will kill this

(Above) Kit surveys the modern southwestern wasteland. Writer-director Terrence Malick had the opportunity to display his unique gift for portraying characters who are dwarfed by their surrounding landscapes in only two films, this and 1978's *Days of Heaven* (courtesy Warner Bros.).

(Left) Apprehended at last. The film was inspired by the real-life Starkweather-Fugate killing spree, though filmmaker Malick employed the tale for personal expression rather than objective docudrama (courtesy Warner Bros.).

young woman, along with her boyfriend, in a matter of moments.

In actuality, after Charles Starkweather and Caril Fugate were captured in 1958, he was tried, sentenced, and executed in the electric chair while she was sent to prison. As there was no evidence that she'd ever actually fired a gun, the jury could not get past her mental density to determine whether she had cooperated or been kidnapped. Malick's film sends Kit to the same fate as Starkweather, though it cynically allows Holly to walk free, perhaps pursuing her marital dream. In her final spurt of quietly crazy antilogic, Holly informs us that before his execution, Kit was "kept in solitary, so he didn't have the chance to get acquainted with other inmates…who would have liked him…especially the murderers."

Spacek reads that line in the same effectively flat tone as the rest of her narration; her character is unaware of the absurdist voice in which she speaks. We certainly do have reason to believe the other inmates would have liked Kit, though. Even the deputy (Alan Vint) who arrests him takes a liking to Kit. "You know who that son of a bitch looks like?" he asks the sheriff. "James Dean, that's who!" Perhaps if he hadn't looked like a rebel, Kit would not have aspired to be one. We last see Kit being interviewed after capture, the small-town boy who couldn't even hold down a garbageman's job at last enjoying his Warholian fifteen minutes: one more variation of the modern gangster as pop celebrity.

FIFTEEN

Chinatown

(1974)

A Paramount Release

CAST:

Jack Nicholson *(J.J. Gittes)*; Faye Dunaway *(Evelyn Mulwray)*; John Huston *(Noah Cross)*; Perry Lopez *(Escobar)*; Diane Ladd *(Ida Sessions)*; Darrell Zwerling *(Hollis Mulwray)*; John Hillerman *(Yelburton)*; Roman Polanski *(Knife-Wielding Punk)*.

CREDITS:

Producer, Robert Evans; director, Roman Polanski; screenplay, Robert Towne; cinematography, John A. Alonzo; editor, Sam O'Steen; music, Jerry Goldsmith; running time, 131 minutes; rating, R.

"Most people never have to face that at the right time and right place, they're capable of anything." That line is spoken in *Chinatown* by John Huston as Noah Cross, aging lion of southern California's capitalist elite who, by film's end, is revealed as far more corrupt than any of the small-time con artists and other assorted gangland figures who, throughout the movie, have menaced detective hero Jake Gittes (Jack Nicholson). Cross, we learn, is a monster, both in his public and private life. In the former, he has manipulated land deals (necessitating the "elimination" of numerous people hailing from various social strata) to control Los Angeles' water rights, thereby determining the economic and political future of the entire region. In the latter, he has violated his own daughter, their incestuous relationship resulting in the birth of his daughter/granddaughter.

Huston's remarkable screen presence—gaunt and garrulous, chilling yet undeniably charming in a strange, seductive, scary manner—gave a frightful edge to a role that might, in the hands of a lesser performer, been nothing other than a cliché villain. That was true of the film itself, which struck the perfect balance between period-piece crime-film conventions and a modern sensibility that redeemed such stereotypes. Moving beyond the obvious limitations of an escapist exercise in nostalgia, *Chinatown* emerged as that rare movie which employs a past era in history and movie mythology to comment on the present political climate. As Penelope Gilliat commented in *The New Yorker,* "it is exempt from the usual romanticism about [bygone historical] Los Angeles, is obviously steeped in knowledge of older Hollywood thriller-masters, but is full of young verve, bowing to no one." The opening titles appear in black and white while soft, sensuous jazz plays; for a brief moment, we might believe we've stepped into a revival house. But as the movie begins, color slowly drains into the image until it's clear this is a modern movie: be it cinema and/or history, the past is inseparable from the present.

At first glance, Robert Towne's story does not seem terribly different from those written by Dashiell Hammett, Raymond Chandler, and Mickey Spillane a generation earlier. Private eye Gittes, specializing in divorce cases, is approached in his office by a well-dressed woman (Diane Ladd) who claims to be Mrs. Evelyn Mulwray. The case seems simple enough: she fears her husband is cheating on her, hiring the detective to learn the truth. But in the world of the crime film, nothing is ever simple, just as nothing is what it initially seems. Shortly, Mr. Mulwray is murdered; Jake meets Mrs. Mulwray face-to-face, discovering she (Faye Dunaway) is not the woman who hired him. Jake realizes he has been duped; he's a minor pawn in some nasty plot. The incident might end there, except that Jake is not content to crawl back to his seedy office and lick his wounds.

Like his famed fictional antecedents—lone wolf Sam Spade, jaded knight Philip Marlowe, temperamental tough guy Mike Hammer—Gittes has got to know who did this to him and why. So he pursues on his own,

John Huston as Noah Cross, representative of the gangsters in contemporary crime films, including period pictures like *Chinatown*. Firmly entrenched in the establishment, Cross nonetheless employs ruthless tactics for his corrupt plans that put Al Capone to shame (courtesy Paramount Pictures).

learning that the case moves steadily up the ladder of society, involving privileged socialites as well as low-life grifters, a Big Con of such enormous proportions that even a sneering cynic like Gittes appears wide-eyed when cognition of its vastness dawns. A drought has hit southern California hard, putting water at a premium. People in the power structure—Noah Cross among them—realize they can use this catastrophe to their advantage through their political positions, diverting water to less developed areas, meanwhile employing their financial resources to purchase those still-cheap areas before the water arrives. This is the world of the crime film, where gangsters—in this case, respectable-looking white-collar WASP "business-men" who would never identify themselves as gangsters, though that's precisely what their actions make them—acquire money not for what it can buy, but for its own sake, and the ever-increasing power that comes with ever-larger sums of money.

Towne based his story (set in 1937) on the real-life Owens River Valley scandal of 1908. The situation, however, proved absolutely timeless: 1908, 1937, and 1974 all run together. This was the age of Watergate, the televised hearings that brought down a presidency owing to corruption, conspiracy, and attempted cover-up, all perpetrated by those trusted patriarchs in power. Those very elements formed the core of this elaborate period piece, brought to the screen by director Roman Polanski with a vivid, clear-eyed awareness of unspeakable acts of greed, lust, and ambition taking place in broad daylight, just behind the façades of respectability. No wonder, then, that Paul D. Zimmerman of *Newsweek* tagged this "Watergate with real water."

Director Roman Polanski also played the part of a diminutive hood who cuts open Gittes's nose. Based on the toady villains once incarnated by Elisha Cook Jr., the role effectively evoked past noir thrillers without ever breaking the believability of the story at hand. Evelyn, who becomes Jake's lover, does indeed revive memories of beloved shady ladies from the past, those classy,

Class distinctions have always been at the heart of crime films, classic or contemporary. Here, the honest working-class hero is set upon by goons in the service of corrupt but rich Noah Cross (courtesy Paramount Pictures).

frayed-around-the-edges glamour girls once portrayed by Lizabeth Scott and Alexis Smith. The key to the film's success, though, is that the cliché is evoked only to be given new dimension and modern resonance. Evelyn is a victim of incest (such a situation would barely have been implied, much less explored, in crime films of yore), a very real woman whose characterization quickly moves beyond the limits of genre. She is also a battered woman, physically abused not only by the villain (father and former lover, Noah Cross) but also by her current lover, Jake Gittes. In the film's most memorable scene, he—desperate to know the truth—slaps her again and again, wanting to know the identity of the pretty lost child she cares for.

"She's my sister," Evelyn says after a harsh slap that forces her face to one side.

Gittes, knowing he has not been told the whole truth, slaps her again.

Director Roman Polanski did double duty as the knife-wielding punk who cuts Gittes on the nose in order to scare off the detective (courtesy Paramount Pictures).

Film noir revisited: as the advertising poster suggests, *Chinatown* was the most successful of the numerous attempts to revive the postwar style for modern moviegoers (courtesy Paramount

"She's my daughter," Evelyn says, her face now sent spinning to the other side.

Jake, sensing he has still not been told the whole truth, slaps her once more.

"She's my sister *and* my daughter," Evelyn exclaims.

At last aware of the ugly truth, Jake is unable to move. As in Greek tragedy, the truth will out; whether it will save or destroy the characters remains to be seen.

Jake Gittes is as much a three-dimensional modern man as he is genre hero played by a popular star of the present. "Bogart for the age of rock 'n' roll," the *Village Voice* insisted, though John Simon emphasized the distinction rather than the similarity: "The hero is played by Nicholson as an emblematic man of today. Unlike the Bogartian hero, he is not coolly sure of himself all the way down the line. Nicholson has never trod with greater assurance the fine line between professional cynicism verging on sleaziness and a still untarnished self-respect and concern for at least the less demanding decencies of life." Disgusted by his capacity for cruelty, Jake attempts to "save" Evelyn and her daughter, spiriting them away from their palatial surroundings and the absolute evil residing there.

The final confrontation takes place in the title demimonde, where Jake once worked as a policeman. He and onetime partner Escobar (Perry Lopez), still on the force, try to protect Evelyn but are unable to. She is shot down by her own father while attempting to escape

Jack Nicholson as J.J. Gittes in a situation from the past that eventually transforms into a commentary on the present: Watergate with real water (courtesy Paramount Pictures).

by car with the semiretarded child. Evil incarnate wins out in the end, as Noah Cross—protected by his vast power—seizes the child and carries her back to his abode for purposes that, apparently, are both familial and sexual; it would not be beyond him to seduce the grandchild he incestuously fathered.

In fact, screenwriter Towne initially proposed a slightly hopeful ending, in which Evelyn shoots her father, then escapes with the child. Polanski insisted the conclusion be changed to the bleaker one we see. It isn't surprising that the man whose pregnant wife, Sharon Tate, was killed in a now-legendary incident would have turned into a pessimist, an artist who perceived the world as a place of moral darkness and portrayed it as precisely that in his films. *Christian Century* insisted that *Chinatown*'s power derived from its uncanny combination of the two abiding evils of that time, effectively objectifying this in the period-piece setting: "Polanski merges Manson with Watergate as elements in the substance that now pervades and stains all of society."

"Come on, Jake," Escobar whispers in Jake's ear while forcefully leading him away. "After all, it's Chinatown." It is the evil that exists on the edges of our seemingly sound, safe, sane civilization, encroaching on our supposedly moral world and quietly absorbing it, until nothing is left but respectable façades, which, in the bright light of day, hide the horror once relegated to the night world. That is the frightful truth of *Chinatown,* and of the modern crime genre it is a part of. Or, as the seemingly unvanquishable Noah Cross puts it: "Politicians, ugly buildings, and whores all get respectable if they last long enough."

SIXTEEN

The Killing of a Chinese Bookie

(1976)

A Faces Distribution Release

CAST:

Ben Gazzara *(Cosmo Vitelli);* Seymour Cassel *(Mort Weil);* Timothy Carey *(Flo);* Robert Phillips *(Phil);* Morgan Woodward *(John-the-Boss);* John Red Kullers *(Eddie Red);* Al Rubin *(Marty Reitz);* Azizi Johari *(Rachel);* Virginia Carrington *(Betty);* Meade Roberts *(Mr. Sophistication);* Alice Friedland *(Sherry);* Donna Gordon *(Margo);* Solo Joe Hugh *(Chinese Bookie).*

CREDITS:

Producer, Al Rubin; director/screenwriter, John Cassavetes; camera operators, Fred Helms and Mike Harris; supervising editor, Tom Cornwall; music, Anthony Harris; running time, 130 minutes; rating, R.

John Cassavetes's worldview and cinematic style proved particularly appropriate for the urban thriller, a world of lone wolves and mean streets upon which he imprinted his singular dark modernist vision in *The Killing of a Chinese Bookie.* Cassavetes was always something of a loner himself: a Hollywood star as well as writer-director of edgy experimental films. As such, Cassavetes provided a bridge between the studio system that reached its peak in the late fifties, and the emerging independent filmmakers who would come to dominate commercial American moviemaking during the early 1970s. Not surprisingly, his richest period, both as an actor and an auteur, was in the 1960s. Influenced by the French New Wave experiments, which were then revolutionizing art-house films, he proposed an American variation of cinema verité.

One of those young Method actors who moved from the New York stage to the West Coast during the 1950s, Cassavetes—with his wild pusher's eyes and angular starving-wolf's grin—looked like John Garfield on junk. Not surprisingly, he was quickly cast in 1950s crime films such as *The Night Holds Terror, Crime in the Streets,* and *Edge of the City,* most often as a psychologically disturbed, clearly doped-up, vaguely menacing young man. An attempt to establish Cassavetes as TV's first antihero, via *Johnny Staccato* (a 1959 series about a Greenwich Village jazz musician turned Beat-generation private eye), was cancelled after a single season. Momentarily, it seemed as if, at age thirty-two, Cassavetes's career was over.

Instead, he scrounged up enough money to make a shoestring budget feature, *Shadows,* shot improvisationally from a blueprint rather than a finished script, with talented but unknown actors winging their way through a then-controversial story of interracial romance. "Formless, crude, but strikingly realistic" is how critic Leonard Maltin described it. Clearly, Cassavetes had found his métier as the first self-styled American auteur. He accepted acting roles in Hollywood films (important pictures like *The Dirty Dozen* and *Rosemary's Baby,* also drive-in junk films including the bizarre biker epic *Devil's Angels* and the Italian-lensed crime flick *Machine Gun McCain*) to finance his personal, uneven, fascinating experiments. By this time, Martin Scorsese and other young talents had caught up with him, influenced by his cutting-edge style, transforming it into nouveau mainstream. Cassavetes was no longer the exception, but the rule.

In *The Killing of a Chinese Bookie* (the title is reminiscent of such earlier film noirs as *The Killers, The Killing,* and *Killer's Kiss*), Cassavetes at last returned to the crime milieu in which, some twenty years earlier, he'd debuted as a film actor. Close friend and regular costar Ben Gazzara played Cosmo Vitelli, a compulsive gambler and owner of a sleazy nightclub on Hollywood's fabled Sunset Strip. Cosmo considers himself something of an artist (and, as such, can be interpreted as a stand-in for filmmaker Cassavetes). He writes, produces, and directs the skits (all notably awful) performed in his club, skits that may be intended to represent the similarly improvisational movies Cassavetes made up until his untimely death.

Though not precisely a gangster himself, Cosmo owes the mob $23,000 in gambling debts he cannot even begin to repay. He incurred this debt one night when, having decided to show his girls a stylish high time ("Not class, but style!" is his constant refrain and apparent philosophy on life), Cosmo rented a tuxedo, hired a stretch limo, and took his strippers along for a night of big-stakes poker at a posh Santa Monica club. In the wee hours of the morning Cosmo handed the mob his IOU, lacking enough cash to tip the chauffeur. Though outwardly self-confident, Cosmo lives in constant fear some of the boys will stop by the club for a pound of his flesh. Instead, mobster Flo (Timothy Carey) brings word from John-the-Boss (Morgan Woodward) that the debt will be forgotten, and all forgiven, if Cosmo performs a simple favor: kill a Chinese bookie. Cosmo must perform this contract murder without being allowed any understanding of who the man is or why he must die. The bookie is, simply, the mark; Cosmo, the shooter. That is all he knows, and all he needs to know. As Jay Cocks noted in *Time,* "Cosmo likes the risk of the proposition. Even

Ben Gazzara as Cosmo Vitelli: the Gangster as existential hero (courtesy Faces Distribution).

Cosmo attempts to discover the difference between style and class as he runs a sordid little club on the edges of organized crime (courtesy Faces Distribution).

more, he enjoys the almost certain prospect of disaster. He has been looking for a way over the brink for a long time."

As much a modern existential man as the heroes of Franz Kafka's *The Trial* or Albert Camus's *The Stranger,* Cosmo sets out on a mission that has no meaning for him other than his own survival. As Cosmo blithely walks through the motions of this nihilistic act, we watch and wonder whether he really is the cold absurdist he appears to be, ready to kill without remorse, or if he's inwardly wrestling with the ultimate moral question that haunts us even in our blatantly amoral age: What right do we have to take the life of another man, whoever he may be, whatever he has done? Cassavetes provides a modernist comic touch: Cosmo (like no other killer-for-hire before him) has a blowout on the way to the gentlemanly bookie's isolated Xanadu-like mansion. Unfazed, Cosmo simply hails a yellow cab to take him the rest of the way. Though the genre may be the crime film, Cassavetes endows it with his pervasive sense of everyday reality.

Cosmo has long since ceased to see himself as having any kind of true identity, which perhaps explains why he all but becomes invisible, walking right past the bookie's tough young relatives who've been hired to guard their boss, completing his mission without regard for the feelings of others, though not necessarily without remorse. However, as in any true modern gangster movie, the criminals' code turns out to be a myth: the mobsters who persuaded Cosmo to perform this hit now plan to kill him themselves so the crime can never be traced back. However horrific his act of murder may have been, an audience cannot help but root for Cosmo as he attempts to evade his pursuers in a darkened warehouse. He—and his film—ends where this all began, in the club, where Cosmo joins his Oscar Wildean drag-queen emcee for one last round of "I Can't Give You Anything but Love, Baby!"—their theme song. Notably, his club is called the Crazy Horse, after the popular (though far classier) French strip joint, which in turn was based on saloons as depicted in American crime and cowboy movies. Only the French really appreciate the purity of American movies, including those by Cassavetes. Besides, reality imitates movies, which imitate reality, which imitates movies.

Cosmo's heart is broken; like Jean-Paul Belmondo in Godard's *Breathless,* a French variation of an American gangster film, Cosmo has finally been spurned by the woman he loved, his black stripper. Cassavetes's movie may be perceived as an American spin on the French variation of an American genre film. We then notice what the others do not see: Cosmo's right-hand jacket pocket is filling with blood from a bullet that hit him during all the confusion. But this being a Cassavetes film, the final credits roll before we learn whether or not he's dead. In a more conventional narrative, the lack of closure might seem a violation, though not here. At the end, the singular Cosmo has finally come to represent Cassavetes's vision of modern man as the walking wounded.

The movie is strikingly shot, vividly capturing the world of Cosmo's sad little club, with its "freaky" emcee (played by Meade Roberts, a screenwriter) and its hope-

Azizi Johari as Rachel, the stripper Cosmo loves well, though not wisely, as she will betray him at the end. The film was one of the first to present an interracial romance within the context of a crime melodrama (courtesy Faces Distribution).

ful, whorish "dancers" who try, with exhausted desperation, to convey a sense of déclassé glamour to jaded customers. An approach such as this elicits strong reactions, both positive and negative. In *Saturday Review,* Judith Crist—a fan of Cassavetes's earlier projects, particularly those starring his wife, Gena Rowlands—complained: "*The Killing of a Chinese Bookie* is a mess, as sloppy in concept as it is in execution, as pointless in thesis as it is in concept. Even an amateur would opt for a bit more credibility in plot, a bit more intelligence in the endless improvised chitchat, a bit more stability in the camerawork, a modicum of coherence in the characterizations." On the other hand, Jack Kroll of *Newsweek* argued that "with *The Killing of a Chinese Bookie,* Cassavetes comes on as a genuine, jaggedly idiosyncratic film artist. The jaggedness will put many people off, which is a shame, because this is a rewarding film that asks only that you stay alert and use your senses. Cassavetes breaks things up (in confusing cinematic fragments) because he wants you to feel, not read. [His] feel for this sleazy world is rich, rueful, totally human. Gazzara is wonderful with his abstract glittering smile, his gutter courtesy, his sense of when to stop moving and take a punch. Visually stunning, stylistically extravagant, this film converts Cassavetes's excesses to a prodigal poetry."

Vincent Canby of the *New York Times* complained that "watching the film is like listening to someone use a lot of impressive words, the meaning of which are just wrong enough to keep you in a state of total confusion, but occasionally right enough to hold your attention. He hopes that if he continues to talk, he may happen upon a truth as if it were a found object." That last phrase is particularly apt. Here, as in other pictures, Cassavetes purposefully chose to confound audiences by drowning out dialogue with encroaching sounds from the streets. Conventional-minded audiences found this off-putting, whereas iconoclasts considered it the cinematic expression of Cassavetes's great theme, that being the death of human communication during our machine-dominated age. One had to concede a great deal while watching such a film, as slickness of style and singularity of purpose were quite impossible. In their place was the adventure of discovering a one-of-a-kind movie that the writer-director had himself discovered while filming it.

The last angry man: actor/director John Cassavetes (courtesy 20th Century–Fox).

SEVENTEEN

F.I.S.T.

(1978)

A United Artists Release

CAST:

Sylvester Stallone *(Johnny Kovak)*; Rod Steiger *(Senator Madison)*; Peter Boyle *(Max Graham)*; Melinda Dillon *(Anna Zerinkas)*; David Huffman *(Abe Belkin)*; Tony Lo Bianco *(Babe Milano)*; Kevin Conway *(Vince Doyle)*; Cassie Yates *(Molly)*; Peter Donat *(Arthur St. Claire)*; Henry Wilcoxon *(Win Talbot)*; Brian Dennehy *(Frank Vasko)*.

CREDITS:

Producer and director, Norman Jewison; executive producer, Gene Corman; assistant director, Andrew Stone; screenplay, Joe Eszterhas and Sylvester Stallone from a story by Eszterhas; cinematography, Laszlo Kovacs; editors, Tony Gibbs and Graeme Clifford; music, Bill Conti; production design, Richard MacDonald; costumes, Anthea Sylbert, Tom Carano, and Thalia Phillips; running time, 145 minutes; rating, PG.

Following three *Rambo*s, five *Rocky*s, and a countless number of failed comedies, it's a strange experience to go back and rewatch early Sylvester Stallone films. Shocking, really, for it forces us to recall that he was once a serious actor/writer. Briefly, Stallone—soon to be a self-styled Superman—was perceived as the perfect proletarian actor, portraying a contemporary equivalent of Marlon Brando's blue-collar hero from *On the Waterfront.* Of all the early Stallone roles, his characterization in *F.I.S.T.* was the one that cemented that comparison.

Like Brando's 1954 film, *F.I.S.T.* dealt with the corruption of labor unions owing to connections with organized crime; like *Waterfront,* it featured Rod Steiger in a key supporting role. Stallone's Johnny Kovak, like Brando's Terry Malloy, is a simple man who finds himself in a position to succeed if he'll accept the dirt and do favors for gangsters. Kovak (a slightly fictionalized version of Jimmy Hoffa) gradually sells himself—and his soul—to organized crime, until he emerges as a gangster/thug who must be eliminated, either legally by the Senate Rackets Committee (with Rod Steiger playing a Bobby Kennedyish character, here called Madison) or illegally by the mob, which has come to believe Kovak knows too much and can no longer be trusted.

Unfortunately for Kovak, the mob gets there first. The final shot depicts a truck, driven by a union member, sporting the bumper sticker "Where's Johnny?"; there really were such stickers asking "Where's Jimmy?" at the time of Hoffa's disappearance. If *On the Waterfront* is an epic—about one man's triumph over evil—then *F.I.S.T.* is a modern tragedy, depicting the fall of a once great man.

The story begins in 1937 Cleveland, when Johnny and best pal Abe Belkin (David Huffman) can no longer tolerate the horrid working conditions for truckers like themselves, or for nearby factory workers including Anna (Melinda Dillon), the tenement-dwelling Old World immigrant Johnny loves. When Johnny stands up to a boss, he's fired; shortly, Mike Monahan (Richard Herd) asks him to work for the Federation of Interstate Truckers as a recruiter. When Johnny proves to be a great communicator, he rivals the national union president, Max Graham (Peter Boyle, basing his character on Dave Beck), in popularity.

But if Abe symbolizes Johnny's angelic side, another old friend, the dapper "musketeer of the streets" Vince Doyle (Kevin Conway), stands as Abe's polar opposite and the dark side of Johnny. Vince is an Irish gangster who offers to help after the union boys decide to strike and are beaten by scabs. Doyle suggests "a little push" wouldn't hurt. Over Abe's loud objections, Johnny lets Vince try his way, and after the gang members blow up nonunion trucks—killing one man during a riot—the bosses finally cave in, sign new contracts, and acknowledge the union's right to exist.

Unfortunately, the union (modeled after the Teamsters) becomes not only an entity to be reckoned with but, in the minds of many, a force of evil. Johnny comes to believe that their union cannot have full impact

Johnny and best friend Abe Belkin (David Huffman) lead fellow workers on a strike against the coldhearted factory bosses who deny them a decent living. Little does Johnny realize that in time, he will be as corrupted by power as the people he at this point fights against (courtesy United Artists).

until every last industry is unionized. When he learns Frank Vasko (Brian Dennehy) and his fellow workers in Chicago don't want a union in their plant (they have been given every concession they've asked for by decent-minded bosses), Johnny and Vince travel to the Windy City, where they enlist the local mafioso Babe Milano (Tony Lo Bianco) to help them. His thugs threaten to rape Vasko's wife; shortly thereafter, Vasko persuades his men to join the union.

Johnny ascends to the presidency of F.I.S.T. by winning ever-larger pay raises for the men (and their undying devotion), but must appease Milano and the mob, to whom he is now in debt. Milano requests one of his "return favors": that Johnny's truck drivers refuse to deliver alcohol to roadhouses that don't have one of Milano's jukeboxes on the premises. Johnny delivers, and in so doing accedes to the first of many corruptions that will set him up for the Senate hearing a quarter century later.

The screenwriter Joe Eszterhas had written a series of magazine articles about the relationship of the labor movement to organized crime. The stories caught the attention of producer Gene Corman, who hired Eszterhas (later to achieve greater fame with psychosexual thrillers including *The Jagged Edge, Basic Instinct,* and *Sliver*) to prepare the first draft of a screenplay. Stallone, riding high on the advance reputation of *Rocky* (the film had not yet been released when he was signed to star in

Anna Zerinkas (Melinda Dillon) joins Johnny for sincere street protests early in his career, then marries him out of respect for the man's ideals. She cannot, however, keep him from slowly but surely selling out to the crime lords (courtesy United Artists).

F.I.S.T.), agreed to star only if he could contribute to the script.

David Ansen of *Newsweek* wrote: "If ambition were enough, *F.I.S.T.* would be a great movie. [*F.I.S.T.*] tries to be *The Godfather* of the union movement, a bona fide American tragedy about the inevitable corruption of power. The outline is there, but the detail and the coloring that could have turned a concept into a living canvas are missing. *F.I.S.T.* is big, bold, and botched…Jewison and his screenwriters have drained the life out of a terrific story to make it conform to some outmoded idea of what a Hollywood [epic] should be."

On the other hand, Vincent Canby of the *New York Times* was one of the film's champions, calling *F.I.S.T.* "a fascinating film…massive, sometimes clumsy and over-simplified but ultimately a very moving melodrama about the rise and fall of a powerful union leader." Canby compared the Johnny and Abe characters, who stumble into union work rather than seek it out for any political or philosophical reasons, to the two brothers played by James Cagney and Eddie Woods in *The Public Enemy,* that granddaddy of all gangster films, arguing that this was essential to *F.I.S.T.*'s appeal. The *Variety* rave likewise praised the fact that the early "portion of

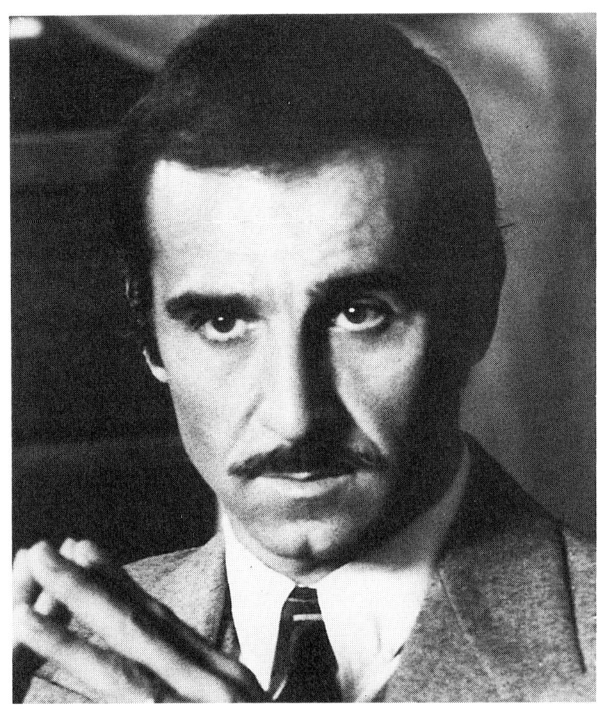

Tony Lo Bianco as Babe Milano, the Chicago racketeer who agrees to help Johnny establish the union, but at a price Johnny could not guess at the time (courtesy United Artists).

Johnny is supported by the members of the Federation of Interstate Truckers for their presidency. Director Norman Jewison angles the shot from over Johnny's shoulder to suggest that, however unconsciously, Johnny has begun to look down on the very men he once walked alongside (courtesy United Artists).

Johnny as an innocent, honest blue-collar youth, full of socialist ideals...

the film strongly evokes Warner Bros. social melodramas of the time; one almost expects Barton MacLane, Pat O'Brien, Ann Sheridan, Cagney, and the rest to appear at any moment." Intriguingly, Ansen likewise argued that *F.I.S.T.* evoked earlier gangster movies, seeing this as a liability: "Perhaps, if you've never seen any of the Warner Bros. social epics of the thirties...this will all seem fresh." For better or worse, *F.I.S.T.* is a throwback to those films, and the way it plays (however unconsciously) with gangster-movie tradition is what's most interesting about it.

Doyle, the Irish gangster, is the flashy dresser, always seen out on the town with flashy women. Our first glimpse of him is at an amusement park, where he has a girl on each arm; they are trophy women, and he likes to show them off. When Kovak appears with Anna, Vince is immediately attracted to her, not knowing how conservative Anna is (she won't even let Johnny touch her hand, much less steal a kiss). Doyle does not praise Anna's looks directly to her (acknowledging her as a human being), but rather compliments her to Johnny, who becomes embarrassed for Anna; she is a woman of substance (however underdeveloped her character may be) and will not tolerate being viewed as a beauty object.

Doyle is the gangster as profligate, the man without home or family, who seems to exist—like the gangsters in so many 1930s melodramas, as well as those on 1950s TV—in some always nocturnal realm, which he inhabits as a calculating playboy. Just as with Capone, Nitti, or any of the other supposedly real gangsters who drifted in and out of TV's *The Untouchables* during its four-year run on ABC (the real Capone and Nitti did indeed have home lives, as did the more realistically rendered gangsters in *The Godfather*), it's hard to picture Doyle going home to anybody. He is the gangster as cardboard cutout, soft-spoken but vaguely menacing at all times. He exists to begin the corruption of Johnny Kovak. As for Johnny, he will exist in a state of denial—he not only tells the senator but himself believes that he's got only the best interests of his union at heart—until the very end. Johnny does not know, cannot grasp, that he has somehow arced downward from proletarian idealist to corrupt gangster.

But Doyle is not powerful enough to complete the corruption of Kovak. Only Babe Milano can do that.

...transforms into Johnny the corrupt, an ally of gangsters who run his union as a crime boss might his empire of evil (courtesy United Artists).

From the moment Vince and Kovak head for Chicago, Milano embodies the film's stereotypical vision of the Sicilian gangster. In comparison to Vince's single-colored suits, made flamboyant only by a jauntily angled fedora, Milano is always seen in knockout pinstripes. He's first encountered in an Italian restaurant, where in between his explanations of how easy it would be to win Vasko over to their way of thinking, he offers elaborate instructions to the waiter as to how his pasta should be prepared. His Sicilian accent is thick and mellifluous.

Unlike the unattached Doyle, Milano is a family man, occasionally speaking of a son who, like Michael in *The Godfather,* has gone off to college. Milano always speaks like a businessman, insisting he and Kovak are merely friendly business acquaintances who do "favors" for one another. Still, he offers to buy Kovak and his new bride a house as their wedding present after the first brief meeting between the two men. Kovak is smart enough to know that if he accepts the present, he will henceforth belong to the mob, even if their Faustian deal is never put into precise words.

Before the Senate committee, Milano denies that organized crime even exists, deflating the senator's probing questions with sly humor. Milano is the coldhearted man of Machiavellian reason who decides that Abe (who has considered testifying against Kovak and, in the process, against the mob) must be silenced; shortly thereafter, he presumably orders the silencing of Kovak as well. At a time when Coppola was attempting to humanize the Sicilian gangster in the *Godfather* saga, Jewison played him as cliché: never glimpsed anywhere but in a restaurant or office, occasionally alluding to a fuller life we are not allowed to see.

In the *Village Voice,* Andrew Sarris nailed the film's significance as a part of the emerging modern gangster movie when he wrote that *F.I.S.T.* "settles down into a lassitude of inevitable corruption as part and parcel of the American success story." This notion—that organized crime is everywhere, just under the surface of everyday life, and that the successful characters are the ones who accept that fact rather than fight it—would characterize the contemporary if cynical spin that has been basic to the gangster film from 1967 to the present.

James Caan as Frank, the first significant crime-film character of the 1980s: an old-fashioned burglar transformed into technically proficient robber for a new decade (courtesy United Artists).

EIGHTEEN

Thief

(1981)

A United Artists Release

CAST:

James Caan *(Frank);* Tuesday Weld *(Jessie);* Willie Nelson *(Okla);* James Belushi *(Barry);* Robert Prosky *(Leo);* Tom Signorelli *(Attaglia);* Dennis Farina *(Carl);* Nick Michaels *(Nick).*

CREDITS:

Producers, Jerry Bruckheimer and Ronnie Caan; director and screenplay, Michael Mann, from the book *The Home Invaders* by Frank Hohimer; cinematography, Donald Thorin; editor, Dov Hoenig; music, Tangerine Dream; sound supervisor, David Ronne; production design, Mel Bourne; art director, Mary Dodson; running time, 122 minutes; rating, R.

During the late 1970s, movies, crime films included, would have to acknowledge the rock-video sensibility, while dispensing with traditional elements, such as lengthy exposition through dialogue, if they were going to catch the attention of ever-younger audiences. The first gangster film fashioned in such a manner was *Thief,* which marked the theatrical directing debut of Michael Mann. He was to bring the rock-video approach to network TV with *Miami Vice.* Music for the film was provided by Tangerine Dream, an electronic-synthesizer band that caught the spirit of the high-tech times. James Caan, searching for yet another gangster role since he'd been rubbed out in the first *Godfather* film, here played Frank, an ultracontemporary thief.

Frank is a career criminal, expert at slipping into seemingly impregnable places with his partner, Barry (James Belushi), and making off with anything he wants. Frank is a thief for his times: forsaking a gun, Frank relies on an electromagnetic drill and custom-made eight-thousand-degree thermal lance. If he can't crack the combination on a safe, he merely blasts through it. Frank can't feel any guilt about taking the jewelry: ultimately, the only people Frank robs are the insurance companies.

Frank can't help being what he is: the product of a difficult childhood, arrested at age twenty for a small theft, killing an attacker behind bars, and ultimately serving eleven years in Joliet. Now he has such an extensive prison record that no one in Chicago will hire him for any honest job. But after four years of successful heisting, Frank's problems are just beginning. Leo (Robert Prosky), a Chicago variation on Don Corleone, decides to transform this ruggedly individualistic thief into a functional part of the current crime establishment. Frank's new wife opposes such a union. The perceptive Jessie (Tuesday Weld) is a former drug smuggler who survived the killing of her then dealer husband and now wants only to go straight, a desire Frank shares.

What Frank learns is precisely what so many crime-film heroes before him have discovered: it's far easier to get into organized crime than to get out. Frank and Jessie are, throughout, striving for some sort of normalcy within the bizarre framework of their life in crime. They would like to move to the suburbs and adopt a child. Frank even carries a game plan for his future that he designed while in prison, including an idealistic vision of a perfect Ozzie-and-Harriet split-level home that he hopes to turn into a reality, qualifying Frank as one more hopeless romantic. Also, he's one more contemporary crime hero in search of family. Frank has a decent (within the film's context) father figure, the cowboyish Okla (Willie Nelson), a former cellmate who gave the young man what guidance he could. But Okla is still on the inside; the film focuses on Frank's wavering between this acceptable foster father and the dangerously alluring Leo.

But Leo's "family" soon proves to be anything but benign to its members. Leo may arrange for Frank and Jessie to get the black-market baby they have their hearts set on (she cannot have children), but at a terrible cost.

James Caan, being beaten by opponents, becomes something of a Christ symbol owing to the way in which his enemies position his arms (courtesy United Artists).

forever alone. Clearly, filmmaker Mann (who adapted Frank Hohimer's novel and also served as executive producer) was as interested in raising existential issues as he was in updating the crime genre. "The setting is in the twilight land halfway between gritty gangster melodrama and that world where writers meditate self-consciously on the sorrows of life," Vincent Canby wrote in the *New York Times,* noting also that, as in the rock videos, "this neon-lit, nighttime Chicago is pretty enough to be framed and hung on a wall.... The camera consistently turns the most commonplace objects into beautiful abstractions of reality."

Mann's desire to include substance as well as style allowed for political interpretation. Andrew Sarris of the *Village Voice* insisted that *Thief* was "the most consciously Marxist American gangster movie since *Force of Evil*" thirty-five years earlier. Critics Al Auster and Leonard Quart explained that "in contrast to the aristocratic thieves of Hitchcock *(To Catch a Thief)* or [Norman] Jewison *(The Thomas Crown Affair),* Frank is a proletarian whose consciousness nudges cautiously close to an understanding of alienated labor." He's a man who takes great pride in his skilled (if illegal) labor, "spir-

Their beloved baby becomes one more "deal," struck with the nouveau devil: an outwardly respectable gangster who steals away something of your soul with each transaction. Frank enjoys a fascinating relationship with the audience watching the movie. They came to see him living life on the edge (the audience's fantasy) owing to boredom with their ordinariness, whereas the hero on-screen wants only to trade places with the suburbanite viewer. In the film, conventional society proves no better than organized crime: the police Frank comes in contact with are corrupt enough to make him appreciate Leo.

The key question is whether Frank will rebel against the inhumanity of modern life and make the commitment to his own imperfect, even dysfunctional family unit; that will necessitate his standing up against the Family itself. Burned by Leo, who double-crosses his new "son" by stealing all the money from a complex heist, Frank turns nihilistic. He burns down his new home as well as the gangster's headquarters, rejecting both family and Family, accepting that he was meant to be

Frank is forced from his car by two unscrupulous policemen (Gavin Mac Fadyen and John Santucci). Like other contemporary crime films, *Thief* insists that those working for the Establishment are inseparable from supposed underworld elements (courtesy United Artists).

The crime-film hero as abusive male in search of enlightenment: Frank forces himself to resist an urge to slap Jessie (Tuesday Weld).

itually cleansed by his dedication to his craft," as Pauline Kael wrote. In this interpretation, Frank views (and rejects) Leo less because he is a ganglord kingpin, more because he is the unfeeling, corrupt boss who wants to make an easy profit. Leo—the gangster as white-collar executive—achieves this without working himself, instead exploiting working-class Frank's labor, promising labor everything but leaving labor with nothing.

"My work, my risk, my sweat," Frank screeches at Leo when he realizes the man wants to steal more than his fair share of the profits from a *Rififi*-like jewel robbery. Ultimately, Frank must give up his long shot at realizing the average American's dream to exact vengeance on Leo for violating Frank's sense of self-worth. However, the film's conclusion can also be interpreted as the polar opposite of Marxism. Frank ultimately rejects Jessie's offer to help him, becoming that conservative hero of both classic and contemporary movies who follows his personal code and ultimately believes in the individual over the collective. His antecedents include not only gangsters but also policemen, from (recently) Clint Eastwood in *Dirty Harry* to (much earlier) Gary Cooper in *High Noon*. Afterward, these lawmen throw away their badges; criminal Frank throws away the only thing he has, that sustaining sketch of a glorious future that he has sentimentally referred to throughout the film. In a Peckinpah-inspired ballet of blood, Frank shoots it out with Leo and his cohorts, eliminates them all, then staggers away, wounded but with his notion of retro-male pride intact. Frank tried to be the family man, in ever sense of the word; finally, he accepts that he is, and always will be, a loner.

The "thief" as hero: James Caan in action (courtesy United Artists).

NINETEEN

The Cotton Club

(1984)

An Orion Pictures Release

CAST:

Richard Gere *(Dixie Dwyer);* Diane Lane *(Vera Cicero);* Gregory Hines *(Sandman Williams);* Lonette McKee *(Lila Rose Oliver);* Bob Hoskins *(Owney Madden);* James Remar *(Dutch Schultz);* Nicolas Cage *(Vincent "Mad Dog" Dwyer);* Allen Garfield *(Abbadabba Berman);* Fred Gwynne *(Frenchy Demange);* Gwen Verdon *(Tish);* Larry Fishburne *(Bumpy Rhodes);* Joe Dallesandro *(Charles "Lucky" Luciano);* Maurice Hines *(Clay Williams);* also, Jennifer Grey, Lisa Jane Persky, Diane Venora.

CREDITS:

Producer, Robert Evans; director, Francis Coppola; screenplay, Coppola and William Kennedy from a story by Coppola and Mario Puzo; cinematography, Stephen Goldblatt; editors, Barry Malkin and Robert Q. Lovett; music, John Barry; music consultant, Jerry Wexler; production designer, Richard Sylbert; running time, 121 minutes; rating, R.

One key theme of the modern gangster movie is the relationship between organized crime and the entertainment business, Hollywood in particular. No film illustrates that theme more vividly than *The Cotton Club.* Fascinatingly enough, this is true not only of the on-screen story about Harlem's legendary nightclub at Lenox and 142nd Street, but also the behind-the-scenes tale of how the movie was made; this cinches that other contemporary crime-movie theme, the relationship of real life to reel life. In the early 1970s, Robert Evans had overseen Paramount's production of *The Godfather,* the monumental gangster film that turned the all-but-unknown Francis Coppola into America's leading auteur. Toward the end of that decade, Evans was inspired by James Haskins's volume of photographs, shot at the Cotton Club a half century earlier, to make a $20-million movie about jazz artists and coffee-colored chorines mixing with movie stars and bootleggers in the late 1920s and early 1930s.

At the time, he planned to cast Al Pacino and Richard Pryor in the leading roles, then direct himself; this was to be Evans's dream project come true. That, of course, meant maintaining total control, financial as well as creative. Turning his back on the studios that had nurtured him, Evans set out to bankroll the movie on his own. Apparently succumbing to the belief that the end justifies the means, Evans made a deal with several Arab arms dealers, then came to his senses and returned the money, in turn becoming involved with Las Vegas casino entrepreneurs, essentially modern counterparts of the shady characters in his story.

With the money (its cleanliness always in doubt) now in his pocket, plus Richard Gere and Gregory Hines signed to replace the intended stars, Evans realized the script he'd commissioned by *Godfather* author Mario Puzo was unplayable. Who else to bring in as script doctor but Coppola, whose magic touch had made *The Godfather* click? Having fallen on hard times owing to self-indulgent bombs like *One From the Heart,* Coppola was eager to accept the $250,000 writing fee, essentially throwing out Puzo's entire approach and starting fresh. Ultimately, Coppola agreed to take control of the directorial reins, which Evans had come to realize he could not handle. Tough-guy writer William Kennedy, all the rage after winning the Pulitzer Prize for *Ironweed,* came on board as Coppola's collaborator. Still, even after shooting began on a Queens, New York, studio set that alone was costing $140,000 a week, Evans and Coppola wrangled over the script. As the budget soared to $47 million and Gere threatened to walk out if someone did not restore a semblance of control, the filmmakers hurriedly completed nearly forty more drafts of the screenplay after principal photography had commenced. At one point, Coppola actually stormed off the set and jetted to Europe. To receive a fast $15 million from Orion (to pay mounting bills and keep the distributor from

Dixie Dwyer, current gangland hanger-on and future film star specializing in gangster roles, develops a romantic fixation on Vera Cicero, a gangster's mistress (courtesy Orion Pictures).

The gangster as movie star: Richard Gere as the George Raft look-alike Dixie Dwyer (photo by Adger W. Cowans, courtesy Orion Pictures).

pulling the plug), Evans finally did the unthinkable: he totally relinquished his control over *The Cotton Club*.

It's doubtful any on-screen story could have matched that one for drama, and sadly *The Cotton Club* is paltry as drama. The script settles for a pair of highly conventional love stories, told in a parallel manner. Gere's character, Dixie Dwyer, is a cornet player who inadvertently saves the life of gangster Dutch Schultz. As a reward, he's given a job as Dutch's "beard": Dixie must pretend to be the lover of Dutch's mistress, floozy-chanteuse-moll Vera Cicero (Diane Lane), whenever Dutch's suspicious wife happens to be around. Dixie's problem is that, despite her hard heart, he really loves Vera and wants her for himself. Vera loves him, too, though she's long since learned to go where the money is. Likewise, dancer Sandman Williams (Gregory Hines) falls madly in love, at first sight, with Lila Rose Oliver (Lonette McKee), a light-skinned blues and jazz singer who dreams of breaking out of the black entertainment industry, going downtown to Broadway, perhaps even pass for white. Though she loves Sandman, her career ambitions threaten to override her best instincts.

The most interesting thing about these characters is the roman-à-clef quality. Dixie, who ends up in Hollywood playing gangsters and modeling them after his old boss, is George Raft as a jazz artist rather than a dancer; while Sandman, who can't decide if he wants to go solo or continue working with his brother (played by real-life brother Maurice Hines), recalls one of the Nicholas Brothers. Vera brings to mind that incendiary blonde Texas Guinan, while Lila stands in for Lena Hornc. Unfortunately, there is nothing else to engage us except what the energetic actors bring to their roles. The characters are nothing more than clichés culled from old movies, skin-deep sketches instead of the in-depth portraits an epic film (such as any of *The Godfather* movies) provides.

There is a major difference between making a movie that references old movies and making a movie that's nothing more than a superficial rendering of stale old movie plots and people. At its rare best moments, *The Cotton Club* offers the former, as when, toward the end, Dixie stands outside a movie theater, peering into his beloved's eyes, speaking cliché words of romantic love. Behind him, we see a poster for his movie *Mob Boss,*

Based in part on the real-life Nicholas Brothers, Maurice and Gregory Hines play the Williams Brothers, who hope their talent as dancers will allow them an escape from life on the streets (courtesy Orion Pictures).

the profile of him in that reel image precisely mirroring his real image, even as Dixie borrows words from his recent film to conquer a woman he might otherwise lose.

Too often, though, *The Cotton Club* borrows familiar images and stale dialogue, but does so uncritically and unimaginatively, as if Coppola somehow convinced himself that a carbon copy would in itself provide some sort of statement. Sandman tells Vera, upon their first meeting, that "I want to take you away from here; let's never be separated, you and me." There's no edge of irony to suggest a necessary distance from such dated dialogue. Later, Coppola shows the passing of time through a montage right out of Raoul Walsh's *The Roaring Twenties:* rapidly edited images of tommy-gunning gangsters and high-kicking showgirls, set against red-hot jazz. The effect of all this verbal and visual nostalgia is, in this expensive and elaborate context, all but incomprehensible: an unhappy halfway point between the serious-minded evocation of gangster-movie mythology in *Bugsy* and the broad burlesque of the Michael Keaton spoof *Johnny Dangerously*.

Despite numerous script problems, filmmaker Francis Ford Coppola did manage to recapture the golden days of the Cotton Club, with its lavish musical acts (courtesy Orion Pictures).

Coppola was apparently influenced by MTV, which had just then made itself felt as a major influence on the nation's young. Many filmmakers predicted rock videos would shorten the attention span of the youthful moviegoer, necessitating the creation of films that played to such an audience through short scenes. Though set in a more relaxed period from the past, *The Cotton Club* breathlessly jumps from one underdeveloped scene to the next. The tragedy of this is that the MTV youth audience didn't care about the film's music or milieu. If targeted at anyone, *The Cotton Club* should have been designed for the last vestiges of the "old" audience that appreciated the chosen period but would have preferred a slower pace and complex characters of the type Evans had provided in *Chinatown*. As Ian Pearson wrote in *Maclean's,* "the music and choreography are consistently breathtaking. But the glorious, inventive music of [Duke] Ellington and his contemporaries only emphasizes the shallowness and banality of Coppola's tale. Although its song and dance sequences are stunning, *The Cotton Club* has little dramatic momentum. Instead, with its frantic, confusing pace and crowded cast of one-dimensional characters, the film resembles an overblown gangster comic strip."

Part of the problem is that Coppola's main characters are peripheral to the story of *The Cotton Club*. A far more effective choice would have been Owney Madden, owner of the club and associate of the varied gangsters—Irish, Italian, Jewish, and African-American—who parade in and out. Though steeped in crime, Owney—like so many modern gangster-movie heroes—only wants to go straight. He is rational and quietly charming when dealing with competing factors, though his wary eyes reveal he can be decisive and deadly when circumstances demand ruthless action. Humble to the point of invisibility, though absolutely regal when push comes to shove, Owney is devious when dealing with criminals yet strikes us as being honest about himself in a way none of the others are. He is, simply, the same essential character Hoskins played three years earlier in the classic British crime film *The Long Good Friday,* which succeeds (on an art-house level) in a way this intended blockbuster does not.

About the actual club, Lena Horne once wrote: "The shows had a primitive, naked quality that was supposed to make a civilized audience lose its inhibitions."

The real and the reel: Gangster Dutch Schultz (*right*, James Remar) confronts Dixie, an actor who plays gangsters in motion pictures (photo by Adger W. Cowans, courtesy Orion Pictures).

That may explain why the decor suggested a jungle: the club allowed upscale whites the cheap thrill of briefly entering the forbidden world, flirting momentarily with the heart of darkness. Which meant, of course, that the club simultaneously exploited the black artists (twisting their talent and culture into a product for the consumption of condescending whites) while showcasing them (without the club, greats such as Horne, Ellington, and Cab Calloway would never have had their big breaks). It was, at best, a mixed blessing, and the film's key failure is an inability to elucidate any of this, merely mentioning the situation in passing, then providing a colorful mosaic of musical routines with fragmentary glimpses of slumming show-business types (Gloria Swanson, James Cagney, and Charlie Chaplin) and the noted criminals of the day.

Dixie's younger brother Vincent (Nicolas Cage) appears briefly as a fictionalized version of "Mad Dog" Coll. Vincent is that recurring character in the modern gangster film, the young hood who begins as minion to a mob boss, then plots his own ascension to power. During one gangland slaying that Vincent oversees on the New York streets, several innocent children are shot down. When the newspapers label him "Mad Dog," Vincent insists to his brother (now a Hollywood star) that the killings were totally unintentional. One more media-created mythic figure, he's the cute kid brother recast as mad-dog killer. Standing up to the Irish gangsters is Charles "Lucky" Luciano (Joe Dallesandro, onetime Andy Warhol star), the Italian gangster who here remains in the shadows until he and Owney decide Dutch might spill all he knows to the new crime commissioner Dewey, necessitating the silencing of Dutch.

Ultimately, though, the most memorable gangster in the film is Bumpy Rhodes, played with a quiet sense of menace by Larry Fishburne. The African American as gangster/activist, he refuses to take the abuse of whites. At one point he tells his friend Sandman, "I'm not a dancer. I'm a pimp, a thief, a gambler. That's what I do. I don't have no talent for dancing to where I want to get in the world. There's only two things I have to do in this world. Stay black, and die. The white man has left me nothing but the underworld. And that's where I 'dance.'" In a film of unrealized potential and unfulfilled ambitions, this brief, classic moment expresses serious thought—which this slick, over-produced creation of the nouveau-Hollywood establishment otherwise sorely lacks—about crime as a social necessity.

Francis Ford Coppola, who had created the legendary *Godfather* films, returned to the world of crime when given the opportunity to re-create the heyday of Harlem's Cotton Club. Here he prepares Diane Lane for an upcoming scene (courtesy Orion Pictures).

TWENTY

Once Upon a Time in America

(1984)

A Warner Bros. Release

CAST:

Robert De Niro *(David "Noodles" Aaranson);* James Woods *(Max);* Elizabeth McGovern *(Deborah);* Treat Williams *(Jimmy O'Donnell);* Tuesday Weld *(Carol);* Burt Young *(Joey);* Joe Pesci *(Frankie);* Danny Aiello *(Police Chief);* William Forsythe *(Cockeye);* James Hayden *(Patsy);* Darlanne Fluegel *(Eve);* Larry Rapp *(Fat Moe);* Amy Rider *(Peggy);* Scott Tiler *(Young Noodles);* Jennifer Connelly *(Young Deborah);* James Russo *(Bugsy);* Richard Bright *(Chicken Joe).*

CREDITS:

Producer, Arnon Milchan; director, Sergio Leone; screenplay Leone and Leonardo Benvenuti, Piero De Bernardi, Enrico Medioli, Franco Arcalli, Franco Ferrini, and Stuart Kaminsky, based on the novel *The Hoods* by Harry Grey; cinematography, Tonino Delli Colli; editor, Nino Baragli; music, Ennio Morricone; art direction, Carlo Simi and James Singelis (New York); costume design, Gabriella Pescucci and Richard Bruno; running times (various): 265 minutes (Italian-TV cut), 227 minutes (European release print), 143 1/2 minutes (American theatrical release); rating, R.

With his spaghetti westerns—*A Fistful of Dollars, For a Few Dollars More,* and *The Good, the Bad, and the Ugly*—Sergio Leone established himself as the great example of a European filmmaking mentality understanding and appreciating Hollywood's golden-age genre films, their artistry and appeal, more so than any American director working today. With the advent of his epic *Once Upon a Time...in the West,* Leone made clear he was not merely a clever copier of past masters but a true artist, able to take half forgotten formulas from old films and blow them up bigger and better than ever on the widest screen imaginable. Leone simultaneously revived and caricatured our collective movie mythology, redeeming the stereotypes by allowing them a vivid, vital new on-screen existence. That remarkable film provided his final word on the western, so Leone understandably moved on to another genre that had always interested him.

Leone's uncut version of *Once Upon a Time in America* begins in 1933, with a brutal hit. Several killers crash their way into an apartment, killing Eve (Darlanne Fluegel), though they are after her boyfriend, Jewish gangster "Noodles" Aaranson (Robert De Niro). But he manages to slip away; we next see him, now aged, in 1968, a prodigal at last returning to the New York of his youth. There, Noodles visits his friend Fat Moe (Larry Rapp) and recovers a briefcase containing the missing money that caused him to be pursued in the first place. As Noodles gazes at the loot, the film leaps back to his oldest memory: In 1922, he and his young friends are growing up on the East Side. Survival of the fittest is the order of the day; in another climate, these bright boys might have turned out to be leading businessmen. But this is the Prohibition era, so they quickly form their own little criminal clique, their only way of making the money they hunger for.

Once Upon a Time in America is to the Jewish gangster what Coppola's *Godfather* trilogy was to the Sicilian: the epic tale of how a group of people went after their share of the American dream, in the only way that bright but uneducated, streetwise males knew how to proceed. "A kosher counterpart to The Godfather" is how *The New Republic* tagged it. The reigning gangster of the area is Bugsy (James Russo), and in time, Noodles and the other young guns go up against him, taking the terrain away. There is no quarter asked or given; they treat Bugsy as he would treat them. This is an asphalt jungle; like primitive beasts struggling for supremacy, there are only victors and vanquished.

Noodles ends in jail after accidentally killing a cop while eliminating Bugsy. He silently serves his time, never ratting on his fellow gang members; they, likewise, follow their code of honor by carefully putting Noodles' share of the take aside so it will be waiting for him when he's released. They also pour a hefty portion of loot into their secret "bank," a piece of luggage (glimpsed in the

Filmmaker Sergio Leone, working in an epic vein, brought the teeming life on the Lower East Side to contemporary movie screens; here young Deborah (Jennifer Connelly) meets the young man who will determine her course in life (courtesy Warner Bros./The Ladd Company).

Now adult gangsters, Max and his companions shoot it out with their enemies. Leone's filmmaking approach was at once true to the crime life of the past and to the genre trappings of Warner Bros. classic crime films (courtesy Warner Bros./The Ladd Company).

movie's early moments), kept in a railroad station locker, the key hidden away in the grandfather clock in Moe's saloon. Their code of honor keeps any of the boys from taking the key and grabbing the money for himself; this is their community treasure, set aside for bad times in the future.

Meanwhile, though, things couldn't be better. When Noodles returns from jail, his friends are no longer rugged street toughs but established gangsters, owning the neighborhood; they wear luxurious suits, smoke expensive cigars. Max (James Woods) runs the business side of things; intelligent but mercurial, he perfectly embodies one aspect of the gangster hero in modern movies, the gangster as corporate kingpin. Max is a businessman, at home in boardrooms. If there are women in his life, we're barely aware of it; while gun molls hang on his arm, they seem ornamental, in no way essential to his life. What Max cares about is money; that money hidden away in the suitcase will eventually erupt in this story like a bomb.

But the gangster as businessman is only one side of the story. Noodles is the perfect alternative hero for a modern mob movie, the gangster as romantic. As a little boy (Scott Tiler), Noodles falls in love with Deborah (Jennifer Connelly) at first sight. This is not just a sexual attraction—we see plenty of that on the part of Noodles and his pals for other women they meet—but pure, platonic love, a romantic vision of a woman who is too perfect to touch, at least in Noodles's mind. She is his dream girl, and he would not sully this by getting fresh the way he would with easily available women.

The recurring theme of betrayal, so basic to modern gangster films, is introduced as Noodles informs the police of a planned robbery, doing this ignoble act for the noblest of intentions. Convinced the heist will end in a bloodbath and unable to talk Max out of the plan, Noodles comes to believe that ratting is the only possible solution. But his hopeful plan leads to horrible results. There is indeed a shoot-out that turns into a bloodbath;

Where the action is: Noodles (Robert De Niro) springs to life during an ambush (courtesy Warner Bros./The Ladd Company).

the gang is wiped out (including, so far as Noodles can tell, Max), while Noodles himself makes a desperate run for his life.

Clearly, his idealism has led to disaster. Noodles tried to be more realisic, but that, too, had disastrous results. He finally takes Deborah out on the date he has been planning ever since he first saw her, the very sort of dream date she desires. The perfect gentleman, Noodles wines and dines her, his manners as close to flawless as could be hoped for. Then, however, he gives in to harsh realism, virtually raping her, and any chance for the happiness he's been dreaming about all these decades is lost in one miscalculated act.

Why does Noddles rape Deborah? Because she broke the platonic spell by leaning over and kissing him; she meant it as a sweet gesture, though he took it quite differently. The masochistic nymphomaniac Carol (Tuesday Weld), who insisted on sex with Noodles and his cohorts when they came upon her by surprise during a robbery, began their relationship with just such a kiss. Noodles merely responded to the gesture as he had before; he assumed that with her kiss, Deborah was trying to make clear that she was, under her ice-princess surface, one more volcano, about to explode. Noodles's tragedy is that, like so many other heroes of modern gangster movies, he cannot understand women.

Men and women feel betrayed by one another; so do men and men. Thirty-five years later, Noodles—living in Buffalo, New York—receives a strange, cryptic, unsigned letter. He senses it is time to go home again and face the past once and for all, knowing he will either be saved or destroyed by the experience. He discovers, as he expected, that Max is still very much alive. As they confront one another in Max's mansion, we realize neither will ever be able to force the other to accept his interpretation of the events. As Richard Corliss summed it up in *Time,* "Leone is less interested in arousing an audience's easier emotions than in presenting, at a dispassionate distance, the horror of two men warily walking toward each other on a tightrope suspended above the snake pit of their deepest compulsions." The characters, according to Leone's vision, are solipsistic; each lives in the world that he creates in his mind, interpreting events according to his inner reality. Noodles and Max lived through the same series of events, at least in the eyes of the world. But what those events mean to Noodles is something very different from what they mean to Max.

Obviously, Leone revived the film noir formulas, but he did so in order to make the kind of intellectualized statement that was never contained in any Hollywood gangster film. Though he worked within a

The McGuffin: Patsy, Dominic, Noodles, and Max hide away a suitcase full of money that will haunt each of them for his entire life (courtesy Warner Bros./The Ladd Company).

Noodles with Eve (Darlanne Fluegel), his last mistress, at the moment of truth when the doorbell rings and his misguided act of betrayal comes back to haunt him (courtesy Warner Bros./The Ladd Company).

A search for respectability: the adult Noodles (Robert De Niro) treats the woman he has always loved (Elizabeth McGovern) to a touch of class...then attempts to create an ideal moment right out of a sheik film. When his naturalistic instincts take hold and he rapes Deborah, Noodles destroys his one chance for happiness in life by tarnishing the dream through vulgar reality (courtesy Warner Bros./The Ladd Company).

genre he knew and loved, his vision is more like that of Fellini, Bergman, or Antonioni, nongenre "serious artists" who employ films to communicate a complicated view of the world. Throughout the film, a telephone is regularly heard ringing; it is the element that cements the varied incidents together. Only at the end do we realize it is the phone call Noodles made to the police, informing on his friends, the phone call he has regretted making all his life, which is why he constantly hears the ringing. We hear what Noodles hears; the movie we are watching is taking place inside his mind.

Significantly, Leone (since deceased) has referred to the gangster era of the 1920s and 1930s as "the second frontier in American history," which helps explain why gangster films, like westerns, have always survived the tumultuous changes that rock the movie industry and cause other genres to fall from favor. Both westerns and gangster films may flourish at times only to seemingly disappear at others, yet they always come back eventually, since they are the uniquely American morality plays, the stories that in broad, basic terms most effectively define our culture, our sensibility.

At one point during the twelve years that Leone planned and replanned this extremely personal film, he had hoped to cast in it as many as possible of those still-living veterans of film noir—Glenn Ford, George Raft, Henry Fonda, Sterling Hayden. The original concept had been to cast three different sets of actors as the same characters at different stages of their lives. That concept may have been scrapped, but Leone was nonetheless able to transform the gangster of American history, long since mythologized by Hollywood, into the hero of a visual legend. His title *Once Upon a Time...* is the key to understanding Leone's great theme: movies in general, and Leone's in particular, have taken such characteristically American stories as the western and the gangster, and transformed them into fairy tales for grown-ups.

Director William Friedkin once again displayed his flair for large-scale action sequences (courtesy M-G-M/UA Entertainment).

The "hero" forces a paroled woman (Darlanne Fluegel) to submit as both a mistress and an informant (courtesy M-G-M/UA Entertainment).

TWENTY-ONE

To Live and Die in L.A.

(1985)

M-G-M/UA Entertainment Company

CAST:

William L. Petersen *(Richard Chance)*; Willem Dafoe *(Eric Masters)*; John Pankow *(John Vukovich)*; Debra Feuer *(Dancer/Mistress)*; John Turturro *(Carl Cody)*; Darlanne Fluegel *(Ruth Lanier)*; Dean Stockwell *(Lawyer)*; also, Steve James and Robert Downey Jr.

CREDITS:

Producer, Irving H. Levin; director, William Friedkin; screenplay, Friedkin and Gerald Petievich, from the novel by Petievich; cinematography, Robby Muller; editors, Bill and Scott Smith; music supervision, Wang Chung; production design, Lilly Kilvert; running time 116 minutes; rating, R.

In 1971, filmmaker William Friedkin reinvented the American crime film with *The French Connection*, for the first time pitting a believable, bigoted cop against an elegant, appealing gangster, eliminating the traditional Old Hollywood dichotomy of obvious goodguy vs. badguy. Nearly fifteen years later, Friedkin attempted to do much the same thing for yet another era, again transforming a well-regarded book about an actual case into a movie that projected precisely the right "look" for its time. Back in 1971, the approach had been gritty NYC mean-streets realism; in 1985, the immensely popular if surprisingly short-lived state-of-the-art style necessitated that Friedkin be influenced by techniques prevalent in the newly popular music videos and in the runaway hit TV series *Miami Vice*. So Friedkin filmed the Los Angeles cityscape in such a way that his camera-eye captured both upscale and downbeat areas in a hazy glow, alternating between pastels and neon; he edited to yoke together images that had no obvious, logical connection; he dubbed in contemporary rock music so the disconcerting shifts in scene would move with the same rhythm as the background beat.

Friedkin defended this approach: "The audience views a motion picture as a series of icons—faces of actors, incidents, a gun, a knife, a flash of sunlight on a road, a sunset, a woman's walk, a fast-moving object, a shadow, a glimmer of light—tight pieces of unrelated information crossing the screen. If these are skillfully combined in an impressionistic way, the audience makes its own film." A fascinating concept, and one that echoes the attitudes of such 1920s avant-garde artists as Luis Buñuel and Salvador Dalí. However, their films were antinarrative. Friedkin attempts to employ this approach to tell a police/gangster flick, as if he believed that by applying a surrealist's technique to what is essentially a familiar genre piece, he would redeem the material.

The film begins with Secret Serviceman Richard Chance and his aging partner, Jimmy, thwarting a terrorist's attack on President Reagan. As played by Chicago stage actor William L. Petersen, Chance initially appears to be a traditional hero, as clean-cut and square-jawed as Dick Tracy. Likewise, the story setup is one of the oldest in the crime books: the cop who will not rest until the death of his partner is avenged. Likable old Jimmy is clearly a doomed man, so this seems a very old story told in a highly contemporary manner.

What's unique, though, is the gangster/villain: Eric Masters (Willem Dafoe), a once ambitious artist who now burns his elaborate paintings of beautiful women. This act of nihilism derives from his cynical belief that his talent should be employed for counterfeiting, as there is nothing that matters anymore but money. While spying on Masters's desert hideaway, Jimmy is caught by Masters's well-armed gang and executed. "Buddy," Masters sighs with characteristic cynicism, "you were in the wrong place at the wrong time." Dafoe's Masters is reminiscent of the wicked gangsters played by Richard Widmark in his film noir days. While most gangster

Eric Masters (Willem Dafoe), serious artist turned counterfeiter and killer, is comforted by his mistress, Bianca Torres (Debra Feuer). Ironically, these "villains" demonstrate more respect for one another in their relationship than do the film's "hero" and his woman (courtesy M-G-M/UA Entertainment).

movies of the eighties concentrated on international drug dealers, *To Live and Die in L.A.* served as an effective reminder that the counterfeiter could indeed serve as an equally dangerous mobster/villain, and that such traditional forms of gangsterism had not disappeared in the age of drugs.

Chance is less than thrilled with his new partner, John Vukovich (John Pankow), a by-the-book cop. Still, the two set out to capture the parties responsible for Jimmy's murder. Chance gets tips from Ruth Lanier (Darlanne Fluegel), a parolee he regularly blackmails into providing information and sex. She sends them to the LAX airport, where they capture one of Master's couriers, Carl Cody (John Turturro). "I'm a businessman," Cody insists as Chance arrests him after a scuffle in the men's room. In a way, he's right, as a dominant theme of modern gangster movies is the blurring of the once-clear distinction between criminal and corporate types.

When Masters visits Cody at the jail, he confronts him with the statement of a man named Waxman, who claims Cody did not make the drop of funny money to his office; Cody swears he did not skim money. Masters employs his girlfriend (Debra Feuer), a performance artist who specializes in bizarre transsexual routines, to help him discover who is telling the truth. Masters sends her to Waxman's office, which is lavishly decorated in fine modern art; all the abodes of the criminals in the film (though not necessarily those of the cops) are exquisitely attired. Friedkin implies that the criminal mind is a creative one; the dogged, plodding police are mundane.

Waxman is a highly interesting character: a lawyer who in the late 1960s donated his services to defend hippies, he's now a prime mover of illegal paper. The implication, though left unstated, is clear; idealists of an earlier generation have become the cynics of today, and though we can only guess at how this happened to Waxman, we will vividly see it happen to the film's only existing idealist. When Waxman comes on to Masters's woman ("I can help you, if you ever get in trouble!"), she makes a semblance of being interested. She opens the front door and, like a throwback to the hippie era, sighs:

> GIRL: I love the rain.
> WAXMAN: Yeah. It's groovy.

For a moment, he reverts back to his hippie-era self, responding to her flower-child role-playing. But it's just that—a role—and as she initiates sex, Masters slips in and holds Waxman at gunpoint. "First you rip me off, then you set up Carl, now you want my lady." Chance and John are on stakeout of Waxman's office, though they've fallen asleep and miss all this. One fascinating theme is that the Secret Service is as bumbling in its investigation as the criminals are thorough and effective in their work. Since author Gerald Petievich was himself a Secret Serviceman, it seems likely he knows what he's talking about.

But when they do finally arrive and discover the body (the police are already there), Chance commits his first criminal act, lifting Waxman's deal book. John is upset—they had no authority to take it—but he can't imagine how much further Chance will go. Chance's loyalty to the deceased Jimmy is the only thing that keeps us rooting for this essentially unpleasant man. His adversary Masters, conversely, has no loyalty toward those who work for him. We next see Masters meeting a black dealer (Steve James), offering to trade a sum of counterfeit dollars if he'll have some of his friends in the prison kill Cody, before Cody can strike a deal with investigators. The man agrees, and there is indeed an (unsuccessful) attempt on Cody's life.

Secret Service agents John Vukovich (John Pankow) and Richard Chance arrest a counterfeiter's bagman (John Turturro) in an airport rest room. Director William Friedkin updated his *French Connection* formula for the post-MTV cinema (courtesy M-G-M/UA Entertainment).

John, meanwhile, meets a lawyer (Dean Stockwell) who represents Masters and has come to resent him. "I don't have to tell you what would happen to my practice if it became known I set up one of my clients," he warns. This yuppie lawyer, perhaps the most seemingly respectable character we meet, is in as deep as everyone else; there's no line where the dirt stops and clean characters begin. The lawyer set up a meeting between Chance and John (posing as visiting Palm Springs dealers) with Masters at the trendy spa where he exercises. Masters demands a hefty $50,000 advance in real money for millions in counterfeit. But Chance and John can't convince their superiors to advance them any more than $10,000 in real money.

Then we realize just how serious Chance is about personal vengeance. He learns from his shady girlfriend that in a totally unrelated criminal enterprise, a man named Thomas Ling is arriving on Amtrak, carrying money to pay for illegal diamonds. "You mean you want to steal real money to buy counterfeit?" John asks in amazement. That's precisely what Chance plans; though John is stunned, even repulsed, by the idea, he goes along to back up the partner he considers wrongheaded, perhaps out of control. At this point, the cops are so clearly fighting fire with fire that they are nearly indistinguishable from the gangster elements they're out to get.

William Petersen as Secret Service agent Richard Chance, another variation on the contemporary crime film's chief anti-hero, the cop who acts like a criminal (courtesy M-G-M/UA Entertainment).

Except for one thing: loyalty to fellow cops, an old fashioned and highly moral idea that ironically causes them to break every law in the book, yet still manages to make

The moment of confrontation: A *Miami Vice*/MTV rock-video approach was employed for the film's mis-en-scène (courtesy M-G-M/UA Entertainment).

them seem better than the amoral world around them.

Chance and John kidnap the hapless Thomas Ling. But the diamond smugglers follow them and, as Chance and John grab the money, fire on them, killing Ling. Chance and John escape by car, pursued by the killers. Filmmaker Friedkin clearly attempts to top his own memorable car chase from *The French Connection* and to a degree, he does. As a finale for the shoot-out between cars on the freeway, there's a knockout getaway as Chance purposefully drives the wrong way up a ramp.

What follows is another of those truth-is-stranger-than-fiction twists that must have attracted Friedklin to the material. At a Secret Service meeting, Chance and John hear the news that Ling, an FBI agent, who was working undercover, has been killed. An all-out search is taking place for the two men who abducted him in a beige car, those two men being Chance and John. The two fugitives are considered more dangerous public enemies than Masters, though no one knows their identity.

Chance tracks down the escaped Cody, forcing him to tell where the counterfeit operation is. In an inferno-like conclusion, Chance and John shoot it out with members of Masters's gang, killing Masters, though Chance is also killed in the crossfire. But the ultimate in cynicism is yet to come. John goes to Ruth's apartment and finds her packing to leave town. She has grabbed $20,000 of the $50,000 the men stole (the rest has been turned over to Masters). John realizes that under the guise of feeding Chance helpful information, Ruth set them up to make her own profit. She is as duplicitous as Masters's girlfriend; it makes sense, then, that filmmaker Friedkin cast actresses in those roles who are all but doubles for one another.

John seems cold and hard-edged when he tells her, "You're working for me now." The only idealist of the early scenes has been transformed through experience into a cop who knows the hard rules of the game and is cynical enough to willingly play by them. He has at last accepted and entered a world in which nothing is what it seems.

TWENTY-TWO

Prizzi's Honor

(1985)

A 20th Century–Fox Film

CAST:

Jack Nicholson *(Charley Partanna);* Kathleen Turner *(Irene Walker);* Anjelica Huston *(Maerose Prizzi);* William Hickey *(Don Corrado);* John Randolph *(Angelo "Pop" Partanna);* Lee Richardson *(Dominic Corrado);* Robert Loggia *(Eduardo Corrado);* Michael Lombard *(Filargi/Finlay);* Lawrence Tierney *(Elderly Cop).*

CREDITS:

Producer, John Foreman; director, John Huston; screenplay, Richard Condon and Janet Roach, from the novel by Condon; cinematography, Andrzej Bartkowiak: editors, Rudi Fehr and Kaja Fehr; music, Alex North; running time, 129 minutes; rating, R

In many respects, *Prizzi's Honor* is the ultimate example of the modern gangster film, intended by its writer Richard Condon and director John Huston as a film that would have it both ways: at once a studious example of the elaborately mounted mob movie, and a satire on all other contemporary crime film beginning with *The Godfather. Prizzi's Honor* is about family vs. Family, the gangster as romantic hero, the postfeminist woman, honor as defined by money, and the inclusion of organized crime as a full-fledged part of the "respectable" Establishment.

The film begins with a prologue, following the birth of Charley Partanna. His mother is apparently inconsequential; Charley's father, Angelo (John Randolph), and the head of the Prizzi clan (William Hickey) gaze at the child admiringly, never making any mention of the woman who did the lion's share of the work. Doing a broad caricature of Marlon Brando's Don Corleone from *The Godfather,* Hickey's Don Corrado gives his blessing to the newborn baby, insisting he will be this boy's "godfather" in more ways than one. "I will be at one with you," he tells the dear friend standing by his side. They are "family" in every sense; the next shot we see is of the child Charley opening a present (presumably from the don) under a Christmas tree, delighted to discover a set of brass knuckles. The image is a gag, but a meaningful one; the film that follows proceeds from the notion that modern mob life has been carefully designed to include the darker elements of their "business" within the conventions of everyday life.

As a teenager, Charley has his finger nicked by a knife that the don wields: "This drop of blood (inducts) you into our family...we are one to the death...protect Prizzi's honor...swear it?" As they become blood brothers, Charley swears yes. He has dedicated himself to the notion of Family honor. He will learn, by movies's end, that honor means money, demanding his willingness to kill anyone—even someone who has become "family" in a far more conventional sense—if deemed necessary.

In the first postcredit sequence, Charley is established as one more variation on the gangster as romantic hero. At a formal wedding in New York, the sounds of "Ave Maria" still echoing in his ears, Charley notices a breathtaking blonde in the church balcony. The look in his eyes makes clear that he is smitten: madly, truly, deeply in love. He dances with her briefly at the reception, but before learning her name, she's called away to answer a phone call and disappears; afterward, he has difficulty learning from anyone present who she was, why she was there.

"The woman in the lavender dress" is how he describes her as he obsessively searches, calling everyone who might possibly know. Then, his phone rings and he's surprised to hear her voice, calling from California, where she lives. Incredibly polite ("I hope you don't think I was rude!"), she introduces herself as Irene, apologizing for leaving so abruptly. She sounds incredibly sincere, so Charley hops on the next plane to the West Coast in hot pursuit. "I was scared I was never gonna see you again," the none-too-bright Charley tells her as

Jack Nicholson as Charley Partanna, a Mafia hit man who falls in love with his mark. Though none too bright, Charley is one more variation on the gangster as romantic hero (courtesy 20th Century–Fox).

The contract killer as glamour girl; Kathleen Turner played Irene Walker as smart, classy, funny, sweet-spirited, supportive…and deadly, a truly complex modern woman (courtesy 20th Century–Fox).

they enjoy drinks at the bar in the chic Bel Age Hotel. Irene explains she's a tax consultant whose husband ran out on her four years earlier, and Charley makes clear this is no mere sexual fascination on his part. In a matter of moments, he pours his heart out:

> CHARLEY: I can't sleep—no one in my life ever affected me the way you make me feel. That's it…that's everything.
> IRENE: I think I'm in love with you, Charley.
> CHARLEY: Not "in love." "In love" is temporary. Just a hormonal secretion.
> IRENE: I…I *love* you, Charley.

He is a dim-witted Gatsby (a role Nicholson has admitted he wanted to play in the 1974 film version), she his inamorata, his dream woman. Or so he thinks. Irene offers a variation on the most characteristic contemporary female crime-film lead, the ambiguous postfeminist woman, projecting an image of upscale normalcy while leading a double life as a deadly lady. Charley inadvertently discovers this when he's ordered by the mob to hit a man who pulled a clever scam in Vegas and made off with $700,000 of the Prizzi family's money. After killing Moxie in his L.A. home, Charley waits for Moxie's wife to return from grocery shopping so he can torture her into telling where the money is hidden, then kill her too.

"Honey, I'm home," she calls happily as she breezes through the door, like Beaver Cleaver's Mom in a 1950s domestic sitcom. But Charley is stunned to realize it's Irene; she not only conspired in the Vegas scam, but was the brains behind the operation. Shortly, Charley will discover that Irene was in New York, at the wedding, for another illicit purpose. She was the outside specialist the mob hired for a hit that their own hit men would all have perfect alibis. Irene is the girl next door who kills people, the all-American hit lady with a soft spot in her heart for Charley. But to the romantic Charley, she remains the dream girl, even in the face of irrefutable facts: "I can't change the way I feel; I love you, and I see what I want to see."

"She's an American," sighs Maerose (Anjelica Huston), Charley's former fianceé and Mafia princess who has become the black sheep of her family/Family. "She saw a chance to make a buck so she grabbed it." Though Maerose initially appears a far more conventional woman than Irene, she, too, has a career, in interior design. And, like Talia Shire's Connie in the third *Godfather* film, she is not nearly so bland as she first seems. Maerose serves as a precursor for Connie by quietly, effectively manipulating everyone and everything to her advantage.

When Charley, in New York, sits in on a decision-making meeting of the mob, listening as head honchos decide whom to whack and whom to spare, the discussion takes place not in a Little Italy eatery but in a brightly lit boardroom; they could be corporate executives, deciding on strategy for the next year. This meeting, like others glimpsed during the film, is conducted not by the aging don but by his son Eduardo (Robert Loggia), who sits at a big executive-style desk and speaks in a subdued voice. Behind him are framed degrees, attesting to his education and, in the conventional sense, respectability. We learn from him that the mob owns a quarter interest in one of the country's most prestigious banks. When he is informed that the "respectable" bank president has been siphoning off money that could well cause the bank to fail, the "committee" discusses whether whacking the man (in order to protect the interests of the mob, as well as the common citizens of America who bank there) is in order. Eduardo will, like his father in days of yore, order hits, even on members of his own organization deemed expendable. But he does so in the cool, calculated voice of an executive. This is the New Mob, new in terms of style if not substance.

For the bottom line remains the same: money. As in almost every modern gangster film since *Point Blank,* the key problem is money that's been wrongfully taken and must be returned, more as a point of honor than greed. The mob never forgets that only half the money Irene stole from them in Vegas has been returned since she took up with Charley. He knows in his heart that he wants Irene to be his "family" though he also knows this will not sit well with his other Family. That's why, in a quiet moment with Maerose, he pours out his heart:

> CHARLEY: Do I ice her? Or do I marry her?
> MAEROSE: Marry her, Charley. Just because she's a thief and a hitter doesn't mean she isn't a good woman in all the other departments.

Charley will marry Irene, and they quickly become a grotesque caricature of ordinary American home life. As Charley and his father discuss strategy for a kidnapping, Irene darts about like the model housewife, brightly making suggestions for their "business project" while putting the finishing touches on a nice dinner. But when she offers to go along on the job and help out, Charley immediately turns into the retro-1950s stereotypical hus-

Don Corrado is a comic variation on the role played straight by Marlon Brando in *The Godfather,* though shortly he would mock his own earlier part in *The Freshman.* Here, Don Corrado addresses a mob banquet meeting with his sons Dominic (Lee Richardson) and Eduardo (Robert Loggia) (courtesy 20th Century–Fox).

The ultimate Machiavelli, Maerose (Anjelica Huston in her Best Supporting Actress Oscar–winning role) insists that Charley pursue his romance, knowing full well she will win him back in the end (courtesy 20th Century–Fox).

Charley and Irene Walker (Kathleen Turner) romance during the daylight hours like any normal upscale couple...

band. "I didn't get married so my wife can go on working," he grumbles. They are frightfully typical as a couple, mouthing all the expected clichés of husband and wife, the only unique twist being that they work for organized crime.

During a hit, they converse about where they should take their honeymoon and how long to wait before having a baby. "See you at dinner," they coo, kissing as they part, Irene having just killed an innocent woman who had the bad fortune to exit an elevator and stumble into one of their illegal operations. Unhappily for them, she turns out to have been the wife of a police captain. An angry old cop (Lawrence Tierney) gruffly informs the mob that the police, like the Mafia, have their code of honor, and will shut down mob operations until someone is turned over as the scapegoat for this travesty. The police do not take their decision lightly; they are in deep with the mob, so this will cost them plenty of money. But honor is honor.

There is Prizzi's honor as well as police honor. There's still the sticky point of the money that hasn't been returned; there's the fact that Charley's wife is Polish rather than Italian Catholic. The police want someone to pay, and the expedient thing to do is give them Irene, which will make everyone happy. Only problem is, the mob doesn't want Irene turned over alive; she knows too much. So Charley is told to hit his own wife. Earlier, Maerose's father—a mafioso who has never liked Charley—tried to hire Irene to kill Charley, unaware they were married.

Charley's feelings for Irene have not dimmed; he remains, at heart, a romantic. Still, there is the matter of that oath, taken in blood; the don reminds him that Charley swore he "would always put the Family before everything else in life; we are calling on you now to keep your sacred oath." He does just that. Like any good modern husband and wife coming together after being separated by business, Charley and Irene happily rush into each other's arms, then head for the bedroom. But she's carrying a pistol, he a knife, and it's a contest to see who can kill the other first. Charley wins, though in fact it is Maerose who wins big. Having used her wiles to great advantage, she now has Charley coming around to her at last, proposing the marriage that should have taken place long ago. Family is finally stronger than family.

...then go about their business of murdering people after dark (courtesy 20th Century–Fox).

The final confrontation between Stanley White and Joey Tai. Many modern gangster films, this one included, resemble old-time westerns as much as they do earlier crime films (courtesy (M-G-M/UA Entertainment).

TWENTY-THREE

Year of the Dragon

(1985)

An MGM/United Artists Release

CAST:

Mickey Rourke *(Stanley White)*; John Lone *(Joey Tai)*; Ariane *(Tracy Tzu)*; Leonard Termo *(Angelo Rizzo)*; Ray Barry *(Louis Bukowski)*; Caroline Kava *(Connie White)*; Eddie Jones *(William McKenna)*; Joey Chin *(Ronnie Chang)*; Victor Wong *(Harry Yung)*; K. Dock Yip *(Milton Bin)*; Pao Han Lin *(Hung)*.

CREDITS:

Producer, Dino De Laurentiis; director, Michael Cimino; screenplay, Oliver Stone and Cimino, from the novel by Robert Daley; cinematography, Alex Thomson; editor, Françoise Bonnot; music, David Mansfield: running time 126 minutes; rating, R

Year of the Dragon was intended as an updating of *The French Connection;* once again a tough, hard-edged, unromanticized cop stoops to the level of the gangster he's up against to win a one-man war. As with the earlier film, *Dragon* was based on a well-regarded book by an author (Robert Daley, of *Prince of the City* fame) who clearly knew and understood his material. Mickey Rourke substituted for Gene Hackman, his Stanley White even wearing a similar hat to "Popeye" Doyle's. In the role of the crime boss, Asian John Lone assumed the place of the earlier film's Eurotrash villain.

Dragon was loudly denounced by Asian-American groups, who insisted the film was racist, portraying Chinese characters as criminals. In fact, not all the film's Asian characters are mobsters; model-turned-actress Ariane (half-Asian, half-Dutch) was cast as a crusading reporter, Tracy Tzu, who joins the Polish police captain in his "war against Chinatown," an unfortunate phrase since the war is less against the vast majority of people living there than a secret criminal empire. A few all-powerful Chinese—the admitted tongs (powerful family-oriented factions) and hidden triads (Chinese equivalent of Mafia Families)—exploit other innocent, hardworking Asians.

Michael Cimino intended the film as a companion piece to his Oscar-winner *The Deer Hunter,* viewing Stanley White as a virtual replay of Michael Vronsky, the Robert De Niro character, recast here as a police captain. White carries emotional baggage from the Vietnam War inside him. ("This is Vietnam all over again," he shouts at superiors who fear he's overstepped his bounds, "and nobody wants us to win.") He is a bigot, viewing Asians as the enemy still. His very name, "White," is significant and symbolic. To emphasize that this man is a symbol for traditional white-male Christian values in a world which the filmmaker views as in danger of being overrun by third worlders, a crucifix and a statue of John Wayne are in White's bedroom. He's assigned to head New York's Chinatown operation when youth gangs begin killing people in public, scaring away tourists. His superiors whisper that he should only go after such punks, keeping his distance from the reigning older gangsters who control the area.

White arrives just in time for the funeral of Jackie Wong, an aged tong leader who has been murdered, seemingly by one of the gang youths. White believes otherwise. He suspects Joey Tai (Lone), Wong's son-in-law, who stands to inherit Wong's dynasty, both the respectable public establishments and the secretive criminal elements. With Wong out of the way, Joey Tai stands as uncrowned King of Chinatown. On the surface, Tai is, like the deceased father-in-law he speaks of in reverential terms, an important community leader. Tai wears thousand-dollar suits, jets back and forth to the Orient for high-level business meetings, and speaks articulately. Tai is the prototypical Asian-American businessman, a perfect role model, the last person anyone would suspect of being a gangster.

Yet that's precisely what White believes Joey to be, so he assigns a young Asian cop to go undercover as a worker at Tai's restaurant. Shortly, the spy reports that Tai will smuggle the largest-ever single shipment of heroin into the country: "the Asian connection." White feeds this information to Tracy, who broadcasts it on her TV show. Tracy also becomes personally involved with White, after his wife tires of his endless absences and throws him out.

"There's a new marshall in town—me," White insists, sounding like an urban Wyatt Earp, a man with a moral mission to clean up the community. White is called on the carpet by his police superiors; they've had a message from the borough president, who receives $100,000 annual campaign contribution from the Tongs and wants White's crusade ended. Organized crime and the political establishment are working together, as in so many modern gangster movies. But White fears an all-out gang war, as the Chinese have been drifting over Canal Street and taking on the Mafia, challenging them on their own turf. Whenever someone suggests he's on the attack against Asian-Americans, White reminds them that tong bosses locked the poor Chinese in sweatshops.

Though the film was produced several years before *The Untouchables* remake, there are notable similarities. Though a far raunchier presence than clean-cut Costner, Rourke's dedicated-to-the-point-of-obsession policeman is a clear predecessor of De Palma's reinvented Ness, ultimately resorting to one-on-one violence against Joey much as Ness will confront Nitti high upon a courthouse roof. White employs illegal methods, including wiretapping, to fight fire with fire and 'get" Joey. Lone's businessman/mobster may be more soft-spoken than De Niro's Capone, but he likewise orders his men to threaten the cop's wife and, in this case, actually kill her in her Brooklyn home.

"The American dream," White says when talking about Joey Tai, echoing the sentiments of *The Godfather, Part II's* conception of young Vito Corleone, coming to America with nothing yet creating a powerful empire (and a respectable image) through mob activities. Likewise, Joey Tai was a street kid in Hong Kong, made his way to America, found a job in a restaurant, married the boss's daughter, then knocked off the boss. Now, Joey—bright young corporate gangster, Asian-American

Mickey Rourke as Stanley White, captain of detectives assigned to crack down on gang violence in New York's Chinatown; even the character's last name suggests his incipient racism (photo credit Stanley Tretick, courtesy M-G-M/UA Entertainment).

Tracy Tzu (international fashion model turned actress Ariane) reports on crime and corruption in Chinatown; an aggressive media professional, she is the film's key positive image of Chinese-Americans (photo credit Stanley Tretick, courtesy M-G-M/UA Entertainment).

A bloody shoot-out in a Chinatown restaurant cinches the connection between the contemporary crime film and the classic western (courtesy Dino De Laurentiis Corp.—M-G-M/UA Entertainment).

variety—stands up to the old mafiosos, who look like weakened dinosaurs, informing them their days are numbered. White adopts the same sort of vendetta mentality as the nouveau Ness shortly will in the final act of De Palma's *Untouchables;* operating outside the law, White roughs up Joey, shoots the two oriental hit women Joey dispatches to eliminate him, then pursues Joey onto a railroad juncture, where the two shoot it out, O.K. Corral style, cinching the long-standing connection of the gangster film to the western.

Joey, defeated and humiliated, does something that Italian gangsters in the movies seldom do, taking his own life, unwilling to live after losing face. It is a notable Asian twist on what otherwise is the oldest and most durable cop-vs.-gangster story. Apparently, Cimino and Stone wanted viewers to accept that a tough but good man has done what had to be done, breaking the rules for the greater good. In fact, though, most audiences saw the scene in different light, failing to cheer White as they had cheered Doyle in *The French Connection,* instead feeling sympathy for the gangster. In part, that may be because the sordid-looking Rourke is unable to invest his cop with the same sort of roughhewn integrity Hackman brought to Doyle. Doyle was a terribly flawed but ultimately worthwhile human being; White is simply a bully and a bigot.

In part, though, the film's problem is that Lone's gangster is a self-made man. More Macbeth than Richard III, he is less a malevolent Machiavelli than a good man who does bad things to succeed. When he hopelessly throws himself into his final shoot-out with White, it's far easier to forgive him his sins and wish he'd win than it is to cheer for the vulgar racist and gloating rapist whose supposed desire to clean up the community seems nothing more than a cover for his need to violently exorcise his postwar demons.

Understandably, then, *Dragon* was not greeted with the same kind of critical excitement that had swirled about *French Connection* some fifteen years earlier. "Cimino has a vivid sense of swirl and motion," Stanley Kauffmann wrote in *The New Republic.* "He knows how to move a camera, and he knows how to move actors within the frame...he is so good at these matters that his besetting flaw comes as a continual shock: he has no sense of proportion. He doesn't know when dialogue gets ludicrous." A perfect example of this occurs long after White's wife has been strangled by Joey's men. Three Chinese gangsters rape Tracy in her apartment in order to "teach her a lesson." Significantly, White has himself raped Tracy, though that apparently is supposed to okay in Cimino's vision, since he's the film's "hero," and according to Cimino's confused/retro ethic, she doubtless wanted him to. At any rate, White mutters, "This time Joey's gone too far!" as if the rape of his current woman is a worse infraction than the murder of his wife.

In the Sunday *Times,* Vincent Canby marveled that

Joey Tai (John Lone) represents the Chinese-American variation on a significant contemporary crime-film character, who reappears in varying races: the supposedly "respectable" businessman who is in fact the dirtiest dealer in drugs (courtesy M-G-M/UA Entertainment).

the film was "arresting to watch even when it goes wrong with a lunatic inconsistency—an elaborately produced gangster film that isn't boring for a minute, composed of excesses in behavior, language, and visual effects that, eventually, exert their own hypnotic effect." The visually spellbinding quality may be due to the fact that the New York scenes were shot in North Carolina, on the sound-stages producer Dino De Laurentis built there. Partially a reproduction of New York's Chinatown and partly an exaggerated distortion, the over-the-top set designs lend the film a surrealistic quality.

Even John Simon, who vitriolically dismissed the film and Cimino's entire career in *National Review,* had to admit that "never has gore been gorier, but also curiously picturesque, almost pretty—manicured carnage, which is Cimino's stock-in-trade." Kael found it to be "hysterical, rabble-rousing pulp, the kind that generally goes over with subliterate audiences—people who can be suckered into believing that the movie is giving them the low-down dirty truth about power...[Cimino] is aiming for a lurid high art. Members of the audience can be hoodwinked because what they see has so many associations with the powerful images and themes that have moved them in the past."

(Below) A new breed of Chinese-American street-punk criminal threatens daily life in Chinatown's mean streets as the more established Tong crime families did not...

TWENTY-FOUR

Tough Guys

(1986)

A Touchstone Pictures Release

CAST:

Burt Lancaster *(Harry Doyle)*; Kirk Douglas *(Archie Long)*; Alexis Smith *(Belle)*; Charles Durning *(Deke Yablonski)*; Dana Carvey *(Richie Evans)*; Darlanne Fluegel *(Skye Foster)*; Eli Wallach *(Leon B. Little)*; Monty Ash *(Vince)*; Billy Barty *(Philly)*; Simmy Bow *(Schultz)*; Darlene Conley *(Gladys Ripps)*; Nathan Davis *(Jimmy Ellis)*.

CREDITS:

Producer, Joe Wizan; director, Jeff Kanew; screenplay, James Orr and Jim Cruickshank; cinematography, King Baggot; editor, Kaja Fehr; music, James Newton Howard; running time, 102 minutes; rating, PG.

Few films have ever been as dependant on the casting as *Tough Guys,* since it was designed as a reunion piece for Burt Lancaster and Kirk Douglas. They were the great male-buddy team of the film noir era, picking up where Spencer Tracy and Clark Gable had left off while preceding Paul Newman and Robert Redford. The two had first been teamed in 1947's *I Walk Alone,* enjoying separate careers but always coming back together for a succession of films—*The Devil's Disciple, The List of Adrian Messenger,* etc.—that effectively exploited their unique chemistry. The most popular among these teaming was John Sturges's 1958 western, *Gunfight at the O.K. Corral.* In it, and each of their other movies together, Lancaster was the tall, intense, soft-spoken, occasionally stiff man of stoicism; his characters, like the actor himself, were "cool" in the McLuhan sense, withholding rather than giving. Douglas, on the other hand, was the short, energetic, bombastic, sometimes out-of-control man of nervous energy; his characters, like the person playing them, were "hot," projecting a remarkable amount of emotional information to the fellow characters in his movie as well as to the audience watching. They worked perfectly together because they were complimentary, the yin/yang opposites that attract.

But even such superstars fade in time. Both were working only irregularly by the mid eighties; the kinds of movies then being turned out didn't offer a great deal for these headliners left over from a notably different era. Indeed, many of the people who had flocked to see them three decades earlier did not go to the kinds of movies now being made, owing to graphic sex and violence. That reality was essential to the "deal" that *Tough Guys* made with its target audience: Kirk and Burt would work together again, for the last time, in a film that allowed them to comment, at least by implication, about the state of screen entertainment today, if only the people who had supported them for several decades would come back to theaters at least one more time. Not surprisingly, then, the opening shot of *Tough Guys* is a black-and-white image, reintroducing the contemporary crime film's focus on nostalgic elements for period pictures.

According to the screenplay by James Orr and Jim Cruickshank, Harry Doyle (Lancaster) and Archie Long (Douglas) were professional train robbers, a twentieth century Jesse James/Cole Younger team nabbed while attempting to rob the Gold Coast Flyer, the last of the haute trains that once crisscrossed the country. After thirty years behind bars, Doyle and Long are finally turned loose, asked to report to a giddily naive young parole officer (Dana Carvey) who idolizes the two legendary old-timers. A stipulation of their parole, however, insists that the two go their separate ways, in order to remain on the straight and narrow. So the youthful-looking Archie (he's a robust sixty-nine) finds himself a demeaning job working in an ice cream shop where he must swallow his pride and take orders from bratty kids. After hours he finds some pleasure by dating a sweet,

Notorious train robber Archie Long must choose between reverting to his old ways…or joining the modern world by romancing an eager disco dancer/aerobics instructor (Darlanne Fluegel) (courtesy Touchstone Pictures, photo credit Christine Loss).

Eli Wallach as the maniacal gun-toting stranger who stalks the film's anachronistic antiheroes owing to a decade-old contract. Though played as comic relief, Leon B. Little is a significant variation on the film's theme, that being the strong sense of commitment on the part of older gangsters, at least in the movies (courtesy Touchstone Pictures, photo credit Steve Schapiro).

sexy, superficial aerobics instructor (Darlanne Fluegel) who finds the tough old guy far more attractive than the bland young bodybuilders she regularly meets. Doyle, meanwhile, heads for an old folks home (he's a weary seventy-two), where he shortly has the sheeplike inhabitants rebelling against the awful spinach-in-mushroom soup they're being fed daily. Also a man with an eye for the ladies, Doyle is soon dating Belle (Alexis Smith), the still-beautiful moll he used to see when he was young and on the loose.

The casting of Smith was, like that of Lancaster and Douglas, significant to the film's meaning. Though her career has all but been forgotten by everyone other than film buffs who savor the noir era, Smith was once as much a queen of the crime film as Lizabeth Scott or Lauren Bacall, specializing in shady ladies with a touch of class and some tawdry secrets, who kept Bogart and other tough guys on their toes in *The Two Mrs. Carrolls, Whiplash,* and *Split Second.* Her presence here is as essential as her high quality performance; like her male costars, she stirs memories of movies past.

Before very long, Doyle and Long brush up against one another. Each is stunned by what he sees on the outside, everything from the mindlessly violent crime on the streets to the open, out-of-the-closet gay lifestyle encountered in the bars, to the tough kids carrying "boxes" and switchblades. The impact of the film resides not so much in the scenes as written (they're extremely predictable

Last of the old timers: Burt Lancaster and Kirk Douglas (in what would prove their final on-screen teaming) as faded film noir tough guys, set against their once and future challenge (courtesy Touchstone Pictures).

and lacking in depth) but in the scenes as played, moving beyond the skill of acting and into that magical realm in which icons automatically bring their entire canon of work with them to this show, and the audience responds in kind. As Walter Goodman put it in the *New York Times*, "we know that when the he-men of *Gunfight at the O.K.Corral* are picked on by a bunch of callow toughs, the toughs are going to regret they started up."

Harry and Archie are romantics at heart, so naturally they're thrilled to learn that as a part of the current nostalgia craze, the Gold Coast Flyer is being taken out of mothballs and sent on one last, glorious run. The boys immediately decide to get the old gang together again, enjoying their second chance at robbing the train; essentially, they get their wish to go back in time and do it over again, only this time maybe get it right. Unfortunately, the old gang members are not what they once were, barely able to get around owing to bad backs and other assorted anguishes of age. Still, they want desperately to return to 1955, or at least an idealized notion of it, by repeating their greatest adventure. The audience watching the film is moved to its own nostalgia, wanting to return to their own youth when they sat watching Burt and Kirk in one of their earlier vehicles.

Throughout the film, the boys must also deal with two near-nemeses: Deke Yablonski (Charles Durning), the mean-spirited cop just itching for a chance to arrest Doyle and Long once again, and Leon B. Little (Eli Wallach), a crazed, nearsighted hit man who constantly tries to shoot them down. Leon took money some thirty years earlier from a now long-dead convict in exchange for shooting the boys, and he's been patiently waiting all these years for their release, so he can come through at last on his hard contract. Though played by Wallach in a wild, broad comic style, Leon furthers a modern gangster-movie theme: values having been a part of the old criminal code, though seeming patently ridiculous in today's jaundiced world.

The great limitation of *Tough Guys* is that it plays off the obvious rather than going for true pathos. Doyle and Long stare in amazement at punk hairdos and light beer, slam dancing and short skirts, stunned at how much the world has changed, less than happy with that situation; they are the Rip van Winkles of the underworld. While that makes for some mildly amusing moments, *Tough Guys* would have benefitted had its writers sought to emotionally explore the situations rather than merely amuse. The film's essential conceit is, in fact, bogus:

Anachronistic Harry Doyle looks up an old flame (Alexis Smith, veteran of so many classic film noirs)...but ultimately prefers to return "to work" (courtesy Touchstone Pictures, photo credit Christine Loss).

nonviolent criminals like Doyle and Long would, while in the penitentiary, have been allowed to watch television and would have been aware of the changes taking place outside. But it's unfair to press such realistic criticism too far; the film is, after all, a fable—indeed, something of a fairy tale—and its fanciful premise works owing to the magnetism of the actors.

"*Cocoon* with *cojónes,*" *Time* tagged *Tough Guys.* The comparison had merit. *Cocoon* had won an audience by showing old folks who break out of stereotyping and learn to enjoy life again by taking some wild risks, in the context of sweet-spirited science fiction. *Tough Guys* presented the same theme as a lighthearted crime caper. Throughout all this, Wallach's nearsighted shooter all but stole the show, bringing a madcap comedy to even the potentially deadly moments. At one point, he and the boys are on board the train, surrounded by policemen. Leon B. Little vows to go out fighting.

> LEON: *(hysterical)* Before they get me, I'm gonna kill a hundred cops.
>
> DOYLE: There's only fifty of 'em out there.
>
> LEON: *(thoughtfully)* Then I'll shoot 'em all twice!

Ultimately, though, the film's great charm comes in watching its two top-billed stars. Though remembered as the best of friends, Douglas and Lancaster have each insisted they always got on each other's nerves; theirs was a love-hate relationship, equally true of their characters, whether in *Gunfight at the O.K. Corral* or here. They argue endlessly, over the pettiest and silliest of things. But we never doubt the depth of their bond. It may not be there in the script, but it certainly was obvious in the twinkling eyes of the two enduring superstars.

TWENTY-FIVE

The Untouchables

(1987)

A Paramount Picture

CAST:

Kevin Costner *(Eliot Ness)*; Sean Connery *(Jim Malone)*; Robert De Niro *(Al Capone)*; Charles Martin Smith *(Oscar Wallace)*; Andy Garcia *(George Stone)*; Richard Bradford *(Mike)*; Jack Kehoe *(Payne)*; Brad Sullivan *(George)*; Billy Drago *(Frank Nitti)*; Patricia Clarkson *(Ness's Wife)*; Melody Rae *(Woman With Baby Carriage)*.

CREDITS:

Producer, Art Linson; director, Brian DePalma; screenplay, David Mamet; cinematography, Steven H. Burum; visual consultant, Patrizia Von Brandenstein; editors, Jerry Greenberg and Bill Pankow; music, Ennio Morricone; wardrobe, Giorgio Armani; costume designer, Marilyn Vance-Straker; running time, 119 minutes; rating, R.

In the 1990s, one significant trend of American moviemaking is the expensive re-creation of cult TV shows: *The Addams Family, Coneheads* (from *Saturday Night Live*), *The Fugitive,* and *The Beverly Hillbillies* were all revived, with varying degrees of success, by aging Hollywood baby boomers who had grown up watching them and sensed the public, like themselves, might want to recapture their lost innocence by seeing contemporary big-screen mountings of much-loved shows. An early significant box-office hit of this new genre came with 1987's *The Untouchables.* The series had flourished between 1959 and 1963, when it won high ratings but sparked controversy, including the first great debate over TV violence, as well as inspiring an outcry over stereotypical depiction of minorities (in this case, Italian Americans) in clichéd criminal roles.

When it was announced that Brian DePalma would direct the film version, there seemed little doubt he would gleefully revive the violence of the original. His horror films *(Sisters, Carrie)* are noted for graphic gore, as was his previous gangster film, a remake of Howard Hawks's *Scarface.* However, the decision to have David Mamet write the screenplay suggested serious ambitions, as the Pulitzer prize winner *(Glengarry Glen Ross)* had his own long-standing interest in the Windy City, he being a Chicago native.

When rising star Kevin Costner was cast as Eliot Ness, it became clear *The Untouchables* might be something special indeed; the quiet, soft-spoken Costner represented a departure from the original TV conception of the character. Gravel-voiced Robert Stack had played Ness as an urban John Wayne: a rugged, no-nonsense, emotionless cop who did not appear to have a life outside the office (in early episodes, his family was in fact fleetingly referred to). Then Robert De Niro, our most important actor, replaced Britain's Bob Hoskins in the role of Al Capone. Was it possible this might emerge as a revisionist version, rather than a retread of the old series? Perhaps the filmmakers had some motivation other than nostalgia in retelling the story of a handful of honest cops, eventually defeating the most seemingly impregnable crime boss of his time.

Sadly, the film is an awkward hodgepodge, combining the complex modern approach to such stories with a value system so simplistic it makes the old TV version seem sophisticated by comparison. Most surprising is that De Niro delivers an operatic performance as the mythic Capone, the larger-than-life character as incarnated by Neville Brand on TV. Anyone who can accept that will find no fault with De Niro's work; it is big, broad, and in its own way beautiful, marked by over-the-top grins and a flamboyant approach that holds an audience spellbound. It is not, however, in any way comparable to the performance De Niro delivered in *The Godfather, Part II,* in which he delivered a realistic portrait of a complex man balancing a traditional family life with a horrifyingly violent criminal career.

Only once does Mamet allude to the fact that Capone had a family. "You insult me in front of my son?" Capone shrieks at Ness, when the T-man enters

Filmmaker Brian De Palma's vision (quite different from that of the famed urban-oriented TV series) portrayed the squad as if they were the Old West's Earp brothers on the way to the O.K. Corral; "I never saw it as a gangster film," De Palma stated, "but more on the order of *The Magnificent Seven*" (courtesy Paramount Pictures).

Sean Connery in the role that won him a Best Supporting Actor Oscar. The fictional Jimmy Malone is an apotheosis of all those Irish cops, beginning with Pat O'Brien at Warner Bros. in the 1930s, who have taken on Italian mobsters in the simplified world of the American mob movie (courtesy Paramount Pictures).

his domain. But that line is all but lost in the confusion of the moment. This film's Capone is in no way a modern, psychological portrait (Rod Steiger attempted to show the man behind the myth in his 1959 docudrama *Al Capone*) but relies on the brilliance, the bluster, the bravura of De Niro as a contrast to the film's understated Ness. If Stack's Ness was a man of few words and swift, decisive action, this movie's Ness has more in common with Robert Young of TV's *Father Knows Best.*

Mamet makes the contrast between Capone and Ness as simple as possible: Capone is the man without family ties, operating his criminal empire from his office-suite in a grandiose hotel, where a red carpet leads up the spectacular stairway lined with gilt, capped by a glittering chandelier. Capone and his cohorts are always surrounded by easy, expensive, expendable women. They guzzle champagne and appear to have no earthly existence other than their criminal pursuits. (The real Capone considered himself a devoted family man, but not the character we meet here.) In contrast, Ness is often seen at home; in the opening scene, his wife serves him breakfast, wishes him luck on his first day at a new job, then proffers a big goodbye kiss. He appears headed for work as a clerk or bank teller; we're surprised to see him at the police precinct, introduced as a Treasury agent sent to clean up the town.

The irony is that while Capone was indeed married, Ness was not; he and his fiancée weren't wed until after the Untouchables were disbanded. In the film, the Nesses already have a little girl, and Mrs. Ness (she has no name, no identity other than "Ness's wife") is pregnant. It's no coincidence the film's villains constantly threaten Ness's family. After Ness's first raid on the Capone empire, he heads home with a birthday present for his child. Outside their apartment, a car sits, ominously parked in the shadows. The monstrous-looking man who will be identified as Frank Nitti (Billy Drago) venomously announces, "Nice to have a family...a man should take care of them—see that nothing [bad] happens to them." Later, an outraged Capone will shout, "I want him [Ness] dead...I want his family dead!"

No wonder Ness insists he only wants single men working for him; he will not put anyone else's family in the same danger as his own. Clearly, Mamet and De Palma strip the story down to basics that communicate their shared values. In real life, there were ten Untouchables, all desk cops; not one was killed, and it's doubtful any—including Ness—ever fired a shot in the line of duty. In the film, there are four; their names (other than Ness's) and personalities are fictionalized; two are killed in violent fighting. At the time of the film's release, DePalma announced he'd read the memoir Eliot Ness had written with Oscar Fraley and considered it unfilmable. Nothing happened in the visceral sense, so De Palma scrapped everything except the concept of a T-man named Ness who comes to Chicago to get Al Capone; Mamet freely invented the story, characters, and situations.

Such as approach has its precedents: that's the way Shakespeare wrote when telling "historical" stories and was the approach of filmmaker John Ford. Understandably, some critics comfortably forgave the film its inaccuracy of detail, such as Terrence Rafferty of *The Nation,* who hailed *The Untouchables* as "a clean, uncomplicated piece of Hollywood entertainment." However, there is in Ford a consistency notably missing from De Palma's *The Untouchables.*

On the one hand, Mamet's script reduces Ness to the straitlaced family man; on the other, it tries to give him dark shadings and colorful edges. During a shootout on the Canadian border, Ness—who has never killed a man before—becomes ill when forced to do so. Shortly thereafter, his second-in-command, Malone (Sean Connery), grabs a helpless gangster, puts a gun in the man's mouth, and blows his head off. Incredibly, Ness laughs cynically when a Canadian Mountie is repulsed by this cold-blooded act.

Nowhere is this inconsistency so clear as when Capone stands trial for income tax evasion, and Ness (after learning that Capone's lieutenant has killed Malone) confronts Nitti atop the courthouse. Nitti is caught attempting to climb down a dangling rope. Ness could let the man drop but stretches out his hand, pulling his archenemy up to safety, grimly announcing he's saving Nitti for the electric chair. When Nitti sarcastically announces he'll beat the rap, Ness tosses him off

"This is a raid!" Treasury agent Ness moves in on one of Capone's distribution centers (courtesy Paramount Pictures).

the building. None of this is historical; in actuality Nitti assumed control of the Chicago mob after Capone went to jail.

Historical accuracy is the least of the problems. It's an awful moment; we might have forgiven Ness for standing by and allowing Nitti to drop. But watching the "hero" consciously throw a man off a building (however horrible that man may be) is a bit much, especially when he later makes glib jokes about it. When Agent Stone (Andy Garcia) asks where Nitti is, Ness answers, " He's in the car." The camera then cuts to Nitti's bloodied body, which went through the car's roof.

No wonder, then, *Commonweal's* Tom O'Brien called this "an evil film—exquisite-looking schlock." The problem is not the amount of violence (though De Palma's decision to shove the camera tight on the blood-

Malone and Ness are threatened by one of Capone's henchmen in the posh Chicago hotel where the gangster seemingly lives as well as conducts business. The film's Ness is a populist hero taking on the corrupt and wealthy Capone, now firmly entrenched in the despised moneyed Establishment (courtesy Paramount Pictures).

ied Malone, dying painfully, seems unnecessary), but the mindless manner in which senseless violence is portrayed. Lacking is the clear moral perspective on violence that elevated Coppola's *Godfather* films to the level of art. When Ness later sits in his office, brooding over newspaper accounts of bloodshed in the city, he sadly intones,"So much violence!" Viewers laughed out loud; how could Mamet give Ness this line—and how could De Palma direct Costner to say it straight-faced—after what we've just seen, which is more violent even than Capone's smashing open the head of one of his henchmen at a lavish banquet?

Mamet's central idea, apparently, has to do with the kind of adherence to the law that has always characterized the traditional American hero. It's important that in the film's first sequence, we see not Ness but Capone from a bird's-eye-view shot. He's in a barber's chair; in addition to a shave, he's also receiving a manicure and shoeshine: a pompous punk emperor. Reporters crowd around, asking Big Al why he sells booze, even though it's illegal. "I'm responding to the will of the people," he insists. "People are gonna drink—all I do is act on it. I'm a businessman." It's doubtful that the real Capone ever said anything quite like this, but the line is highly effective in establishing him as the hero of a modern gangster film, even if it is a period piece. He has more in common with Gordon Gekko of Oliver Stone's *Wall Street* than the Al Capone of TV's *Untouchables*.

Street gangster Frank Nitti (Billy Drago) whispers a message to his boss Al Capone (Robert De Niro), decked out in white tie and tails for the opera. The revisionist portrait of the gangster is of an ambitious, aspiring man attempting to leave his déclassé background behind and to finally achieve respectability (courtesy Paramount Pictures).

Indeed, in his lifetime, Capone was not thought of as a criminal by most Americans, but as a Robin Hood, a noble thief who got them the booze their misguided government unaccountably decided to deny them. Shortly thereafter, we see Ness at his first press conference; when asked his position on booze, he answers, "I'll tell you how I feel about Prohibition—it's the law of the land."

At no point does he suggest he's morally opposed to liquor; yet Ness insists his men be "pure" and never take a drink, staying within those (current) laws of the land. (We could more easily forgive him slipping an occasional drink than we can his illegal killing

A movie about movies: during the final shoot-out in Union Station, a baby carriage slips down the stairs, allowing De Palma to reference Sergei Eisenstein's 1925 Russian masterpiece *Potemkin* (courtesy Paramount Pictures).

of a criminal.) The breaking of some laws are easier to deal with than others, and the film's Ness seems a tad ridiculous expressing moral outrage at drinking while shrugging at the murder of unarmed suspected criminals.

At the end, a cub reporter confronts Ness on the street, mentioning that the Volstead Act will probably be repealed soon, wondering what Ness will do. "I think I'll have a drink," the agent says as he walks off into the sunset. On one level, it's the film's final glib gag; on another, it's a summation of Ness's personal morality. He never opposed the Capone mob and its import of Canadian whiskey because he agreed with the principle behind the law, rather because, as a career lawman, he felt the need to obey the letter of the law. If the filmmakers had managed to convey the irony between their Ness's willingness to suspend his morality on the big, even biblical laws—Thou shalt not kill—while insisting minor and unpopular ones—Thou shalt not drink—be obeyed, they might have turned out a film worthy of the accolades Richard Schickel of *Time* unaccountably heaped on their uncertain project: "A masterpiece of idiomatic American moviemaking."

WALL STREET

TWENTY-SIX

Wall Street

(1987)

A 20th Century–Fox Film

CAST:

Michael Douglas *(Gordon Gekko);* Charlie Sheen *(Bud Fox);* Daryl Hannah *(Darien Taylor);* Hal Holbrook *(Lou Mannheim);* Terence Stamp *(Sir Larry Wildman);* Martin Sheen *(Carl Fox);* Sean Young *(Kate Gekko);* John C. McGinley *(Marvin);* Josh Mostel *(Ollie);* Millie Perkins *(Mrs. Fox);* James Spader *(Yuppie Lawyer);* painter James Rosenquist, art dealer Richard Feigen *(themselves)*

CREDITS:

Producer, Edward R. Pressman; director, Oliver Stone; screenplay, Stone and Stanley Weiser; cinematography, Robert Richardson; editor, Claire Simpson; music, Stewart Copeland; production designer, Stephen Hendrickson; running time 120 minutes; rating, R.

Any mention of the crime/gangster genre automatically brings to mind the Italian, Irish, and Jewish mobsters of the 1930s, shooting each other on the streets of Chicago's South Side, or their contemporary counterparts, the African-American gangstas and Hispanic gang-bangers doing much the same thing in today's East L.A. But there are white-collar criminals as well, the nonviolent gangsters for whom "takeovers" are now accomplished with computers and international banking accounts rather than antiquated tommy guns or state-of-the-art Uzis. Roman Polanski's *Chinatown* depicted the nefarious doings of an earlier generation of white-collar criminals during the Great Depression of the 1930s. *In Wall Street,* our most ambitious muckraker, Oliver Stone, presents the story of Noah Cross's modern counterparts, those Reagan-era corporate raiders whose unscrupulous antics were ignored, even applauded, during the height of the bull market, only to be loudly criticized when stocks crashed on October 19, 1987, forcing mainstream Americans to note that people who should have been considered villains were, in fact, lauded throughout the Greed Decade as heroes.

In short order, such characters as Ivan Boesky and Michael Milken were under investigation for fraud and on their way to jail. Ordinary people who had idolized them and others of their ilk now vilified these very characters, once the debacle drove home the reality that insider trading could prove harmful to the public at large. That infamous date was the Reagan-era equivalent of the St. Valentine's Day Massacre, the 1929 inci-

Promotional art for *Wall Street*: The gangster as white-collar criminal (courtesy 20th Century–Fox).

Michael Douglas as Gordon Gekko, flashing the power sign of the Reagan era (courtesy 20th Century–Fox).

The protégé: just as Douglas's Gekko was drawn from real-life stockbroker/racketeer Ivan Boesky, so was Charlie Sheen's naively cynical Bud Fox based on Michael Milken (courtesy 20th Century–Fox).

dent that finally turned the public against the Chicago gangsters they'd previously romanticized as "musketeers of the streets." Difficult as it is to grasp today , mobsters had, during the 1920s, not been vilified but deified as urban American Robin Hoods, daring to rebel against the unenforceable Volstead Act. Just as Capone had been transformed overnight, in the public imagination, from hero to villain, in the light of sickening violence that went beyond any sense of propriety, so, too, was the point finally driven home that Boesky and Milken were not fiscal saviors but slick, superficial examples of upscale slime: older and younger nightmare visions of that eighties phenomenon, the yuppie.

In one of those remarkable examples of uncanny timing that occasionally accompany a film's release, Black Monday occurred a week after *Wall Street* predicted that event. Stone had closely observed our economic situation, the sleazy financial doings that could only lead to disaster, fashioning a film that warned against the coming crisis. He could not have guessed how soon it would happen. Intended as a cautionary fable for a future inevitability, *Wall Street* turned out to be a behind-the-scenes glimpse of what was right then happening, though fashioned before the fact.

Despite Michael Douglas's obvious playing of Gordon Gekko as the villain, some first-week moviegoers managed to accept his snarling reading of the line "Greed is good!" at face value. Those who saw the film after October 19 grasped that his philosophy—an economic nihilism summed up in the three most devastating words since Nietzsche pronounced "God is dead!"—stood for everything we ought to fear, a horrific vision of what, as a country, we had unconsciously become during the previous seven years.

Stone, always applauded as strikingly forceful though never accused of being subtle, schematized his film as an updating of the medieval morality play. Gekko, the white-collar Reagan-era answer to the gangster of yore, is Mephistopheles, the devil tempter. The innocent Everyman, overanxious to sell his soul for a piece of this pie, is Bud Fox (Charlie Sheen), youthful broker, clearly the film's counterpart to Milken, as Gekko is Boesky's. Since Bud's father (Martin Sheen) is a decent, hardworking airline mechanic, Bud is privy to insider information that can facilitate Gekko's hostile takeover of that company. Throughout the film, Bud wavers between his biological father, an admirable bas-

The morality play, Oliver Stone style: Faustian yuppie Bud is torn between two father figures, his decent blue-collar biological dad (Martin Sheen) and his white-collar mentor/Mephistopheles, Gekko (courtesy 20th Century–Fox).

tion of old-fashioned, blue-collar middle-American morality, and Gekko, symbol of the nouveau upscale-sleaze amorality. Bud realizes too late that he's gone over to the side of darkness, as *Wall Street* transforms into a redemption saga. So Bud makes up for past mistakes by allowing authorities to wire him and monitor Gekko's illegal activities. This results in a lighter prison sentence for Bud, though Gekko will do hard time.

Vincent Canby of the *New York Times* applauded the Stone-Douglas collaboration that resulted in Gekko, noting that this is "a good character. He's ruthless, ironic and, under the circumstances, completely practical, and Mr. Douglas, in the funniest performance of his career, plays him with the wit and charm of Old Scratch wearing an Italian-designer wardrobe." Indeed, that performance would shortly win Douglas the Academy Award as Best Actor of the Year. However, Canby also noted *Wall Street's* weaknesses, owing to Stone's belief that his overtly didactic message is of more significance than the creation of a truly sophisticated human drama: "The movie crashes in a heap of platitudes that remind us that honesty is, after all, the best policy. *Wall Street* isn't a movie to make one think. It simply confirms what we all know we should think, while giving us a tantalizing, Sidney Sheldon–like peek into the boardrooms and bedrooms of the rich and powerful."

The last muckraker: director Oliver Stone at work (courtesy 20th Century–Fox).

Though Stone wanted to make a populist film (as evidenced by his blue-collar hero, the elder Sheen), he conversely did not want to make an anti-capitalist film (as evidenced by Holbrook's white-collar good guy). Still, Stone found himself in the same awkward situation that plagued the anonymous authors of medieval morality plays: it's far easier to make the devil a charismatic character than to do the same for symbols of good, who often appear unintentionally sappy. Too often, Bud and the others merely appear to be puppets, feeding questions to Gekko that allow him to deliver stunningly wicked retorts:

> BUD: Why did you wreck this company?
> GEKKO: Because it was wreckable!

As Tom O'Brien noted in *Commonweal*, "like Satan in *Paradise Lost*, [Gekko] gets all the good [wicked] lines. But his is a strength that unbalances the film."

Whatever its limitations as drama, there was never a moment's doubt that the film worked well enough at accomplishing Stone's first priority: allowing the average American moviegoer a better understanding of the way white collar criminals undermine our economic structure. "I create nothing," Gekko gleefully announces, acquiring vast personal wealth through takeover and liquidation of existing companies rather than creating true wealth (beneficial to the working man and the country at large as well as to himself) by forming new companies to produce new products. The Gekko-Boesky approach, on the other hand, diminishes the number of products for sale, services provided, and ultimately available jobs, the very elements that lead to a healthy economy for all rather than a financial bonanza for the select few.

In addition to the undeniable power of his moral, there is also Stone's stylistic dexterity. If his story is a redemption saga, it's worth noting that Stone's visual technique redeems many problems in his writing by taking old melodramatic clichés and giving them such a fresh appearance, we can accept what might otherwise have been perceived as too trite. Stanley Kauffmann in *The New Republic* noted the take-your-breath-away style, a view of the stock market and contemporary conglomerates that could only have come from a man who knew this world firsthand: "Fiery voluntaries are off to hazard new fortunes in these computerized, neon-lighted beehives.... The editing is like machete strokes, clearing a way through the jungle for the advancing camera. Texture [is] the strongest element in *Wall Street*. The dynamics are in its rhythms and context more than its personified drama. Stone reminds us that the gold standard is gone only technically: these people would make Nibelungs look serene."

TWENTY-SEVEN

Married to the Mob

(1988)

An Orion Picture

CAST:

Michelle Pfeiffer *(Angela De Marco);* Matthew Modine *(Mike Downey);* Dean Stockwell (*Tony The Tiger Russo); Mercedes* Ruehl *(Connie);* Alec Baldwin *(Frank De Marco);* Joan Cusack *(Rose);* Ellen Foley *(Theresa);* Anthony J. Nici *(Joey De Marco);* Oliver Platt *(Ed);* Nancy Travis *(Karen Lutnick);* Al Lewis *(Uncle Joe);* Paul Lazar *(Tommy).*

CREDITS:

Producers, Kenneth Utt and Edward Saxon; director, Jonathan Demme; screenplay, Barry Strugatz and Mark R. Burns; cinematography, Tak Fujimoto; editor, Craig McKay; music, David Byrne; production designer, Kristi Zea; running time, 103 minutes; rating, R.

It isn't surprising that David Byrne provided the music for Jonathan Demme's gangster opus *Married to the Mob;* the two artists working in complementary mediums share a singular vision. Demme films have always looked the way Talking Heads music sounds: playfully intellectual and inoffensively irreverent, projecting a sense of loving satire for the garishness of the American pop-culture environment. While endless example of our kitsch culture are always on prominent display—our expensively garish cars and clothes, our extravagantly sentimental songs—they are presented with enough of an edge to let us sense that the artist studying them doesn't take such items at face value, understands that they are junk, rejoicing in them on that level. It is purposefully impossible to tell whether Demme's films are intense dramas always threatening to transform into broad comedies, or exuberantly silly items that suddenly spill over into high seriousness.

The supermarket sweep: Jonathan Demme's dark humor derived from the contrast between gangland's nefarious activities by night and the attempts of all involved to appear absolutely "normal" during daylight hours (photo by Ken Regan, courtesy Orion Pictures).

Married to the Mob initially appears to be a contemporary crime film, dealing in a relatively straightforward manner with how the once roughhewn organized-crime world has shifted from the inner city to the relative safety of the suburbs, leaving the urban mean streets open for newer mobs of varied ethnicity. Shortly, though, it will shift gears, becoming a surprisingly soft-spoken and emotionally rewarding film about one woman's physical journey from the disquieting comfort of her routine life, accompanied by an inner journey toward self-knowledge and self-fulfillment. Then, in its final act, the movie makes one more abrupt transition, wildly but effectively leaping to bedroom farce. Here, Demme neatly combines the screwball antics of an assortment of people in a tastelessly posh hotel, bouncing from bed to bed with temporary partners they have no right to be with even as

Michelle Pfeiffer as Angela DeMarco: the Mafia princess as all-American wife and mother (photo by Ken Regan, courtesy Orion Pictures).

Director Jonathan Demme is famous for his eclectic casts: Al "the Worm" (Gary Klar), Nick "the Snake" (Frank Gio), Connie (Mercedes Ruehl), Tony (Dean Stockwell), Angela (Michelle Pfeiffer), Mike (Mathew Modine), "Stevarino" (Steve Vignar) (courtesy Orion Pictures).

infuriated spouses rush to the scene, with the deadly serious agendas of the mob.

The film's opening introduces and effectively illustrates one key theme of the modern gangster film, the inability of our ever separating mob subculture from everyday suburban life. We see a group of men, all in conservative business suits, standing on a Long Island Rail Road platform, waiting for the morning commuter train that will take them into the city. All are bleary-eyed, including Frank (Alec Baldwin) and Tommy (Paul Lazar), casually discussing a third man who has not yet arrived. Presumably, they are talking about an acquaintance who cuts it close every morning. Sure enough, the big bald fellow does drive up, just in time to catch the train. Frank and Tommy sit behind the man, reading the paper and blending into the background of seemingly like persons. Then, as the train enters a tunnel, Frank (in fact, a hit man for the mob) draws a pistol and, with silencer attached, calmly puts a bullet through the head of the "businessman" ahead of him, himself a gangster whom mob bosses wanted eliminated. Once the train is out of the tunnel, the man appears to be sleeping in his seat. Frank and Tommy rise and join other commuters as they exit the train, a mob hit—once upon a time an outrageous "hail of bullets" on some déclassé city street—now quietly blending into the texture of daily life.

There is more of the same in Frank De Marco's handsome suburban home, where his wife, Angela (Michelle Pfeiffer) vainly attempts to raise their little boy, Joey (Anthony J. Nici), with the wholesome values that supposedly accompany such an existence, though the task is made difficult by her husband's profession. Little Joey is running an extortion racket at the school and a three-card-monte game in his backyard. How could he do otherwise when his dad casually reaches for his pistol on the way out to work even as other men might reach for a briefcase? We're made aware that Angela—who looks the part of a Mafia princess—does not really fit in. She avoids the company of the garishly coiffed mob brides, even turns down dinner invitations from the virtual queen of their crowd, Connie Russo (Mercedes Ruehl), despite the fact that Connie is married to mob boss Tony "the Tiger" (Dean Stockwell), whom Frankie must impress.

Demme plunges us from such exposition into the drama at hand when Frankie makes the mistake of visiting Karen Lutnick (Nancy Travis), the hatcheck girl known to be Tony's mistress, at the expensively chintzy motel (decorated in a mock-medieval fashion, with hot tubs in every room) where Tony has just bedded her. Tony kills Frankie and Karen, leaving the two entangled in the bubbly water. Tony then follows the well-known gangster's pattern of leading the trail of mourners at Frankie's funeral. Frankie's mother, like so many gang-movie Italian mothers before her, threatens to join her son in the coffin, only this time the character actually lives out that threat. Then Tony attempts to seduce Frankie's widow, making pretenses of concern for her fate (Angela has no idea it was Tony who made the hit on her husband), interested only in sating his lust while enacting further vengeance on the deceased Frankie.

When Tony attempts to grab Angela in her backyard even as the wake continues inside, he's spotted by various Mafia princesses, who report it back to Connie. Mercedes Ruehl managed to make audiences believe her character was Medusa-like enough to strike fear into her husband's heart, even though he thinks nothing of shooting it out with various gangland competitors at the local hamburger stand. The tryst is also spotted by a pair of observant FBI agents, Mike (Matthew Modine) and Ed (Oliver Platt), who incorrectly assume Angela is doing the seducing, though in actuality she attempts to fight off Tony's advances.

When Mike's FBI boss makes clear the Bureau will put Angela behind bars (she obliviously cosigned illegal papers her husband had put in front of her) if she doesn't become an actress herself, giving in to Tony's entreaties and providing information to the Bureau, the dialogue that follows is significant:

> ANGELA: God! You people are just like the mob. There's no difference.
> FBI AGENTS: The mob is run by cheating, murdering psychopaths. We work for the president of the United States!

Or, to coin a phrase, the end justifies the means. Of course, it doesn't, and the audience is smart enough to know that. However buried under the nuttily appealing surface of this seemingly lightweight gangland entertainment, Demme's theme is there for the taking. The theme connects this to numerous other examples of the modern American crime film, in which gangsters and the forces pursuing them are no longer viewed in a black-and-white moral scheme. In our age, it's ever harder to tell the good guys from the bad guys.

The gangster as woman, the woman as gangster: Angela De Marco (Pfeiffer), experienced shooter, shows naive FBI agent Mike Downey (Modine) how it's done (courtesy Orion Pictures).

Tony "the Tiger" Russo (Stockwell) orders the death of Angela's husband, then immediately moves in on the lonely lady. Jonathan Demme characteristically played his film on a fine line between serious crime drama and outrageous dark comedy (courtesy Orion Pictures).

The film, though quirkily charming, lacks the final impact of some of Demme's other works. Though the texture is rich, there is simply not enough of it on-screen, and a closing-credit montage includes provocative glimpses of other sequences presumably shot, then eliminated during editing, including Angela and Mike, out on a late-night Manhattan date, spontaneously breaking into a sensuous rumba in the deserted city. In the film, their romance occurs too quickly, with their first sparks taking place offscreen. Our fleeting glimpse of what might have been the properly magical moment to cement their growing feelings, and our conviction that their romance is indeed something special, make clear that this movie deserved a longer running time, avoiding what Janet Maslin of the *New York Times* rightly referred to as the film's "amiably thin" quality. Nonetheless, *Married to the Mob* remains one of the best modern gangster films to present criminal activity within the context of comedy, while also approaching life in the mob from a decidedly female point of view.

Christopher Lloyd as Bill Burns: His fixing of the World Series marks the beginning of the end of American innocence (photo credit Bob Marshak, courtesy Orion Pictures).

"Read all about it!": the "big fix" becomes the subject of tabloid journalism (photo by Bob Marshak, courtesy Orion Pictures).

TWENTY-EIGHT

Eight Men Out

(1988)

An Orion Release

CAST:

John Cusack *(Buck Weaver);* Clifton James *(Charlie Comiskey);* Michael Lerner *(Arnold Rothstein);* Christopher Lloyd *(Bill Burns);* John Mahoney *(Gleason);* Charlie Sheen *(Hap);* David Strathairn *(Eddie Cicotte);* D. B. Sweeney *("Shoeless" Joe Jackson);* Michael Rooker *(Chick);* Bill Irwin *(Eddie Collins);* John Anderson *(Judge "Kenesaw Mountain" Landis);* Nancy Travis *(Lyra);* Studs Terkel *(Hugh Fullerton);* John Sayles *(Ring Lardner).*

CREDITS:

Producers, Sarah Pillsbury and Midge Sanford; director and writer, John Sayles from the book by Eliot Asinof; cinematography, Robert Richardson; editor, John Tintori; music, Mason Daring; costume design, Cynthia Flynt; running time, 119 minutes; rating, PG.

If Francis Coppola's *The Cotton Club* stands as the most ambitious effort to make a period-piece picture about the connection between organized crime and the entertainment industry, then John Sayles's *Eight Men Out* is that film's natural companion piece, the most uncompromised and important motion picture ever to focus on the relationship between the dark criminal subculture and its seeming opposite, the world of sports. That distinction is significant: whereas crime and show business appear to go naturally hand in hand, their respective glitz and glamour completely compatible, crime and sports would seem the polar opposites of American popular culture. Crime is the negative extreme, the deep, dark secretive side of our society, the compendium of all evil things that happen only at night. Sports supposedly stand for the clean-cut incarnation of simple American values, a brightly lit day world in which agreeable athletes compete in wholesome, fair-and-square fashion.

Which makes the connection all the more deplorable, while adding to the contemporary crime film's key theme, a devastating realization that nothing is pure and untainted. No sport has ever represented American purity in our national collective unconscious quite so effectively as baseball, while no one element of baseball has ever captured the American imagination so completely as the World Series. Which helps explain why the 1919 fix has, over the years, taken on mythical proportions. In *Maclean's,* Brian D. Johnson rightly tagged it "baseball's moment of original sin." This was more than just a sorry incident to be dealt with, then have done with, like once-notorious/now-forgotten boxing setups, outrageous in their time but of little true significance in the grand scheme of things. But the "Black Sox" scandal destroyed the faith of millions of Americans then and since, not only in the team in question and that year's Series, but the World Series as a national ritual and baseball as an American institution.

The notion that an era of American innocence—a vision of ourselves as fundamentally decent and simple in the best sense—was forever lost resulted from the subsequent trial, itself apparently as fixed by gambler-gangster Arnold Rothstein as the Series had been. Though no one was physically harmed, the 1919 Series fix can be considered (at least up until the 1963 assassination of President Kennedy) the crime of the century, the single seminal act that precipitated an ever-escalating sense of widespread cynicism. The fix marked not only the end of baseball's golden age, but our country's as well.

"Say it ain't so, Joe!" That, according to legend, was what a little boy called out to "Shoeless" Joe Jackson as he exited the Chicago courthouse where he and seven other members of the White Sox were on trial for conspiracy. In writer-director John Sayles's *Eight Men Out,* that line appears near the end; throughout, Sayles employs this child and several others as a modern equivalent of the ancient Greek chorus, commenting on all that happens. At first overawed by the players, perceiving them as epic heroes, the boys later express shock and finally condemnation as the athletes fall from grace and must therefore be sacrificed so that social institutions can survive. Sayles's version offers twentieth-century history tinged with Sophoclean tragedy.

George "Buck" Weaver (John Cusack), who was not in on the fix but was vaguely aware of it, is tried along with Jackson and Felsch (courtesy Orion Pictures).

"Most films about athletics are untrue both to sports and life," Tom O'Brien wrote in *Commonweal.* "They emphasize sensational plays and leave out or trivialize the social context of sport itself. *Eight Men Out* presents baseball not as momentarily glorious but consistently intense; it also raises issues of integrity and class warfare in the mode of moral tragedy." In doing this, *Eight Men Out* served as a companion piece to Sayles's 1987 *Matewan,* concerning a West Virginia coal miners' strike likewise set in 1919. A similarly independently produced, serious-minded motion picture emphasizing artistic vision over entertainment, *Matewan* also focused on the plight of labor at the hands of capitalists, portraying individual working men as manipulated—and, in the end, destroyed—by the bosses who exploit them for their own ends, by turning the ordinary person's American dream of success through hard work *(Matewan)* or God-given skills *(Eight Men Out)* into a bogus myth rather than a workable reality.

Not surprisingly, then, Sayles takes a highly compassionate view of the Chicago players who sold their souls to gambler Arnold Rothstein by agreeing to throw games to Cincinnati. In his interpretation, they were motivated not by personal greed, which would qualify them as the lowest villains, but by a need for vengeance. Though the public perceived them as celebrities and golden boys, White Sox players were criminally underpaid, receiving less than $5,000 a year at a time when other pro-ball players received more than $10,000. Uneducated hillbilly youths who signed contracts without reading the fine print (or, in the case of illiterates like Jackson, were unable to read altogether), they'd been thrilled to play big-time ball until realizing they'd been betrayed at every turn. When Charlie Comiskey promised a bonus if the team qualified for the Series, he did not come through with the cash players were counting on, instead serving them cheap champagne—flat champagne at that.

Gangsters "Sleepy Bill" Burns (Christopher Lloyd), Billy Maharg (Richard Edson), and Smitty (Jim Desmond) prove instrumental to master criminal Arnold Rothstein's scheme to fix the World Series (courtesy Orion Pictures).

However unconsciously, taking the bribe was a form of embittered political action. The class war then raging in society at large was here crystallized within the sacrosanct demimonde of sports. Significantly, this all occurred a mere two years after Russia's Bolshevik Revolution; corporate America was in the grips of a Red scare, now long forgotten but at the time as intense as the subsequent 1950s McCarthy-cra panic. Judge Landis was picked to head the baseball commission, not owing to any love for sports or sense of fair play but because of his strong antilabor rulings. It was believed then that to be "pro-American," one had to be pro-boss and antiworker, whether that worker labored in a bleak coal mine or achieved status on the playing field. Though a jury found the accused players "not guilty" in a court of law, Landis chose to banish them forever from professional baseball. Team owner Comiskey had hired lawyers to represent the players (not out of generosity, but so that he could control their "defense" to his own best interest) while testifying for the prosecution. Though his greed was the catalyst that created the fix, he escaped unscathed, as did the prime fixer, Rothstein. The Establishment and the criminal establishment were already weaving a web of mutual cooperation in the century's early years. Also noteworthy: the players were as abused by the gambler/gangsters (who paid only a portion of the promised money) as they had been by "legitimate" society, reintroducing the revisionist theme that there is no honor among thieves, just as the supposedly "honorable" people are themselves thieves.

Eddie Cicotte (David Strathairn) contemplates the big fix. Filmmaker John Sayles sided with the players, interpreting the event as a struggle between powerless, uneducated blue-collar boys and a system that promised them a road to the American dream only to betray their trust, logically causing them to turn against that system (courtesy Orion Pictures).

Another key theme of contemporary crime films is the notion of acting. Here, a group of young actors pretend to be ballplayers who are themselves "acting" in that they pretend to be playing their best to win the game, causing the concept of "performance" in *Eight Men Out* to widen like ripples in a pond. *Eight Men Out* is, like all of Sayles's films, filled with a marvelous integrity that derives from his insistence on working outside the Hollywood establishment, which he views as being as corrupt as the varied establishments depicted in his films. Made without commercial compromise, *Eight Men Out* offers a rich, epic portrayal of the historical events. Ironically, it fails to achieve true greatness owing to a lack of a strong dramatic through-line that Hollywood studios would have insisted on. His movie is structured as an ensemble piece, attempting to cover all the players, owners, gambler-gangsters, journalists, and other assorted characters who waltzed in and out of the disastrous incident. But it would have been wise to de-emphasize such a docudrama approach, allowing John Cusack as Buck Weaver—a totally innocent athlete who was tried with the guilty and, as such, the obvious choice for tragic hero—to be first among equals. Sayles attempts to imitate Eliot Asinof's 1963 book on which the film is based, but such a broad canvas is far more effective in a literary endeavor than as part of a mainstream motion picture.

As David Denby put it in *New York:* "By instinct an observant, rather than circumspect director, [Sayles] doesn't whip up the noisy confrontations that a hack would rely on. But unfortunately, he doesn't do what good directors do, either—shape the material dramatically and intellectually, so that all the little bits of observation add up to something." In trying to avoid emotional excess, Sayles may consistently err in the opposite direction. Denby rightly concluded, "I'm beginning to feel that Sayles's fear of melodrama may be simply a fear of drama." Despite any such limitations, *Eight Men Out* still stands as the strongest film ever on the subject of organized crime's infiltration into sports.

Sean Penn as Danny McGavin (photo by Merrick Morton, courtesy Orion Pictures).

The mean streets of L.A.: an update of the topical, sociological crime films of the past for today's realities (photo by Merrick Morton, courtesy Orion Pictures).

TWENTY-NINE

Colors

(1988)

An Orion Release

CAST:

Sean Penn *(Danny McGavin)*; Robert Duvall *(Bob Hodges)*; Maria Conchita Alonso *(Louisa Gomez)*; Randy Brooks *(Ron Delaney)*; Grand Bush *(Larry Sylvester)*; Trinidad Silva *(Frog)*; Don Cheadle *(Rocket)*; Gerardo Mejia *(Bird)*; Glenn Plummer *(High Top)*; Rudy Ramos *(Sy Richardson)*; Damon Wayans *(Gangsta)*.

CREDITS:

Producer, Robert Solo; director, Dennis Hopper; writer, Michael Schiffer, from a story by Schiffer and Richard Dilello; cinematography, Haskell Wexler; editor, Robert Estrin; music, Herbie Hancock; production design, Ron Foreman; running time, 120 minutes (theatrical) and 127 minutes (director's cut, videotape); rating, R.

The classic gangster films of the 1930s were torn from the headlines, featuring real-life incidents and actual people altered at a screenwriter's whim to conform with what had quickly emerged as the conventions of a genre. So audiences for Warner Bros. crime epics soon became accustomed to seeing wise old Pat O'Brien and cocky young James Cagney as G-men inevitably getting the goods on the likes of Humphrey Bogart. Similarly, contemporary crime movies are derived from factual material, with anecdote and information made palatable to mainstream moviegoers by being fitted into a popular narrative form. If the approach to period-piece crime stories has, in recent years, been to modernize such material by playing it against the grain of genre or even spoofing that tradition, then the modern gangster stories are pulled in the opposite direction, reality reduced to genre.

Colors was just such a film. The movie is of great significance in any serious study of the modern gangster film, since it was the first to deal with the gang-banger or the gangsta, ethnic street criminals of our contemporary cities. Particularly, the film focuses on the Bloods and the Crips of Los Angeles, who identify themselves through the red and blue items they respectively wear, thereby lending the film its title. At the time, some seventy thousand L.A. street youths had become gang members. The bloody turf war between the two most famous gangs, often cited as proof positive that today's society is quickly crumbling into absolute chaos, was in fact eerily similar to the territorial wars of a half century earlier between Al Capone and Dion O'Bannion on the South Side of Chicago.

The truth is, nothing had changed but the locale, the firepower, the skin colors of the criminals, and the spelling of the word *gangster/gangsta*. Apparently, one key element that had not changed was the depiction of dedicated police officers attempting to stop, or at least slow down, gang violence. Pat O'Brien's wise, soft-spoken, on-the-edge-of-retirement senior character was here aptly embodied by Robert Duvall. He played Bob Hodges, nineteen-year veteran of the force, hoping only to walk quietly through his final year before retirement, when he will slip away to some peaceful place with his wife and children. He is of course doomed, by the overriding convention of the genre, to a sorry end. James Cagney's role as a hyped-up, combative, antagonistic younger officer, who believes he knows everything until he learns different from harsh experience, was assumed more or less intact by Sean Penn as Danny McGavin. The crazed street criminal they set out to nail, the modern equivalent to the mad-dog killers Humphrey Bogart played early on in his career, was embodied by Glenn Plummer as High Top, a drug-age Duke Mantee.

In *Time,* Richard Corliss complained that "a movie might focus on the seductive psychopathy of gangland brotherhood, on the loyalties and vengeance, the frightening energy. In *Colors,* though, the hoods are supporting phantoms, refracted through the agonized idealism of a pair of cops." That situation would be corrected in such later films as *New Jack City* and *Sugar Hill,* both starring

The 21st Street Gang: Filipe (Romeo De Lan), Buddah (unidentified extra player), Spanky (Bruce Beatty). Frog (Trinidad Silva), Larry/Looney Tunes (Grand Bush), Bird (Gerardo Mejia), two extras, and Whitey (Courtney Gains)...take on the Bloods: High Top (Glenn Plummer, *second from left*) and his fellow gang members (courtesy Orion Pictures).

Wesley Snipes as the focal gangsta. In the meantime, though, old-fashioned storytelling served as the uncertain framework on which ultramodern material was loaded. Stanley Kauffmann of *The New Republic* noted that this was "a well-made movie but traditional, taming unruly material with familiar patterns." Janet Maslin of the *New York Times* agreed: "What *Colors* does best is to create a sense of place and a climate of fear, to capture the vivid mark that gang life has left upon the downtown Los Angeles landscape. The look of this film, with its hard-edged, brightly sunlit urban settings and its constant threat of unanticipated motion, is genuinely three-dimensional.... *Colors* is less notable for its plot than for its chilling urgency and its sense of pure style."

The style was provided by director Dennis Hopper. As an auteur, he had, back in 1969, sided with the outlaw element while cowriting, directing, and acting in the seminal hippie-era road movie *Easy Rider*. But times had changed and, with them, so had Hopper; the onetime radical and legendary drug-overdoser openly admitted that he had transformed into an ultraconservative supporter of Ronald Reagan and George Bush. That shift in personal politics was reflected in Hopper's artistic attitude: now, he sided with the cops he would have damned two decades earlier. Still, there were fascinating parallels. The street people in *Colors* use the term *home* (short for *homeboy*) at the end of almost every sentence (to describe the person being addressed) much as the street people in *Easy Rider* employed *man*.

Hopper and his colleagues were immediately charged with "glorifying" the street-crime scene, just as the filmmakers responsible for *Super Fly* had been attacked for romanticizing nouveau gangsters in the early seventies. That charge seems far more understandable in the case of *Super Fly*, in which an appealing movie star (Ron O'Neal) played a drug dealer as the title character, an abiding "hero" who survives unscathed at the end. Conversely, in *Colors,* the gangsters, glimpsed briefly, are portrayed as monstrously unpleasant characters, shot down by the good-guy cops before the film is over. Likewise, the charge of racism (good cops vs. bad black drug dealers) is untenable. The film's most sensitive, intelligent police officers (though not, notably, the leading police characters) are black. Several whites, and a number of ethnic women, are liberally mixed in with the Hispanic and black gang-bangers so that the "evil" on view here is not perpetrated solely by men of color. Significantly, we see not only the bad black gangsters, but also the majority of good black citizens, threatened by the gangstas even as the fine folk pray in their storefront church.

The unlikely romance of Danny and a princess of the barrio, played by the gorgeous Maria Conchita

Danny struggles with a gang member. Though some critics complained that the film glorified the gangs, it in fact is a tribute to the imperfect but dedicated cops who combat them (courtesy Orion Pictures).

Alonso, stood out like the proverbial sore thumb. Still, however contrived and unlikely the plot, the film's writers had clearly done their homework, then fitted all the key elements of urban-ghetto life into their script, however fleetingly. The film begins with a drive-by shooting in which the Crips kill a Blood for no reason other than that he is a member of the competing gang who may have been standing too close to their turf. The decent people living in the neighborhood who witnessed the killing are unwilling to say anything to the police for fear of gang reprisals. Young gang wanna-bes are shown spray-painting graffiti on walls, covering over the names of opposing gang members earmarked for death. Older drug dealers set up franchise tables in front of their homes, then employ "peewees" (too young to be charged as adults if apprehended by the police) to run their drugs down the street to customers. Older gang veterans complain about the random violence of the current cowboy-style kill-crazy kids—glimpsed carrying beepers and high on either crack or PCP—shaking their heads while, without irony, commenting on the sorry state of the new generation.

"Venture capitalists, underworld style," Corliss called the gang-bangers in *Time.* A key element of the modern crime film was reintroduced when, at a gang meeting, one member explains to a visiting social worker that the gang is the only family he's ever had, and that he will always be loyal to it for providing that. The gradual disintegration of the traditional American family, and the parallel attraction of gangs as alternative families for young, vulnerable, impressionable people, desperately in need of the support only a family unit (biological or makeshift) can provide, are as basic to this scene as it is to the emerging genre. Hopper and Wexler captured the gangs' antics, and the frantic attempts of the police to curtail them, vividly and, at moments, dazzlingly. One particular shot stands out: Bloods and Crips, arrested and jailed in separate cells, move toward one another (halted only by the bars) as if immersed in a frightful tarantella, a breathtaking dance of death, even as the camera washes over them.

In her *New Yorker* review, Pauline Kael complained that "as a director, [Hopper] isn't inside the material; he doesn't bring us to a fuller consciousness of gang life (or of police life, either). He's a visual aesthete—less a director than an artistic arranger of people in the frame. We're turned into passive voyeurs; we get a look at gang violence without being asked to become emotionally involved. *Colors* is like an art tour of ghettos and barrios." Still, Kael admitted that "the picture belongs to an honorable tradition of melodramatic muckraking," and like those earlier crime epics from which its plot mechanics are derived, *Colors* did indeed drive home the harsh realities of contemporary crime to the mainstream moviegoing audience.

Danny "Pac-Man" McGavin romances Louisa (Maria Conchita Alonso) as they play with his partner's daughter. As is so often the case, the love story proved to be the least convincing element in the film (courtesy Orion Pictures).

CLUB
Sugar Ray

THIRTY

Harlem Nights

(1989)

A Paramount Picture

CAST:

Eddie Murphy *(Quick);* Richard Pryor *(Sugar Ray);* Redd Foxx *(Bennie Wilson);* Danny Aiello *(Phil Cantone);* Michael Lerner *(Bugsy Calhoune);* Della Reese *(Vera);* Lela Rochon *(Sunshine);* Arsenio Hall *(Crying Man);* Berlinda Tolbert *(Annie);* Stan Shaw *(Jack Jenkins);* Jasmine Guy *(Dominique La Rue).*

CREDITS:

Producers, Robert D. Wachs and Mark Lipsky; director/writer, Eddie Murphy; cinematography, Woody Omens; editor, George Bowers; music, Herbie Hancock; production design, Lawrence G. Paull; running time, 115 minutes; rating, R.

Eddie Murphy's sudden ascension to superstardom (his first seven movies grossed $1 billion worldwide) allowed him, in the personality-dominated world of today's Hollywood, an all but free hand at choosing projects, so long as they continued to make money. Murphy worked on the writing and preparation of several films, then chose to singly write and direct *Harlem Nights,* his dream project about the African-American experience during the late 1930s, that post-Prohibition era of rampant gangsterism. The film combines elements of *The Cotton Club* and *The Sting,* with touches of *Prizzi's Honor* thrown in for good measure. Any edge of originality was due to the largely black cast, as well as the point of view of minority members relegated to supporting roles in previous pictures.

That Murphy's movie is not just about the late thirties, but about films of that era as well , is clear from the title sequence. Opening credits roll over an image of elegantly rumpled satin, precisely as they would in a noir produced a half century earlier, even as soft jazz (by Herbie Hancock, self-consciously evoking Duke Ellington themes) plays. The subject of this revisionist work is less Harlem in the historical 1930s than the Harlem of Hollywood's thirties; we sense at once the "world" we are being cinematically dropped into is a world of movie mythology.

Eddie Murphy as Quick and Richard Pryor as Sugar Ray: the *Sting*'s buddy-buddy team, re-created by an African-American artist, writer-director-star Murphy (courtesy Paramount Pictures, photo credit Bruce Talamon).

A brief prologue, set in 1918, makes clear that Murphy intends to revise as well as revive stereotypes. A black child runs through Harlem streets and into a seedy club where Sugar Ray (Richard Pryor) runs a backroom crap game, surrounded by unsavory characters. The child delivers Sugar Ray's cigarettes, but one particularly nasty gambler grows furious that a little boy is present, insisting children bring him bad luck. Sugar Ray attempts to calm the man, but nothing works. The fellow grows ever more violent, threatening to kill the child and Sugar Ray. We notice a pistol hidden beneath a table, and Sugar Ray's face as he cautiously reaches for it. Then, suddenly, we see a bullet strike between the unpleasant man's eyes.

We assume that we know what happened; either Sugar Ray managed to grab the gun, or his trusted croupier Bennie (Redd Foxx) rushed to his aid. Filmmaker Murphy cuts to a shot of the child, casually holding the gun. The image is shocking, not because a child has killed an abusive man (we see that on the TV news) but because a child in a movie (and a period movie at that) has killed, violating a no-no of 1930s Hollywood. We are informed, by the incident, that things are not going to work in this period-piece world in the manner that they once did.

Still, conventions of the past are continuously evoked. Murphy decided on a story structure not unlike those in many old Howard Hawks historical films *(Red River, Land of the Pharaohs)* in which we meet a father figure and young adopted son, then cut to the main story

Dominique La Rue (Jasmine Guy) enters the club and charms Quick, as a mobster (Miguel Nunez) and Tommy Smalls (Tommy Ford) gaze on. Dominique will never join the positive black "family" at the Sugar Ray because she has sold out to the white Establishment (courtesy Paramount Pictures, photo credit Bruce Talamon).

twenty years later, after they have created their empire and must defend it. Pryor's Sugar is thus joined on-screen by Murphy as Quick (even the characters' names are Hawksian), the onetime ward now full partner in running Harlem's most popular nightspot, featuring booze, music, dancing, gambling, and prostitution, attracting both the local gentry and whites who go uptown, crossing 110th Street to do a little slumming.

The threat to their empire comes from Bugsy Calhoune (Michael Lerner), a white gangster who runs the competing Pitty Pat Club (similar in concept to the Sugar Ray, only fabricated, without heart and soul) and plans to drive them out of business. Calhoune sends a policeman in his employ, Sgt. Phil Cantone (Danny Aiello), to inform Sugar and Quick that henceforth they will be expected to fork over two-thirds of their proceeds. Knowing this will bankrupt them, Sugar and Quick devise a complex scheme to defeat their adversaries through an elaborate sting, in which they will steal all the betting money Calhoune collects for an upcoming fight between black champ Jack Jenkins (Stan Shaw) and a white contender.

The details of their scheme, in which Quick manipulates everyone into believing the champ plans on taking a fall, are considerably more predictable and less intriguing than the themes Murphy marbles through his genre piece. Essential to his revisionist approach is a reversal, whenever possible, in our expectations of characters' clichéd identities. Bugsy, the overweight mob boss, looks and sounds like the Italian gangster characters from so many previous movies, though his last name—Calhoune—suggests he's of English descent. Contone is clearly an Italian name, though Aiello's characterization is modeled on the smiling, soft-spoken, evil, and corrupt Irish cops who have inhabited movie screens in the past.

Interestingly, several of the film's most offensive

Crooked cop Phil Cantone (Danny Aiello), who actually works for mob kingpin Bugsy Calhoune, gives Quick and Sugar Ray an ultimatum. Though presented as a lavish period piece, the film actually conveys a radical philosophy on race relations in America (courtesy Paramount Pictures, photo credit Bruce Talamon).

Bennie "Snake Eyes" Wilson (Red Foxx) listens as the aging club owner Sugar Ray considers giving in to the Establishment, while Quick—the gangster as arrogant youth—refuses; even within their solid "family" there is room for dissension (courtesy Paramount Pictures, photo credit Bruce Talamon).

characters are black, ranging from the gambling-hall crazy in the film's prologue to Dominique (Jasmine Guy), amoral mistress of Bugsy, to Tommy, loudmouth archenemy of Sugar Ray who, like Dominique, is in Bugsy's employ. On the other hand, not all whites are as wicked as Calhoune or Cantone; the white couples briefly glimpsed in the club are pleasant enough, while a couple of white males who aid Quick in his scheme are portrayed as nice guys.

Most intriguing, though, is Murphy's take on man-woman relationships. Elegant creole beauty Dominique seduces Quick in the lavish suite Bugsy provides for her. Hoping she's in love but intuiting she may have murder on her mind, Quick hides a pistol under his pillow while Dominique is in the powder room, donning boa and teddy, readying herself to kiss, then kill the man her white "master" has targeted for execution.

The gangster as romantic hero: though Quick worships his idea of what Dominique could be, he will eventually kill her when he realizes that the reality is something else altogether (courtesy Paramount Pictures, photo credit Bruce Talamon).

Before she can pull the trigger, Quick—unruffled by what's happening—asks, "Is this business or pleasure?" Perched above him, aiming right between his eyes, the ice princess answers, "Business." Then she fires—and the gun does not go off. We—and she—realize he removed the bullets before she joined him in bed the previous night. What we expect, from moviegoing memory, is for Quick to gently wrest the gun away, then seduce her into joining his team. "This is personal," he coldly says, pulling out his pistol and blowing her away.

There was an outcry that this action was antifeminist. Brian D. Johnson of *Maclean's* complained that "the humor in *Harlem Nights* is cruel, clichéd, and misogynist—nothing new in an Eddie Murphy movie." Such an argument misses the point; if Quick were to forgive Dominique not only her betrayal of her people but also her betrayal of him, he would be treating her differently than he treats men, a patriarchal view. With equality come responsibilities as well as rights.

What's presented here, then, is a total acceptance of feminist thinking on a tough, no-nonsense street level. It's an attitude that also extends to female friends such as Vera (Della Reese), madam of Sugar's whorehouse. When Quick has reason to believe Vera's been skimming profits, he confronts her as he would any male employee. She's outraged that he could charge her thusly and hits Quick. His reaction is simple: he hits her back. He will not fall back on "old" thinking. If women are equals, then in the modern gangster film (even one played in period setting) they must get what they give. Despite such mayhem, there remains a sense of family—if something of a dysfunctional family—at the Sugar Ray.

Vera (Della Reese) is in charge of the club's "working girls." Though some critics would charge that Quick's harsh treatment of her was sexist, it in fact represents a rough-hewn equality between men and women that exists at the Sugar Ray, though not at the white clubs (courtesy Paramount Pictures, photo credit Bruce Talamon).

Such scenes contrast those at Bugsy's, where skimming of profits is also suspected. When Tommy, their black mobster, is believed to have stolen, one of Bugsy's soldiers is assigned to kill Tommy, which he and cop Cantone brutally do. First, Bugsy blames that very soldier for hiring Tommy, bringing a piano lid down on the man's hand and breaking it as punishment. Since this sequence is juxtaposed with the parallel skimming situation at Sugar's, we are made aware through effective contrast of the nasty brutality within Bugsy's Family (in the Mafia sense of the term) as compared to the egalitarian violence within Quick's family (in the other sense of the term). This notion of loyalty to a clique (based on youth, race, long-term friendship, blood ties, or what have you) opposing the adult mobsters who have become part of the Establishment is basic to the workings not only of *Harlem Nights* but of the modern gangster film in general.

In addition to all the seriousness, entertaining sequences ricochet off expectations inherited from traditional crime films. The best features Arsenio Hall as the Crying Man (though whining would be more correct), who mistakenly believes Quick killed his brother Tommy and goes all out for revenge. A well-staged car chase, culminating in the trapping of Quick in a warehouse that's soon riddled with tommy-gun bullets, ends when Quick fires three rapid shots and is stunned to realize that, by sheer luck, he's eliminated the entire trio of would-be assassins. On those rare occasions when things do happen as they did in old movies, the hero of a modern gangster film is stunned.

Clearly, Murphy enjoyed reviving the trappings—clothes, cars, music, and atmosphere—of late-thirties films. But he also employs the period-piece settings to make an anachronistic statement about young black radicals of the 1990s, their refusal to knuckle under (as Sugar is ready to do) to the corrupt white Establishment in which cops and crooks have formed a system excluding people of color. When Sugar reminds Quick that the other side has a virtual army, Quick, though wearing period clothes, sounds contemporary when he utters the film's most frightful statement: "It's not how many people you shoot. It's who you shoot."

Alone among A-list critics, Vincent Canby of the *New York Times* approved of all this: "Murphy's effort is distinguished by his own singular presence as an actor, and by the delight he takes in appearing with his various costars.... The characters in *Harlem Nights* talk dirtier than movie characters used to. Vulgarity has become a principal means of communication. Yet the movie remains an essentially innocent fantasy.... This is no update of the sort of arrogantly unfunny, self-referential films made by Frank Sinatra and his Rat Pack pals in the 1960s. At the center of *Harlem Nights* is one of the great young talents of the day in the process of seeing just how far he can go."

THIRTY-ONE

The Freshman

(1990)

A TriStar Picture

CAST:

Matthew Broderick *(Clark Kellogg);* Marlon Brando *(Carmine Sabatini);* Penelope Ann Miller *(Tina Sabatini);* Bruno Kirby *(Victor Ray);* Paul Benedict *(Prof. Arthur Fleeber);* Bert Parks *(Himself);* Maximilian Schell *(Chef Larry London);* Frank Whaley *(Steve);* B. D. Wong *(Edward the Houseboy);* Jon Polito *(Chuck Greenwald);* Richard Gant *(Lloyd);* Pamela Payton-Wright *(Liz Armstrong).*

CREDITS:

Producer, Mike Lobell; director and writer, Andrew Bergman; cinematography, William A. Fraker; editor, Barry Malkin; music, David Newman; production designer, Ken Adam; running time: 102 minutes; rating, PG.

The Freshman is in part a comedy that spoofs gangster films, in part a gangster film that embraces old-fashioned screwball comedy. Deconstructionist critics had a heyday analyzing the film's once-in-a-lifetime casting coup, while popular audiences simply sat back and enjoyed Marlon Brando playing the part of the Mafia don who is constantly told that he looks, acts, and sounds like Vito Corleone, Brando's Oscar-winning *Godfather* character. The screenplay by Andrew Bergman is so insistent on this key character's similarities to Brando in that role that it wouldn't have been worth making the movie had the elusive actor not agreed to do it.

The role presented Brando with a unique acting challenge to create several layers of performance. Carmine Sabatini is, on one level, a unique person with a "back story" all his own. At the same time, though, Brando had to show the qualities of the movie character Corleone that others saw in the "real life" Sabatini. We must accept Sabatini as "real" and Corleone as "reel" though we're always aware, on some level, that both are in fact movie characters.

For this reason, it would have been disastrous for Brando to repeat the Corleone mannerisms precisely. Sabatini is not Corleone, real or reel, and that makes it necessary to alter those famed gestures in certain significant ways, while adding elements that individualized Sabatini without in any way negating the resemblance. To do this effectively, Brando had to both revive the Corleone character and at the same time spoof it. Yet that parodying quality could not get out of hand, for if it did, *The Freshman* would border on the ridiculous, and Bergman's film was not intended as a flat-out *Blazing Saddles* burlesque (though Bergman did indeed contribute to the script for Mel Brooks's legendary over-the-top western spoof) but rather to involve audiences emotionally while also making them laugh. The film, while clearly comic, had to remain within the possibilities of everyday reality, however exaggerated.

Brando had to make clear that Sabatini was a man who, to a degree, relished the comparison to Corleone. Though years earlier the resemblance may have been mild, Sabatini has, perhaps unconsciously, heightened the parallels bit by bit (he can't help looking like Corleone, but dressing precisely like him had to be a conscious decision) until he has become virtually indistinguishable from the movie icon. It is to Brando's credit that he pulled all this off quite marvelously; what might superficially seem nothing more than a goof is in fact one of the most intricate and complex characterizations of the two-time Oscar winner's career. Yet it's also to his credit that he made this riff seem easy; audiences had a grand time watching Brando outdo the endless impressionists who like to do Brando as Don Vito.

As Terrence Rafferty remarked in *The New Yorker,* Brando "seems to be in a bizarre and wonderful world of his own. When he's on-screen, he makes Bergman look like a genius. Brando's first few scenes, in which he's seated, a massive presence, at a special table...are lit (by

Gentlemanly crime boss Carmine Sabatini (Marlon Brando) waxes playful with college freshman Clark Kellogg (Matthew Broderick). A dozen other films had parodied Brando's Don Corleone characterization, but this time Brando did the honors himself (courtesy TriStar Productions).

A movie about movies: Clark is a film student who realizes his life is turning into an imitation of the gangster movies that he loves (courtesy TriStar Productions).

William A. Fraker) in the rich brown tones of Gordon Willis's cinematography for *The Godfather*.... Brando plays along.... All the *Godfather* trademarks are trotted out: the whispery voice, the noble tilt of the head, the delicate, courtly gestures of the hands. It's a spectacular turn. His effects are timed with Jack Benny precision, and they're always surprising; every joke arrives like a little gift, individually wrapped. In his scenes the movie seems less frantic; its lunacy takes on an air of serenity—a deeper, more inexplicable, and much funnier weirdness. Brando's performance begins as parody and gradually, almost imperceptibly, transcends its jokey origins; Carmine Sabatini develops from a revue-sketch version of Vito Corleone into a real and strangely original character."

The ostensible star of the movie, though, is Matthew Broderick, playing a mild-mannered young man from Vermont named Clark Kellogg. The comparison of his first name to Superman's alter ego is as unavoidable as that of his last name to a wholesome cereal company. Clark is an unlikely hero for a crime movie, having just moved from his middle-American home to Manhattan, where he's enrolled as a film student at NYU. His connection to the analysis of motion pictures also adds to the deconstructionist approach of the script. Clark is even more impressed by the relationship of film to reality than most other people around him, quite unable to grasp when his life is transforming into *The Godfather* or if Don Vito has stepped out of the movie and into his life.

Broderick as Clark is himself as much a variation on a film icon (if less obviously so to the general viewer) as is Brando playing Sabatini playing/resembling Corleone. As Richard A. Blake noted in *America*, Clark "is a direct descendant of the screwball comedy heroes of the 1930s...a latter-day Mr. Deeds come to town,

"The Family": as he falls under Carmine's spell, Clark grows disaffected from his all-American family back home (courtesy TriStar Productions).

Like so many other (alleged) crime figures before him, Carmine insists there is no Mafia, and he is merely an "importer." His daughter Tina (Penelope Ann Miller) and small-time hustler Victor Ray (Bruno Kirby) conspire to draw Clark ever deeper into their semisurreal world (courtesy TriStar Productions).

although a bit younger than the Gary Cooper character in Frank Capra's classic of 1936....Screwball comedy demands not only a clash of cultures, but an element of romance. Clark has Tina (Carmine's insistent daughter), a byzantine mixture of Shirley Temple and Jean Harlow." Few people missed the insider's gags about Brando, though few picked up on Clark's echoes of past pictures.

Likewise, Clark's teacher, Professor Fleeber (Paul Benedict), furthers this theme. He is the author of various deconstructionist analyses of films, including his unreadably brilliant masterwork, *And the Wheels Go Slow: Form and Function in 42nd Street.* Whenever he shows classic films (including *Godfather II*) to his students, he unconsciously lip-synchs the dialogue, so much a part of him have the old films become. So Fleeber shares the dumbfounded fascination of Clark when a man who appears to be a living, breathing incarnation of a celluloid gangster-movie icon actually walks into their sacrosanct academic world. Though the film is relatively realistic in its approach, it comes close in terms of theme to Woody Allen's fantasy *The Purple Rose of Cairo,* in which Mia Farrow—playing a 1930s movie addict—was stunned to see the leading man of a melodrama hop down from the screen and ask her for a date.

On his first day in New York, Clark runs afoul of a little weasel named Victor (Bruno Kirby), who feigns friendship and steals the naïf's belongings. Shortly, Clark spots Victor from a school office window and pursues; to make amends, Victor promises Clark a job with his uncle. Victor is ushered into a Little Italy "social club" that appears lifted from Martin Scorsese's *Mean Streets,* another intended movie reference; Professor Fleeber has a poster of Martin Scorsese (himself an NYU grad) on his wall. There, Clark is introduced to a professional "importer" named Sabatini.

"He looks just like...like—" Clark says, and one of the film's brightest running gags is that no one who observes Sabatini is ever allowed to finish this sentence.

Clark is given a high-paying job as delivery boy, soon realizing he's working not only for a man who looks like a mobster, but who in fact is one. One of the film's sharpest ironies is that, as in most mob movies, no

Carmine and chef extraordinare Larry London (Maximilian Schell) plan the ultimate filmed feeding frenzy. The two Oscar-winning actors had been teamed years earlier, in 1958's *The Young Lions* (courtesy TriStar Productions).

one will admit there is a mob, or that they work for it, though an unspoken assumption of the organization's existence and vast power permeates every business transaction and human relationship. Another irony is that Clark, like so many guileless young men in previous dramatic gangster films, is drawn into mob activity without ever realizing it, gradually comprehending that he—the least likely mobster in the world—has in fact become a mob member, though he's unable to grasp just when or where (or, for that matter, how).

Whereas previous pictures showed businessmen, lawyers, and the like discovering they were owned by the mob, here a film student discovers the same thing. Bergman's comedy is based on discovery of one's identity; Clark must face who he is and what he has become, particularly painful whenever he has to call home to his parents, who look as if they've just stepped out of a Norman Rockwell painting. Clark gradually grasps that the growing relationship between him and Carmine's daughter, who makes no bones about the fact that she plans to marry him and that he would be wise to go with the flow, is no accident; beginning with the stealing of his clothes, he has been manipulated by arch-Machiavellians for that very purpose.

"Someone called my father to say how intelligent you are," she confides to him at last. "Perceptive and gentle. If you weren't all those things, do you think my cousin would be out getting you a gun?"

Besides having been picked as a perfect mate for Tina, Clark has other duties. Early in the film, Clark and a friend, Steve (Frank Whaley), are assigned to drive to Kennedy airport and pick up an immense, live Komodo dragon. The sequence in which it slips away and runs wild at an elaborate New Jersey mall, diving into an indoor pool and wreaking incredible havoc until it is recaptured, resembles one of those remarkable Laurel and Hardy comedies in which a minor mishap gradually, and hysterically, escalates into complete chaos. Initially, this seems nothing more than a clever set-piece, to be enjoyed in passing then forgotten. In fact, it is the film's neatly disguised setup. Sabatini's actual scheme, for which the "honest import business" is nothing but a cover, is an elaborate smuggling operation that brings endangered species, such as the lizard, into America through secret channels. Then, the creatures are turned over to a master chef, Larry London (Maximilian Schell), who resembles a mad scientist right down to his Igor-like assistant (B. D. Wong). This serves as yet another neatly planted film-on-film reference; London transforms the creatures into forbidden delicacies for jaded millionaires to dine on.

Once a month, the members of an upscale/illegal gourmet club pay $1 million a plate to devour the last existing member of some species that becomes extinct even as they eat, while Bert Parks emphatically sings "Tequila" and something that closely resembles the Miss American theme song. At the appointed moment, men arrive in black tie and tails, the women bedecked in jewels and sequined gowns, as if they were attending one of the Reagan inaugurals. They are the pillars of society, and they are corrupt beyond conception. What we see, then, is not only a great gag but a comic restatement of that key modern gangster-film theme, the mob having over the years become inseparable from society's supposed "elite."

Though *The Freshman* may ultimately be more a comedy than a pure gangster film, it certainly embellishes many of the modern crime genre's key elements.

The old and the new: Marlon Brando as Carmine Sabatini with Matthew Broderick as Clark Kellogg (courtesy Tristar Productions).

THIRTY-TWO

Miller's Crossing

(1990)

A 20th Century–Fox Film

CAST:

Gabriel Byrne *(Tommy Reagan);* Albert Finney *(Leo O'Bannion);* Marcia Gay Harden *(Verna);* John Turturro *(Bernie Bernbaum);* Jon Polito *(Caspar);* J. E. Freeman *(Eddie Dane),* Steve Buscemi *(Mink);* Mike Starr *(Frankie);* Al Mancini *(Tic-Tac);* also, Michael Jeter and Frances McDormand (Secretary, unbilled).

CREDITS:

Producer, Ethan Coen; director, Joel Coen; screenplay, Joel and Ethan Coen; cinematography, Barry Sonnenfeld; editor, Michael Miller; music, Carter Burwell; production design, Dennis Gassner; running time, 115 minutes; rating, R.

The Coen brothers, Joel and Ethan, leaped from virtual obscurity to the big leagues with a single film: 1984's *Blood Simple,* a bloody, stylish throwback to old-fashioned film noirs, done with edgy humor that lent their sordid crime tale a contemporary quality. Shot in Texas on a budget so tight even minor "names" were beyond reach, *Blood Simple* won film-festival accolades, though a few critics demurred. Stanley Kauffman of *The New Republic* tagged it "a crushingly unclever murder story laden with spurious style," suggesting those cineasts who sang the Coens' praises were falling for a scam. These young movie mavens were unquestionably able to grandstand with virtuoso camerawork, though their approach made some wonder if perhaps they lacked the necessary soul for the kind of honest art that can touch an audience deeply.

Miller's Crossing (1990), their contribution to the plethora of gangster films that flourished in the early nineties, only added to the controversy. This sleek, self-assured film (picked to open that year's New York Film Festival) contains moments as visually memorable as anything to appear on-screen in recent memory. Still, the film leaves one with a sour aftertaste, a sense of having been had rather than satisfied. Some former fans came to see the Coens as a pair of grifters not unlike those in the film itself, meticulously practicing their art of deception. As Vincent Canby wrote in the *New York Times,* "*Miller's Crossing* is about movies...old gangster movies....The real world impinges on the movie only by accident."

Lovers, each sensing betrayal by the other, confronting one another on a dark and rainy night, form a key noir motif. Here, Verna turns on Tom when she realizes it is he who killed her brother Bernie (courtesy 20th Century–Fox, photo credit Patti Perret).

Though the credits suggest this is an original screenplay, the brothers actually drew their inspiration from a pair of Dashiell Hammett novels. In *Red Harvest,* Hammett wrote of an unnamed American city in which the political bosses curry favor with whichever of the warring crime lords appears likely to gain the upper hand. In *The Glass Key,* he told the tale of a ganglord in love with a younger woman, who was double-crossing him with the young man he treated as a son. The Coen version—part homage, part rip-off, part straight-faced satire—was mounted as a grim burlesque of old Warner Bros. films, featuring over-the-top humor. Which is why, in *Miller's Crossing,* it's often difficult to tell whether the Coens are kidding, serious, or trying for a middle ground.

As the film opens, a gang war rages in an unidentified American city, circa 1929. The major combatants are Leo O'Bannion (Albert Finney), leader of the Irish gang that for years controlled the city, including its corrupt mayor and chief of police, and Johnny Caspar (Jon Polito), an Italian mob boss who believes O'Bannion has grown complacent and vulnerable. For the time being, Caspar insists, he'll back off, if O'Bannion will eliminate a pesky Jewish gambler, Bernie Bernbaum (John Turturro), who has welched on bets.

O'Bannion's second-in-command, Tommy Reagan

(Gabriel Byrne), advises his boss to do as Caspar says; Bernbaum is hardly worth all-out war at this difficult juncture. However, O'Bannion cannot bring himself to order the hit because—as in "The Gangster as Tragic Hero," which Robert Warshow wrote about a generation earlier—he has a single flaw of a romantic order. O'Bannion's mistress is Bernbaum's sister Verna (Marcia Gay Harden), and he's fallen deeply in love with her. He will not do anything that might drive Verna away, even at the risk of his empire. Tommy Reagan is so incensed at this blindness that he insists he'll leave O'Bannion if he doesn't do what has to be done. Complicating matters, Tommy has been sleeping with Verna behind his boss's back.

When the choice finally comes between personal and professional, Tommy does not hesitate to tell O'Bannion that Verna is unfaithful: he knows for sure because he's the man she has been unfaithful with. Tommy reckons this may be the means of persuading O'Bannion to eliminate Bernie, though O'Bannion—lost in his love/lust for Verna—turns his wrath on Tommy, beating him from one end of their posh hotel headquarters to the other. This scene—strikingly edited, remarkably visceral, a dazzling set piece—is one of the film's highlights. But whether it is true style—an approach designed to communicate the filmmakers' point of view—or merely a clever, gimmicky stunt was the bone of contention.

The war between men and women: The shady ladies of film noir are revitalized for the post-feminist era in contemporary crime films (courtesy 20th Century-Fox).

In *Commonweal,* Richard Alleva unfavorably compared the sequence to the parallel one in *GoodFellas* in which Ray Liotta and Lorraine Bracco rush through a restaurant. Alleva argued that Martin Scorsese is a true artist whose attitude determines his camerawork, whereas the Coens are upscale con artists, show-offs who take our breath away in hopes we'll overlook that their technique is imposed on the material, rather than deriving naturally from it. Said Alleva, "The Coen brothers...have taken Hammett's excellent crime novel, exchanged its tense, logical action for gory special effects, dissolved its grimy urban poetry with overblown photography and forgettable sets, and substituted cheap ethnic stereotypes for Hammett's cruelly veracious characterizations."

Tommy's loyalty never shifts; if he does have an arc, it's in his emotions. The great irony is that Tommy, who begged O'Bannion to hit Bernie, is assigned to do just that after joining Caspar's gang. But alone in the

Johnny Caspar (Jon Polito), ill-tempered mob leader, hires Tommy Reagan when the antihero has been tossed out of his old gang by Leo. Old or new, gangster films deal with the complex issues of loyalty and betrayal, and the thin red line between the two (courtesy 20th Century-Fox, photo credit Patti Perret).

Albert Finney as Leo O'Bannion, defending himself and his home even as delicate feathers from the throw pillow ironically fly about. Filmmakers Joel and Ethan Coen updated noir for the nineties (courtesy 20th Century–Fox, photo credit Patti Perret).

woods—with Bernie on his hands and knees, begging for his life—Tommy can't pull the trigger. "Look into your heart," Bernie sobs; Tommy fires in the air, then lets Bernie run off. The scene is central to the film, and to the film's problems. It's difficult to believe Caspar's goons, waiting for Tommy back at the car, could be dumb enough that they'd fail to check to make sure this significant job has been done.

Bernie—the nastiest of the varied dislikable characters in the film—returns to haunt Tommy, blackmailing him. Either Tommy takes care of Bernie for life, or Bernie will tell Caspar he's still alive. Finally, when Bernie has killed Caspar, Tommy takes a gun and once more points it to Bernie's forehead. When Bernie again falls on his hands and knees, repeating his plea for mercy, he makes the mistake of again appealing to Tommy's emotions ("Look into your heart!"). "What heart?" Tommy asks before pulling the trigger. The problem is that Tommy's transformation isn't believable; since he was the cleverest of the characters, he should have been able to deduce that Bernie would pull such a stunt. Besides, Tommy seemed so cynical from the first frame that it's difficult to grasp how Bernie's actions could possibly have made Tommy any colder than he originally was.

No scene was more self-conscious than the tour de force in which O'Bannion's home is invaded by Caspar's mobsters. He is glimpsed in bed, smoking his cigar while listening to a recording of "Danny Boy"; enemies slip in, kill his guard downstairs, then head up to finish the big boss. But he's waiting; there's an exchange of gunfire, a wild chase, then a bloody shoot-out, all paradoxically set against the rich baritone of an Irish tenor singing the most hoary of old folk tunes. The sequence concludes with the magnificent presence of Finney firing a machine gun at a retreating car, still calmly smoking, apparently oblivious to the hail of bullets, continuing his own fire until he brings them down.

It's a big, bold moment, if a patently dishonest one, dramatically speaking, the kind of sequence naive critics, who adore the more operatic aspects of cinema, tend to overrate. In *Rolling Stone,* Peter Travers hailed *Miller's Crossing* as "a jewel of a gangster film." Certainly, Marcia Gay Harden did offer a jewel of a performance, midpoint between past caricatures of women in crime films (she's a mistress, the conventional kept woman) and contemporary values (Verna stands up to every man she meets, whether it's her keeper

A sense of the absurd: A bemused child lifts the wig off a dead gangster in the Coen Brothers' *Miller's Crossing* (courtesy 20th Century–Fox).

The gangster film as modern tragedy: *Miller's Crossing* and other recent crime films deal with betrayal between fathers and sons, biological or adoptive, as vividly as such key works of literature as *Oedipus Rex* and *Hamlet* (courtesy 20th Century–Fox, photo credit Patti Perret).

O'Bannion, lover Tommy Reagan, or homosexual hoodlum Dane). Fascinating, too, is that even in the most intense sexual scenes between Verna and Tommy, she remains dressed, if scantily so. This effectively conveys the sleazy sensuality of a gang moll's relationships while avoiding the graphic exploitation that might have invited attack by feminist critics.

The one element that suggests the Coens may be serious cinematic artists rather than dazzling con artists is the symbolism of Tommy's hat, consistently developed throughout the movie. In the opening sequence, we see a pastoral stretch of woods, later identified as Miller's Crossing, the place where people face their ethical tests of character. Early in the film, Tommy has a dream in which his fedora is blown away; we know—and he will later learn—that the place is the woods from the opening. "Where's my hat?" Tommy asks nervously as he wakes; his hat is the one part of him he most fears parting with, but which can easily be removed from him.

Throughout, Tommy will be buffeted by natural forces, always anxious because he cannot guess which way the wind will blow. Tommy wanders to Verna's apartment, demanding that she return his hat. "I won it," she insists, referring to Tommy's drunken gambling binge the night before. His hat, apparently, represents his masculinity as well as his morality. When they make love, the Coens' camera focuses on Tommy's hat, perched on her dresser, nestled among various female objects. Symbolically, she has confiscated the dearest, most private part of him.

Tommy will tell Verna about his dream; her analytic Jewish mind will attempt to decode the symbolism of the hat, Freudian style. Tommy, the rugged Irishman, quickly rejects the notion that either his values or his masculinity (or both) were in danger of blowing away, though his eyes suggest he grasps her drift and fears she may be right. Every time the two meet for lovemaking, Tommy's hat is center stage; later, when Leo beats Tommy and throws him out, he tosses Tommy's hat out after him. Caspar accuses Tommy of giving him "the high hat" last time they met, while Tommy, after telling Caspar where he can find Bernie, admits that if the little weasel isn't there, "I'll be facing the coroner in a funny *hat*."

Shortly thereafter, Tommy is taken to Miller's Crossing and discovers it's the place he pictured in his dream. When told he'll be the one to shoot Bernie, he immediately pulls his hat brim down low over his eyes. Back in the city, when Tommy is beaten in a phone booth by mobsters trying to collect his gambling debts, his hat falls off. When Tommy finally confronts Bernie over the dead body of Caspar, the sequence is shot over a discarded hat. Is the missing hat the "heart" that Bernie begs Tommy to look into? Perhaps; whether it is heart or mind, morality or masculinity, the hat—a powerful, persuasive visual symbol, open to various interpretations but clearly a sustained metaphor—suggests that the Coens may be something more than colorful show-offs.

THIRTY-THREE

State of Grace

(1990)

An Orion Pictures Release

CAST:

Sean Penn *(Terry);* Ed Harris *(Frankie);* Gary Oldman *(Jackie);* Robin Wright *(Kate);* John Turturro *(Nick);* John C. Reilly *(Stevie);* Burgess Meredith *(Finn).*

CREDITS:

Producers, Ned Dowd, Randy Ostrow, and Ron Rotholz; director, Phil Joanou; screenplay, Dennis McIntyre; cinematography, Jordan Cronenweth; editor, Claire Simpson; music, Ennio Morricone; production designers, Patrizia von Brandenstein and Doug Kraner; running time, 130 minutes; rating, R.

The film that most clearly attempted a delicate balance between Hollywood's classic gangster films and the harsh realities of our own time was twenty-eight-year-old director Phil Joanou's wildly uneven *State of Grace.* Though hardly a fully successful enterprise, *Grace* does feature fascinating subtexts in a story of modern Irish gangster life. Sean Penn's Terry Noonan returns to his old neighborhood after a dimly explained absence of twelve years, and discovers that Frankie Flannery (Ed Harris), older brother of both his best buddy Jackie (Gary Oldman) and onetime girlfriend Kate (Robin Wright), has emerged as local mob boss. Terry resembles Cagney in a number of Warner Bros. films from the 1930s; Penn's final shoot-out with Frankie is so stylized that it echoes a western gunfight more than a mob movie. But the film is contemporary not only in language (rough, even for films of this type) and violence but also theme. Where in the old gangster films did we ever experience the notion of Hell's Kitchen being invaded not only by competing Italian mobsters but also by yuppies who want to gentrify the area?

Screenwriter Dennis McIntyre relied heavily on an audience's appreciation for basic elements of the traditional gangster saga: the hero with a terrible secret, unspeakable betrayals within the family structure, characters torn apart by conflicting loyalties. But the filmmakers also drew (as had the writers of WB thirties films) from newspaper headlines. The gang here is closely modeled on the Westies, a brutal Irish mob that so feared infiltration by yuppie elements that they did indeed sit down and hack out a deal with their longtime rivals, the Gambino Italian crime Family.

No wonder, then, that David Ansen of *Newsweek* applauded the movie for its blending of the literary tragic with the realistic temporal: "This fictionalized account (of recent events) turns the downfall of the Westies into an electrified Irish tragedy." At times, the film sticks frightfully close to reality. In both real and reel life, the union of Irish and Italians, in Ansen's words, "was an uneasy partnership, for the Westies were wild men, unreliable 'cowboys' prone to drinking and chaotic explosions of violence. They didn't play by the old rules," certainly not the rules of the Mafia, with its strict, succinct code. What caused the filmmakers to want to make the picture was the three-way stretch between social elements involved. The best moments in their sometimes muddled melodrama occur when cool mafiosi, out-of-control Westies, and laid-back yuppies clash in ever-escalating conflicts.

The key gangster on view here is Frankie Flannery, a surprisingly soft-spoken but devious and ruthless man who puts personal ambition above all else. Harris—a gentle-looking actor—may have seemed an odd, even inappropriate choice for the part, if only because he does not embody anyone's cliché notion of a gangster, Irish or Italian. In fact, that's precisely what makes him such a marvelous choice, allowing the introduction of another staple of ancient tragedy, the appearance-and-reality theme. Flannery appears a quiet businessman, making his horrid power plays even more horrific. Without hesi-

Jackie Flannery (Gary Oldman, *second from left*, Terry, and Stevie (John C. Reilly, *center*) confront several members of the established Italian mob. The film was based on actual events involving the Irish gang known as the Westies (photo by Brian Hamill, courtesy Orion Pictures).

Kate can't help herself. A prisoner of her emotions—and her upbringing—she starts sleeping with Terry, fully aware Frankie and Jackie have made him a member of their gang. What she does not know—like the gang and, for the first half of thc movie, the audience—is that Terry is a cop, working undercover to infiltrate and expose the Westies. In the film's opening, we see (or think we see) Terry involved in a drug deal gone bad, shooting a dealer (John Turturro), thereby proving to the old neighborhood he's still one of them. Halfway through the film, Terry meets with that man, very much alive, causing us to realize this is the police superior Terry regularly reports to.

Terry—at first seeming to be a Flying Dutchman, wandering back from some nebulous netherworld—is a far more realistically drawn and psychologically complex person than he at first seems. He's every bit as Machiavellian as Frankie, with whom

tation, Frankie manipulates his drug-and-alcohol-addicted younger brother, as well as his kid sister, who has moved out and up, attempting to put her background behind her by working as a concierge at a posh mid-Manhattan hotel.

This theme is reminiscent of the social dramas of the early twentieth century, those works by Theodore Dreiser and Frank Norris that insisted such an escape from the asphalt jungle is impossible. In the survival-of-the-fittest world of social Darwinism, those born on the bad side may try to reach beyond their humble origins, but will be pulled back into the mire by their basic instincts. That's what happens to Kate when Terry returns; he was Kate's first boyfriend, and though he disappeared without a word, Kate is soon drawn back into the affair, though she consciously realizes she's risking everything she worked hard and long to achieve.

Terry confronts a local bartender. In filmmaker Phil Joanou's vision, the Westies' absurdist sense of dignity derived from their entrapment between the older, more established mafiosi and the new yuppie element attempting to gentrify their neighborhood (courtesy Orion Pictures).

he has a great deal in common. Both are willing to manipulate Jackie and Kate to their own ends, the difference being that Frankie's ends are those of a crime boss while Terry's are those of a policeman. Still, the two are doppelgängers (or, to yield to the irresistible pun, doppelgangsters): Terry exploits Jackie's friendship, as well as Kate's love, to achieve his ends. When, at the end, Terry finally shoots it out with Frankie, it's clear Terry is not merely a cop trying to kill his archenemy, but a man attempting to eliminate the dark side of himself.

Director Joanou desperately attempts to use razzle-dazzle technique to redeem the basic artificiality of this sub-Rambo gun battle. This patent artificiality wouldn't seem so offensive were it not for the rough-hewn realism of the earlier episodes. The big battle at the end of an old B western takes place after an hour and a half of cartoonish characterizations. Here, the shoot-out is preceded by nearly two full hours of kitchen-sink realism, which cries out for something more believable, less kitschy. It's as if Joanou and his screenwriters had a marvelous idea for a movie but were unable to come up with a satisfying ending.

The gangster as contemporary anachronism: Frankie Flannery surrounded by henchmen Jackie and Nicholson (R. D. Call) (photo by Brian Hamill, courtesy Orion Pictures).

The overly familiar romantic plot involving Kate Flannery, who has moved uptown, and her first love, Terry, recalls Warner Bros. gangland films of the 1930s (photo by Brian Hamill, courtesy Orion Pictures).

On the other hand, it would be wrong and unfair to deny the raw power of many scenes, including one in which members of the gang (Terry included) get drunk while waiting for Frankie to call them from a restaurant where he's meeting with the Italians. As the gang members gradually emerge from their stupor, they can't for the life of them recall whether they're supposed to rush to that restaurant and kill all the Italians if Frankie calls them requesting reinforcement, or to do the deed only if Frankie does not call them. Their debate—which starts humorously and escalates into hysteria—is remarkable, if only because it's such a one-of-a-kind scene, new to movies in general, gangster movies in particular.

It's fascinating that the filmmakers could make an audience sympathize with these petty, pitiable gangsters, anachronistic in that they want to keep the spirit of their neighborhood alive, even if that spirit happens to be sordid. The tradition of Hell's Kitchen may be less than honorable (to say the least), but at least it is a tradition, which counts for something in a world in which all traditions are fast disappearing. On the other hand, the yuppies cleaning up the area appear to us, as they do to the

Frankie (Ed Harris) confronts Terry. Harris's soft-spoken characterization effectively cut against the grain of crime-film clichés (courtesy Orion Pictures).

Westies, as a threat.

Kate is conceived as the prefeminist heroine of a 1930s crime melodrama, gussied up with some postfeminist notions about independence that she quickly surrenders the moment that Sean Penn gazes into her eyes. They could as easily be Jean Harlow and James Cagney, and in a sense they are, or at least reasonable facsimiles thereof. Just as Cagney's tough Irish character in *The Public Enemy* needed to learn the concept of respect from more traditional mobsters, so, too, does Frankie. Respect is the key issue in this film, as it is in so many other gangster movies, classic or contemporary. In the quiet, classy (at least in comparison to the Westies' digs) social club that the Mafia boss (Joe Viterelli) runs, Frankie must bide his time, watch the Italians dine on cannelloni and sip designer coffees, while he receives a lengthy discourse from his "betters" on the necessity of respect.

Frankie will glumly agree to kill his own brother, who has violated the truce between the two gangs. Frankie will rationalize the act, indulging in psychologically convenient denial to believe he's doing the right thing. He also earns the undying hatred of Terry, who knows Frankie has given up his basic Irish blood loyalty to assuage the rumpled feathers of organized crime. In hopes of appeasing the Family, he has violated his own family. Men locked into codes of honor that are in opposition, thereby causing those men to be torn apart by conflicting loyalties, was—and is—basic to the lasting appeal and undying impact of gangster films. They inform *State of Grace,* insuring a patina of interest to this less than successful venture.

THIRTY-FOUR

GoodFellas

(1990)

A Warner Bros. Release

CAST:

Robert De Niro *(Jimmy Conway);* Ray Liotta *(Henry Hill);* Joe Pesci *(Tommy DeVito);* Lorraine Bracco *(Karen Hill);* Paul Sorvino *(Paul Cicero);* Frank Sivero *(Frankie Carbone);* Tony Darrow *(Sonny Bunz);* Mike Starr *(Frenchy);* Gina Mastrogiacomo *(Janice Rossi);* Frank Vincent *(Billy Batts);* Catherine Scorsese *(Tommy's Mother);* Samuel L. Jackson *(Shanks);* Sandy *(Debi Mazar);* Henny Youngman, Jerry Vale *(themselves).*

CREDITS:

Producer, Irwin Winkler; director, Martin Scorsese; screenplay, Scorsese and Nicholas Pileggi, from his book *Wiseguy;* cinematography, Michael Ballhaus; editor, Thelma Schoonmaker; production design, Kristi Zea; costumes, Richard Bruno; running time, 146 minutes; rating, R.

In *GoodFellas,* Scorsese returned to *Mean Streets* territory and reevaluated it from his more mature point of view, once again bringing a group of young people into middle age. *GoodFellas* cynically demonstrates the way in which youth-cult loyalty would, under pressure, quickly crumble, as in the world of crime the notion of honor among thieves proves to be nothing more than a quaint, curious myth. The ugly reality, ultimately, is survival of the fittest: everyone for himself, dog eat dog, may the worst man win.

Henry Hill (Ray Liotta) narrates this narrowly focused chronicle of crime in the second half of the twentieth century. Henry is one of a trio of musketeers of the street, along with the incurably greedy, quietly paranoid, ever-calculating career criminal Jimmy Conway (Robert De Niro) and the darkly comical, kill-crazy Tommy DeVito (Joe Pesci). In contrast to his companions, Henry appears passive and submissive. Henry is repelled by Tommy's sudden bursts of bloodthirsty violence. Having shot a teenage waiter in the foot for delivering a drink too slowly, Tommy later casually kills the boy for expressing anguish at his hobbled foot. Likewise, Henry is a follower, not a leader, whenever Jimmy concocts some complex scheme to steal money, including the famed Lufthansa heist from Kennedy airport, which netted them more than $6 million, the largest single caper in the history of American crime up to that point. Henry appears the noninnocent bystander, always around for the ride, never actually doing anything.

In time, though, Hill will do the others in. Tommy has long since been executed by fellow mobsters; he committed the one intolerable act, murdering "made-man" Billy Batts without proper permission. But Henry betrays Jimmy and Paulie (Paul Sorvino), the local mob boss Henry has idolized since childhood and perceived as an alternative father, his own dad having been a simple working man. In Henry's eyes, mentor and best buddy can no longer be trusted. Jimmy, who accompanied Henry on a cocaine-smuggling operation, fears Henry will talk to the feds; it is Jimmy who tells Henry, on the day they first meet, that the only unbreakable rule is "you don't rat on your friends." Paulie, on the other hand, is one of those old-fashioned, anachronistic noble elder gangsters so prevalent in modern mob movies. Paulie refuses to have anything to do with drug dealing.

Paulie warned Henry against such horrible "modern" activity, hoping Henry would prove a throwback to an earlier, presumably more gentlemanly era in crime. Henry rewards Paulie for his naïveté by pretending to be the man his mentor would like to believe he has molded (Henry is the gangster as improvisational actor), then does precisely what he wants, what needs to be done to survive as a gangster in today's urban battleground. When push comes to shove, Henry assumes that each lifelong friend will betray him and, before either can, strikes first, telling everything he knows. Henry sits calmly in court, watching as his Family members are convicted by his testimony, then heads west with his family, wife Karen (Lorraine Bracco) and their kids, assuming a new life through the Witness Relocation Program.

Jimmy Conway (Robert De Niro) introduces young Henry Hill (Christopher Serrone) to young Tommy DeVito (Joseph D'Onofrio) in hopes they'll all be "family." In time Henry will betray that relationship with each man, illustrating the film's premise that there is no honor among criminals (courtesy Warner Bros.).

Paul Cicero (Paul Sorvino), the local godfather, wants to believe he and Jimmy can raise Henry Hill to be a man of respect, though Henry proves to be self-interested and superficial, the nightmare vision of the contemporary criminal (courtesy Warner Bros.).

In *GoodFellas,* the last time we see Henry, he stands in front of his suburban home in a wholesome heartland neighborhood, picking up the morning paper. "The hardest thing for me was leaving the life," we hear him sigh on the sound track. "We [good fellas] were treated like movie stars with muscle." This statement serves as a bookend that completes the theme introduced in his opening line of narration, as poor kid Henry (Christopher Cerrone) glanced out the window at Brooklyn's mean streets below, while we heard the man he would eventually become muse, "As far back as I can remember, I always wanted to be a gangster. To me, being a gangster was better than being president. I knew I wanted to be a part of it." The year was 1955, but there is no subtitle to tell us this; respecting his audience's intelligence, Scorsese allows us to intuit such information from snippets of songs we hear on the sound track or the styles in clothes and cars.

No film has ever allowed an audience to understand such criminal thinking as effectively as *GoodFellas.* Scorsese fashioned a film that, through words and images, allows us not merely to observe but to share the rush of life in the fast lane as Henry, and then Karen, experience it. Through crackerjack editing, bizarre narrative leaps backward and forward in time, fluid camera movement, and emotionally effective angles that express the characters' ever-changing take on their world, Scorsese thrusts us full throttle into the lifestyle. We experience the bizarre contrasts between sordid "business" in the back alleys and raucously glitzy good times in the Copa. Scorsese allows us inside the mind of Henry Hill, a functioning schizophrenic able to rush back and forth, several times in a single day, between the intricate setup of a Family cocaine delivery and the equally intense simmering and stirring of spaghetti sauce for that evening's family dinner, always approaching the two activities with equal intensity. Scorsese allows us to grasp how a nice Jewish girl, Karen (Lorraine Bracco), could be swept up in the excitement, so much so that she abandons her parents and becomes a Mafia princess.

Whenever Henry enters a Mafia den, the camera does not show his arrival, rather presenting the scene from his point of view. As compared to one of Coppola's *Godfather* films, which combine epic, tragedy, and opera, Scorsese's approach might be tagged the cinema of immediacy, allowing us to simultaneously experience excitement and revulsion at the criminal subculture. Perhaps the single sequence that most perfectly reveals Scorsese's method occurs near the end, when Henry has been arrested, then released on bail. First, his wife, Karen, visits Jimmy, who graciously offers Karen money to hold them over, then suggests she walk down an alley to pick up an item of clothing from his warehouse. As she steps away, Karen becomes convinced Jimmy is sending her to her death, having her killed to keep her from talking. Moment by moment, she grows more frightened until, finally, she bolts and heads for her car, speeding away. We are never told, for certain, whether Jimmy was or was not doing what Karen feared; her fear is never expressed in words, instead implied from film-making techniques that allow us to share the growing sense of malevolence. This is a world where such anxiety is the order of the day, so it would ruin the effect if we learned for certain whether or not Jimmy had set her up. The paranoid ambiguity is what the movie is all about.

Joe Pesci as Tommy DeVito, who ironically can become a full member of the mob owing to his birthright, and despite his obvious insanity; Pesci won a Best Supporting Actor Oscar for his performance (courtesy Warner Bros.).

A little while later, Henry meets with Jimmy at a diner to discuss what they ought to do next. Though Jimmy acts no different from before, calmly explaining his attitudes, Henry's voice-over allows us to grasp his own all-consuming paranoia. On-screen, we see two men, old friends calmly sharing coffee and conversation in the booth by the window. What we hear is totally contrapuntal: near hysteria, as a barely controlled Henry reads horrible implications into Jimmy's friendliest remarks about their ongoing loyalty. Is Henry paranoid or perceptive? Again, we're never told. Since we are not viewing the film from the usual moviegoing objective perspective, but subjectively sharing Henry's worldview, we cannot know this, as he never finds out for certain. When asked to sum up the wiseguy philosophy in words, Scorsese (who grew up in Little Italy and knows his material from the inside out), responded, "Want. Take. Simple!" Though his movie's meaning is to share that frightful, fascinating demimonde with us, *GoodFellas* can also be said to project a message on a more literal level: there is no criminal code, any more than there ever was a code of the Old West. Those were only the twin myths of old gangster and cowboy movies; the modern ones tell a different story. Richard Corliss of *Time* wrote: "Watching *GoodFellas* is like going to the Bronx Zoo. You stare at the beasts of prey and find a brute charisma in their demeanor. You wonder how you would act if you lived in their world, where aggression is rewarded and decency is crushed. Finally you walk away, tantalized by a view into the darkest part of yourself, glad that that part is still behind bars."

Once again, the contemporary crime film employs Mafia activity as an allegory for the American dream, or at least its dark side. As David Ansen noted in *Newsweek*, "living in a totally self-enclosed society, these wiseguys and their wives and mistresses are an upside-down parody of untrammeled consumerism." Henry's abodes attest to this: the house he shares with his wife and, shortly thereafter, his children looks like a caricature of normalcy, with expensively tasteless decor, while the apartments he provides for his mistresses (Janice, who is without explanation replaced at a certain point by Sandy) are an ignoramus's misconception of a classy cathouse. Since childhood, Henry has hungered for upward mobility. The great stumbling block in his life is that Henry, like Jimmy Conway, is half-Irish, which means neither man can ever become a full-fledged member of a "crew," no matter how apt they prove to be at Family business. The great irony is that their maniacal pal Tommy, pure Sicilian, is eligible to be a made man, a status Henry or

Ray Liotta as Henry Hill: the youth cult depicted in Martin Scorsese's *Mean Streets* has given way to the amoral 1990s, and an antihero who betrays his friends so that he can survive (courtesy Warner Bros.).

French (Mike Starr) gives inside advice to the aspiring gangsters. By pushing his camera in as close as possible, director Martin Scorsese allows the viewer to feel an active participant rather than cool observer (courtesy Warner Bros.).

Jimmy are far more qualified to hold. There is class distinction in organized crime as well as society at large; the deck is stacked, making the netherworld a fitting representation for the larger, all-encompassing American dream surrounding it.

It's also a movie about movies, about the gangster as twentieth-century cowboy, reinventing the asphalt jungles as his final frontier. Only moments before shooting that hapless waiter in the mob's cellar club, Tommy asks his card-playing companions to identify that "Bogart movie, the only western he ever made." Someone recalls it was *The Oklahoma Kid;* at that point, Tommy whips out his gun and does a wild imitation of the actor best known for playing gangsters. We see an actor (Pesci) playing a gangster (Tommy) playing an actor (Bogie) who ordinarily played gangsters but here played a cowboy, precisely the word Paulie will later choose to describe Tommy. Not surprisingly, Joe Pesci received an Academy Award as Best Supporting Actor for his performance, which always threatened to go way over the top, yet appeared believable owing to Scorsese's sense of conviction. Things had to be big and broad because, we realize, that is precisely how it is in such people's lives. No wonder, then, that David Denby of *New York* hailed *GoodFellas* as "the greatest film ever made about the sensual and monetary lure of crime."

Though the conversation is kept quiet as they discuss mundane matters, Jimmy and Tommy realize during their last meeting that there is nothing left between them but a shell of their onetime trust. The youth cult from *Mean Streets* has disintegrated as such characters move into adulthood (courtesy Warner Bros.).

The family tradition: An aging, Lear-like Michael Corleone (Al Pacino, *far left*) oversees his brood (courtesy Paramount Pictures).

THIRTY-FIVE

The Godfather, Part III

(1990)

A Paramount Picture

CAST:

Al Pacino *(Michael Corleone);* Diane Keaton *(Kay Adams);* Andy Garcia *(Vincent Mancini);* Sofia Coppola *(Mary);* Talia Shire *(Connie Corleone Rizzi);* Raf Vallone *(Pope John Paul I);* Joe Montegna *(Joey Zasa);* Richard Bright *(Al Neri);* Franc D'Ambrosio *(Anthony Corleone);* Donal Donnelly *(Archbishop Gilday);* Bridget Fonda *(Grace Hamilton);* Eli Wallach *(Don Altobello);* George Hamilton *(B. J. Harrison);* Don Novello *(Dominic Abbandando);* Vittorio Duse *(Don Tommasino).*

CREDITS:

Producer/director, Francis Ford Coppola; screenplay, Coppola and Mario Puzo; cinematography, Gordon Willis; editors, Barry Malkin, Lisa Fruchtman, and Walter Murch; music, Carmine Coppola; production designer, Dean Tavoularis; running time, 161 minutes; rating, R.

With *The Godfather,* Francis Ford Coppola reinvented the gangster film for modern audiences. Scant years earlier, moviemakers desperately clung to old clichés. Roger Corman's *The St. Valentine's Day Massacre* (1967) was nothing but a compendium of stereotypical situations (George Segal enters a speakeasy and roughs up the owner, much as Cagney had done in 1931's *The Public Enemy*), now presented in garish color that seemed all wrong. Coppola recast the gangster film as a *Gone With the Wind* family saga, the complexities of underworld life now effectively dramatized. Men who, in their solemn offices, coldly give orders to kill are the same men who attend marriages and baptisms. The gangster as a dual personality became the subject of this Best Picture Oscar winner and of gangster films to follow.

Amazingly, Coppola managed to outdo himself with his sequel. Considerably darker than the original, *G II* allowed Coppola to distance himself from the first film's romanticized view of Michael Corleone (Al Pacino). His boyish charm gone, Michael emerged as a man able to maintain his power only by cutting himself off from all love and emotion. In the final scene, Michael sits on his private island, his wife having long since deserted him, his brother Fredo dead at his own command. As he stares glumly into the camera, Michael bears no resemblance to the heroes of classic gangster films. Yet he certainly does recall the nihilistic characters in Ingmar Bergman art films. In the contemporary existential cinema, every man is an island.

Over the years, Coppola and Pacino were endlessly offered the opportunity to add yet another installment to their *Godfather* saga, though each declined. Serious artists first and commercial filmmakers second, they cared less about the amount of money such a film might make than the aesthetic challenges open to them. Unfortunately, they suffered more failures than successes. Coppola made one controversial masterpiece (1979's *Apocalypse Now*) but too many of his films—*One From the Heart, Rumble Fish, Gardens of Stone, Tucker*—were critical and commercial busts. Pacino starred in a few solid hits—*Serpico, Dog Day Afternoon*—but following what appeared to be an endless string of bombs—*Bobby Deerfield, Cruising, Revolution*—he dropped out of films for five years, retreating to the New York stage.

By 1990, Coppola and Pacino—in danger of being forgotten by the public at large—were quite willing to mount another *Godfather* film, so long as they could do it with the artistic integrity that marked their earlier efforts. The great hope was that *The Godfather, Part III* might prove a perfect final chapter for the trilogy, perhaps even winning one more Best Picture Oscar. The abiding fear was that it would be a bust, further diminishing the careers of the once-promising director/star team, downgrading what had been a great undertaking. In fact, the film would turn out to be somewhere in between; though not in a league with the first two, *G III* was certainly respectable, featuring many moments that seamlessly mesh with the first two installments. Sadly, a few casting mishaps, as well as a lack of the narrative drive that pro-

"The *Gone With the Wind* of gangster films," as one critic called it. Whereas previous movies portrayed Mafia bosses as solitary men with molls instead of wives, *The Godfather* offered an alternative vision of a loving father and his three dutiful sons (Al Pacino, Brando, James Caan, John Cazale) (courtesy Paramount Pictures).

pelled the first two films, reined in the impact of an extremely ambitious work.

As *The New Yorker* reported, "in the first two *Godfather* pictures Coppola took opportunistic, sensationalist material and turned it into drama. In *G III* you catch glimpses of news stories...the package deals with the Vatican recall the Sindona affair. But Coppola doesn't transform the sensationalist material; he just presents it, with an aura of solemnity....The internal force has vanished from his work...the quality of feeling—what gave the films their lyricism and made the public bond with them—is gone....Trying to make a masterpiece, he resorts to operatic pyrotechnics that don't come out of anything." In fact, they come from old movies. Without question, the best sequence in the film is the last: an extended amalgam of opera and cinema in which various assassins skulk about the Palermo opera house even as Michael's son is onstage, playing Turiddu in *Cavalleria Rusticana.* It is a masterfully shot and edited conclusion, yet devoted movie fans know it is hardly original; the sequence is derived from Alfred Hitchcock's *The Man Who Knew Too Much.*

In *The Godfather, Part II,* Robert De Niro assumed the role of Don Corleone and, like Brando before him, won an Oscar for his performance (courtesy Paramount Pictures).

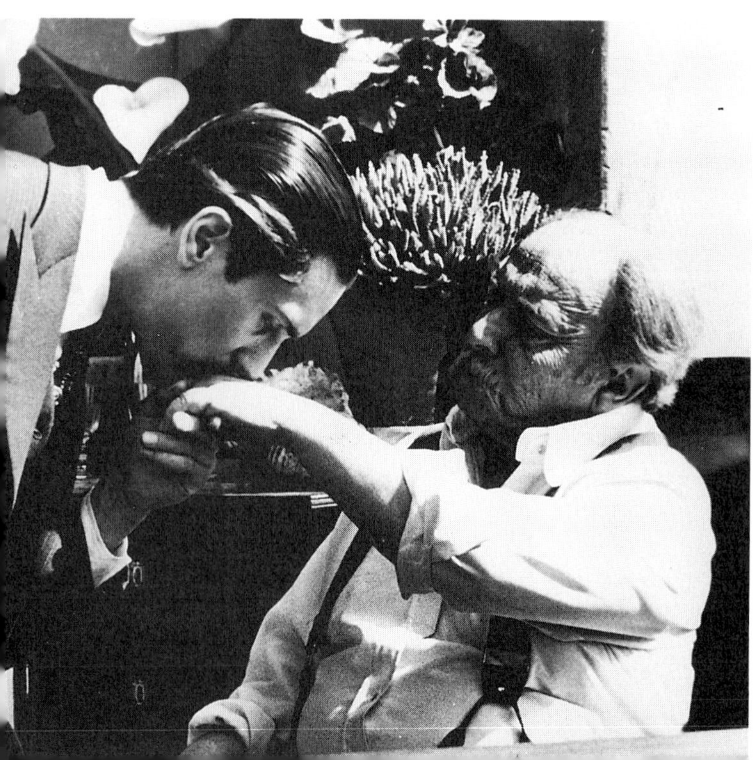

One of the most impressive aspects of *G III* is that Coppola and coscreenwriter Mario Puzo were able to come up with a story that neatly has it both ways. While fans of the earlier films sensed that the new story built on the groundwork set by the first two, anyone who had not seen *G I* and *G II* would nonetheless easily be able to follow the current story, as it in no way insists on familiarity with its predecessors. Twenty years have passed since we last encountered Michael; in 1979, he has entered the third stage of his life. In his youth *(G I),* he resisted his family "business" as long as possible, then succumbed to the pressures and finished on top. The middle-aged Michael *(G II)* maintained his empire and power at all costs. Now, the aging Michael—like the heroes of so many other modern gangster films—senses his final reckoning drawing close. He wants to achieve the social sense of "respectability" (as compared to the brutal underworld "respect" of his earlier years, the fear and loathing that kept enemies at bay), then be remembered as a fine human being, however horrific his past actions may have been. He is not so different from corrupt business kingpins who, in old age, pour vast amounts of money into philanthropic enterprises to insure that their "good" names will carry into the future.

Much to the chagrin of other mobsters, Michael wants to divest himself of the gambling casinos and mob-related enterprises, then spend his salad years as a dignified international financier. Surrounding gangsters see this move toward social respectability as a sign of weakness; in this, Michael is not unlike the hero of Edward James Olmos's *American Me* and other modern gangster films. Michael sues for papal knighthood from the Vatican establishment. One high point of the film is the elaborate ritual in which he's awarded the Papal Order of St. Sebastian, the pretentiousness of the ceremony effectively undercut by the film's cynicism that such a horrible person could receive such a majestic honor, owing to a single fact: the obscene amount of money he lavishes on the Vatican.

He discovers, to his surprise if not ours, what the antiheroes of so many other modern gangster films discover: the supposedly "clean" bankers he will work with are far dirtier than he. The key to understanding not only *G III* but most modern gangster films is that they redefine the notion of "gangster." The very people who, in earlier films, were beyond suspicion (the good, solid citizenry of America or the world) turn out to be closet gangsters themselves. As Michael pales in comparison to them, the film features a neat feminist twist: Michael is now overshadowed by his sister Connie (Talia Shire). Now a wild-eyed combination of Lady Macbeth and Lucrezia Borgia, she manipulates, controls, and kills with the ruthless effectiveness once demonstrated by her brother and, before that, her father, Vito Corleone.

A tale of two gangsters: as in so many other contemporary crime films, Coppola's third *Godfather* installment offers a contrast between the anachronistic, "noble" old gangster and the young, amoral criminal of tomorrow (photo by Favian Cevallos, courtesy Paramount Pictures).

Since *The Godfather* saga is based on a sense of continuity, Coppola necessarily introduced a young character who related to Michael much as Michael, in his youth, related to Don Vito. This is Vincent Mancini (Andy Garcia), illegitimate son of Michael's long-deceased brother Sonny (James Caan). Vincent insinuates himself into the family and the family business, eliminating enemies like Joey Zasa (Joe Montegna) while seducing Michael's daughter (Sofia Coppola). Garcia, just then making headway toward becoming a superstar for the nineties, was all anyone could have hoped for as Vinny. On the other hand, Sofia Coppola proved to be the key casting flaw. The brilliant young actress Winona Ryder had been signed to play Mary, but when she dropped out of the project for personal reasons, Coppola was desperate to move on at once, casting his daughter. Sadly, she lacked both the physical beauty and natural acting ability so necessary for the part.

Also notably absent was Robert Duvall, who had played the family lawyer and adopted son, Tom Hagen. When he held out for an impossible fee, Duvall was at last replaced with George Hamilton, who gave a competent performance, but could not fill the shoes of Duvall. On the other hand, Montegna and Eli Wallach were perfectly cast as competing gangsters. Other performers—John Savage as Tom Hagen's priestly son and Bridget Fonda as a nosy journalist—were wonderful in small, unrewarding parts; they are carefully introduced, then play no role at all in the emerging drama.

Like so many other modern gangster films, *G III* takes sacred-cow institutions and makes them appear no better than organized crime. Other films did this to government, the banking industry, and big business, but *G III* went further, insisting that the Catholic Church is knee-deep in dirt. Not only does Michael Corleone easily buy himself a place of honor by donating laundered money; Machiavellian Vatican characters are here seen plotting, counterplotting, even sanctifying murder in the pursuit of their self-interests. As John Simon noted in *National Review*, "the story is alert to recent history: the Vatican's involvement in international finance and the sudden death of Pope John Paul I one month after his election, with concomitant rumors of foul play. Capitalizing on this, Puzo and Coppola achieve a modicum of originality by making the Catholic Church come out grayer than in any other American movie." Shortly after the film's release, the Church would be rocked by accusations including rampant pedophilia by priests. *G III* offered an extremely savvy presaging of the virulent attacks on this once sacrosanct institution, demonstrating that ambitious Hollywood movies are often ahead of their time.

In addition to social comment, Coppola also employed *G III* for self-expression, creating an analogy in which Michael's losses mirrored his own, though in organized crime rather than show business. Indeed, the two institutions have always been closely related; Coppola's earlier film *The Cotton Club* was about that very relationship. The filmmaker who had at an early age risen to the top of the Hollywood heap thanks to *G I*, paralleling Michael's swift rise to mafioso kingpin within that movie, now saw his entertainment empire slipping through his hands, owing to one too many box-office bombs. His studio, bought with *Godfather* profits, had long since been sold; by showing Michael similarly losing control, Coppola could express his own trauma, presenting it

A rare moment of tranquility; shortly, Coppola will take his saga to its tragic conclusion (photo by Emilio Lari, courtesy Paramount Pictures).

The love story between Michael's daughter Mary (Sofia Coppola, *right*) and Sonny's illegitimate son Vincent Mancini (Andy Garcia) proved the least-rewarding element in *Godfather III.* Note, though, that director Coppola strikingly frames the couple (who mistakenly believe themselves to be free) through window bars, visually setting up and presaging the tragic end to their semi-incestuous Romeo and Juliet romance (photo by John Seakwood, courtesy Paramount Pictures).

within an entertaining gangland story. More telling still, Coppola had lost his beloved son in a bizarre boating accident; so when Michael's beloved daughter (played by Coppola's daughter) is accidentally killed, the Mafia don's scream of anguish is Coppola's own.

"The film is a slow fuse with a big bang," Richard Corliss wrote in *Time,* "one that echoes through every family whose own tragedy is an aching for things past and loved ones lost. It is here, in the ruined face of such a man, that *G III* locates an emotional gravity rare in American movies." Michael, at this point, is the ultimate example of the gangster as tragic hero: intended as Coppola's contemporary version of King Lear, he cradles his dead daughter Cordelia in his arms. The tragedy of the film itself: the impact is blunted, owing to a belabored setup and the inadequacy of Sofia Coppola in a role that must mesmerize an audience if the full catharsis is to take place. Indeed, in at least one theater, a cruel but not necessarily incorrect voice was clearly heard calling out, "Thank God somebody finally shot her!"

Though the film had a strong opening weekend during the year-end holiday season of 1990—indeed, a record-breaking one—it quickly faltered at the box office, proving a disappointment (if in no way a disaster) financially. Why? In *America,* Richard A. Blake argued that the tepid tone and tedious pace were only part of the problem. Missing (along with Duvall and the edge of audacious energy that had motored *G I* and *G II*) was a key theme: "Americans are always fascinated by a reworking of the Horatio Alger myth, especially if it involves gradual corruption. We enjoyed seeing a poor boy like Vito Corleone rise from the slums to the top of his profession and an apparently weak man like Michael Corleone consolidate his power. This current film shows us a tank of financial piranhas in $800 suits devouring one another. The fun of watching upward mobility is absent. The story makes it difficult to sympathize with anyone, and as a result the film lacks that familial intimacy of the first two sagas." In all fairness, though, *G III* is as much a film of the early nineties as *G I* and *G II* were of the seventies. Had *G III* been made a few years after *G II,* Vinny Mancini would have had a more likable personality. He would probably have been played by Robert De Niro, who did express some interest in portraying the grandson of the character he'd won an Oscar as in *G II.* Instead, this was a film by, for, and about the post-Reagan era, when cutthroat attitudes toward financial success had replaced any earlier sense of idealism.

Vinny is precisely the right person, at least from this perspective, to assume control of the Corleone dynasty. Cool, clever, and calculating, he seems the very sort of man who would be completely comfortable engineering the savings-and-loan scandals. One dramatic weakness in the film derives from this approach: when Vinny romances Michael's daughter, it is totally impossible to tell whether he is sincerely in love with her, manipulating a naive young woman for his purposes, or a bit of both. In his earlier years, Coppola was able to direct a scene so that his audience understood the psychology of each character simply by observing body language and listening closely to the tone of voice. Here, the seduction sequence is ambiguous, causing us to fear the filmmaker himself doesn't completely understand what's transpiring between his characters.

Still, there was at least one great line of dialogue, which sums up the theme not only of this single movie but of the modern gangster film in general: "Finance is a gun, and politics is knowing when to pull the trigger."

THIRTY-SIX

The Grifters

(1990)

A Miramax Film Release

CAST:

Anjelica Huston *(Lilly);* John Cusack *(Roy);* Annette Bening *(Myra);* Henry Jones *(Simms);* Pat Hingle *(Bobo);* Charles Napier *(Hebbing);* J. T. Walsh *(Cole);* Billy Ray Sharkey *(FBI Man).*

CREDITS:

Producers, Martin Scorsese, Robert A. Harris, and Jim Painter; director, Stephen Frears; screenplay, Donald E. Westlake, from the novel by Jim Thompson; cinematography, Oliver Stapleton; editor, Mick Audsley; music, Elmer Bernstein; production designer, Dennis Gassner; costumes, Richard Hornung; running time, 118 minutes; rating, R.

No survey of the modern crime film would be complete without at least one digression for Jim Thompson, the pulp novelist who died in 1977 frustrated, to a degree even despairing, since none of his lurid little stories had been turned into the Hollywood film noirs for which he believed they were destined. *The Killer Inside Me* and *A Hell of a Woman* stand as throwbacks to the lusty potboilers of the preceding generation. An anachronism, Thompson might be thought of as the last scribe still working in a once-flourishing, now all but forgotten, déclassé genre, the bus-station pulp paperback. Thompson never lost faith that his novels, all written with screen adaptations firmly in mind, would eventually bring in a great deal of money, though he'd long since grown pessimistic, convinced he'd never see a penny of it in his lifetime. On his deathbed, the destitute cynic promised his wife that he'd be "famous after I'm dead about ten years." That's precisely what happened. In the late 1980s, one after another of his tawdry thrillers were optioned by Hollywood companies, including *After Dark, My Sweet, The Kill-Off,* and *The Grifters,* the last referred to by Pauline Kael as "a bitter, somewhat repellent book with a misanthropic integrity."

Typical of Jim Thompson's work, *The Grifters* features seamy settings, steamy sex, a lurid and barely comprehensible plot, peopled with unsavory characters who will do anything to survive. Taken together, they represent all-American rugged individualism at its absolute nadir. In the 1963 book and 1990 screen adaptation overseen by Martin Scorsese (no stranger to this netherworld, certainly, considering *Mean Streets, Taxi Driver,* and *GoodFellas*), we meet a triad of sleazy con artists. Scorsese, working with British director Stephen Frears, insisted on emphasizing the ugliness and squalor of his film's grifters, viewed simultaneously in the striking opening sequence via a three-way split-screen device of the type popular when Thompson's book was written, though rarely used today. Indeed, the very presence of such a device now serves not only to facilitate the storytelling but to deconstruct the viewing experience, calling attention to it and reminding us this is in fact a movie.

Lilly, working for the Baltimore branch of the mob, visits a racetrack and makes heavy last-minute bets (with Mafia money) to abruptly alter the odds and benefit her clients. Roy, supposedly a salesman in L.A., visits downscale saloons where he offers to pay for a beer with a $20 bill, slipping the bartender a ten-spot and pocketing the "change." Myra, onetime assistant on some major-league S&L scams in the Southwest during the 1980s, now trades her sexual favors for the next month's rent on her grubby little apartment. We watch as they—involved in these diversified scams in far-flung places at the same precise moment—turn toward the screen and don dark sunglasses just before beginning the latest grift. The simultaneity visually informs us that they share the art, craft, lifestyle, and mind-set of the grifter.

Still, there are as many differences between them as similarities. Whereas Roy lacks any ambition to move beyond the small con he learned from a long-ago mentor, Myra desperately wants to get back into the big abusive treatment he suffered during childhood, doesn't want a cent of her money, much less her tender loving care. Myra quickly realizes if she's ever going to convince wary Roy to leave his penny-ante activities and join her in the kind of risky but rewarding big con she and her partner Cole used to pull off, it will first be necessary to eliminate the intrusive Lilly.

To facilitate this, Myra places a call to Bobo (Pat Hingle), Lilly's already suspicious Mafia boss, letting him know about all that skimmed loot Lilly's hoarding. A horrified Lilly goes on the run. When she discovers Myra is following with plans to kill her and steal the dough, Lilly strikes first, strangling the girl in a shabby back-road motel, then hurrying back to her son, hoping to beg, borrow, or steal his scam money, hidden in his shabby apartment behind a garish black velvet painting of a clown. When Roy refuses, Lilly plays off his human instincts

The intense emotions of grand opera and classic tragedy are found nowhere in modern motion pictures except crime and gangster films. Here, Roy and Lily struggle, though each is uncertain whether the feelings are familial or sexual (courtesy Miramax Films, photo credit Suzanne Hanover).

time. Lilly, on the other hand, makes small-time plays for the big boys, while skimming money off their profits and storing it away in the trunk of her gold Cadillac. Quickly, the three come crashing together in a bizarre variation of the oldest of American movie conventions, the romantic triangle, though with a most unconventional twist. Myra is Roy's current girlfriend, while Lilly is his mother. She clearly resents the adorably naughty babe her son is dating (Stuart Klawans of *The Nation* called Myra "a Kewpie doll with a dirty mind") not for the normal reason (she's not good enough for him), but because Lilly just barely represses incestual desires for Roy.

Making matters more complex, and more interesting, is that none of the characters initially knows the others are con artists. They play their social roles for one another even more intensely than they do for their marks, until it gradually becomes clear to each that the others are in the same line of work. Likewise, they will betray each other even more viciously than they do the targets of their cons. The catalyst for the escalating drama is the hospitalization of Roy, after he's caught in the middle of an attempted con by a burly bartender who hits the young man square in the gut. Lilly, visiting at the time, whisks her son off for medical care and insists on paying for everything. Roy, resentful for the

Lily has been skimming off the top of proceeds that are marked for her godfather, Bobo (Pat Hingle). Truly "married to the mob," Lily is caught in a film that's anything but a gangland comedy like the one bearing that phrase as its title (courtesy Miramax Films, photo credit Suzanne Hanover).

John Cusack as Roy: the con man as antihero (courtesy Miramax Films, photo credit Suzanne Hanover).

Grifters in love: John Cusack and Annette Bening (courtesy Miramax Films, photo credit Suzanne Hanover).

of trust in one's mother, however unpleasant that woman may be, handing her son a drink, then smashing the picture frame against him, the glass breaking as it strikes his neck, killing Roy. Though she cries in anguish at what she's done, Lilly nonetheless scoops up the bills between sobs and embarks on her flight. Richard Corliss of *Time* described Lilly as "a mother consuming her young, for the same reason a mama scorpion does: she's hungry."

"Actors are con artists," Kael noted in her *New Yorker* review, "and our entertainment is in watching them get away with things." One way of viewing the film, then, is as (by implication) a movie about acting: three professional actors effectively portray three people quite different from themselves, making the illusion totally convincing, though importantly the people they play also happen to "act" in their everyday lives, convincing everyone around them (even bed partners and soul mates, if indeed they have souls) that they are something other than what they really are. The filmmakers likewise attempt to create an illusion, in that they hope the audience will buy the idea that this story is taking place in present-day L.A.

Certainly, the cars and the clothes are all contemporary, while Myra's flashbacks to her adventures with Cole (who "acted" as a supremely self-confident man, though ironically he ended up institutionalized owing to his secret insecurities) are properly set in the 1980s. However, Roy's flashback to his days on the road learning the big con looks as if it could be set during the Great Depression, appearing to happen in the middle of the dust bowl, visualized as an outtake from *Bound for Glory*. Likewise, a scene in which Roy scams several sailors on a train is played as though it were set during the early 1940s, when such good-spirited servicemen really did ride the rails. The basic situations, then, were already anachronistic when Thompson wrote them thirty years ago. Now, they seem doubly so, a Kennedy-era writer's memories of the golden age of the grift, passed through a time warp and reset in the present. The effect

John Cusack as Roy: The modern man as forties' grifter (courtesy Miramax Films, photo credit Suzanne Hanover).

is of watching a film noir designed not as a period piece but as a fighting document that insists nothing has changed since 1947, though of course it has. The tension created between Lilly, an outward dominatrix who is in fact inwardly nothing more than a frightened little girl, and Myra, who pretends to be a little girl but has the sharp killer instincts, is heightened by the fact that the man they fight over is so low-key. Perhaps most important, the script by Donald Westlake (himself an old pro at the noir genre) is true to Thompson's most characteristic element, a refusal to provide the redemptive moment at the end that has been basic to film noir ever since *Out of the Past.* That was Thompson's unique contribution to the genre: in Hammett and Chandler, there had always been a guarded sense of optimism as the jaded hero performed some positive action that belied the meaninglessness of the ruined world around him. In Thompson, it's strictly dog-eat-dog, a pessimistic portrait of amoral animals darting about our asphalt jungles.

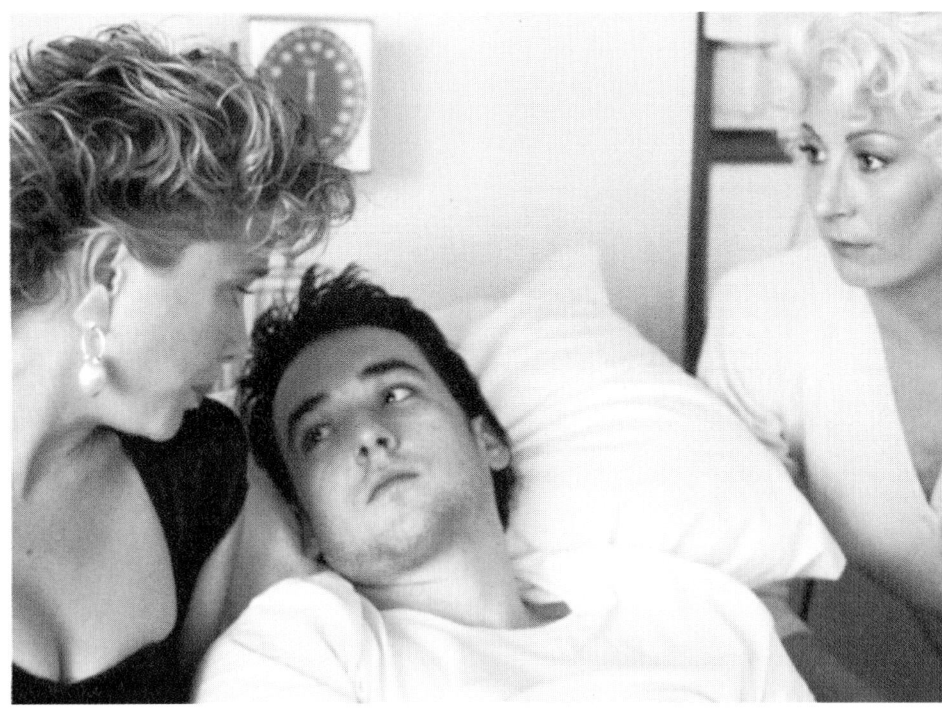

Torn between two women: Roy finds himself in bed with both his current girlfriend, Myra (Annette Bening) and his own mother, Lily (Anjelica Huston) (courtesy Miramax Films, photo credit Suzanne Hanover).

One scene stands out as significant about the role of women in contemporary film noir. In it, Bobo—the movie's key gangster—confronts Lilly after she has failed to do her job at a racetrack owing to her attentiveness to the hospitalized Roy. Bobo calmly tells Lilly of his concern, and clearly fearful, she attempts to humor the seemingly calm capo. Then, Bobo suddenly hits her as hard as possible in the stomach. The scene, though repulsive, is nonetheless toned down considerably from the book (and the working screenplay), eliminating Lilly's wetting herself while writhing on the floor. Bobo then instructs Lilly to fetch a towel and fill it with oranges, all the while making her recite as if by rote the basis of this form of torture. When he beats her with the toweled oranges, she will, like people attempting to scam insurance companies, look ravaged but not be seriously hurt. We finally get to see the harsh, cold Lilly's vulnerability as she becomes hysterical in the middle of her recitation, though she continues with it while shaking in fear. Importantly, Bobo does not beat her; he lets Lilly off comparatively easy, though we do not forget the punch to the gut. Clearly, she is a slave to the mob, however strong and willful she may appear in other situations. She is being punished within the constrictions of a carefully conceived criminal code, a code she has violated. She appears to be a strikingly independent woman, though on closer examination she is a possession. Yet the mob, in the person of Bobo, treats her with a kind of rough-hewn streetwise belief in the equality of women. She is given equal responsibilities to the men and, when she fails, must face equal punishment. Like the film noir women of the 1940s, the women of the modern crime film who choose to walk the dangerous path of the urban lone wolf must accept that they will be given no quarter should they fail.

Many critics were intrigued the final results. In his *Time* review, Richard Corliss called the film a "gem—small, cold, bright, brilliantly crafted. [Yet] the book was minor Thompson, lacking the snaky obsession [of his better work]. And Frears has turned it into a minor movie. Its characters are too small and twisted for sympathy, the pace is too studied, a little too in awe of its artfulness, to pack a wallop." In *Maclean's,* Brian D. Johnson complained that "Frears mimics the flat, amoral tone of Thompson's novel without getting beneath its glib surface. Rejecting the dark, brooding style that pulp fiction has traditionally assumed on-screen, he moved its period setting into the sun of contemporary California. And anachronistic shards of Thompson's original dialogue tumble through the script with the counterfeit clink of lead slugs. Westlake faithfully retypes fragments of Thompson's hard-boiled dialogue but fails to mend the cracks in its narrative."

THIRTY-SEVEN

Billy Bathgate

(1991)

A Touchstone Picture

CAST:

Dustin Hoffman *(Dutch Schultz);* Nicole Kidman *(Drew Preston);* Loren Dean *(Billy Bathgate);* Bruce Willis *(Bo Weinberg);* Steven Hill *(Otto Berman);* Steve Buscemi *(Irving);* Noira Kelly *(Rebecca);* Billy Jaye *(Mickey);* John Costelloe *(Lulu);* Tim Jerome *(Dixie);* Stanley Tucci *(Lucky Luciano).*

CREDITS:

Producers, Arlene Donovan and Robert F. Colesberry; director, Robert Benton; screenplay, Tom Stoppard from the novel by E. L. Doctorow; cinematography, Nestor Almendros; editors, Alan Heim, Robert Reitano, and David Ray; music, Mark Isham; production designer, Patrizia von Brandenstein; costumes, Joseph G. Aulisi; running time, 106 minutes; rating, R.

Dutch Schultz (aka Arthur Flegenheimer) was manipulative and mean-spirited, clever and strangely charming, dangerous but enigmatic; he was among the most deadly of the 1930s-era gangsters, ripe for revival during the comeback for the period-picture crime film that swept Hollywood in the early 1990s.

Dustin Hoffman reteamed with Robert Benton, his *Kramer vs. Kramer* director, for a classy production of an acclaimed 1988 novel by E. L. Doctorow *(Ragtime).* With a script by Tom Stoppard *(Rosencrantz and Guildenstern Are Dead)* and cinematography by the esteemed Nestor Almendros, the film was a high-profile undertaking for Disney's Touchstone Pictures, intended as their prestige release during the summer of 1990. But much-publicized production problems (reportedly, Hoffman and Benton argued bitterly, and a new ending had to be hurriedly filmed) caused the film's release to be put off until the following fall.

In fact, the classy quality works against this film's overall effectiveness. Watching *Billy Bathgate* is like watching *Bonnie and Clyde* (cowritten by Benton) by way of *Masterpiece Theatre, Little Caesar* as it might be remade by Merchant and Ivory *(Howard's End).* There's something subdued, even soft, about the production, suggesting that Benton felt the need to make clear he was concerned with more thematically weighty things than mere genre. Watching *Billy Bathgate,* we get the impression we're watching a gangster film made by a man who would be embarrassed at the thought of doing a gangster film.

Todd McCarthy summed this up in his *Variety* review, stating that "this refined, intelligent drama about thugs appeals considerably to the head but has little impact in the gut, which is not exactly how it should be with gangster films....Its center is hard to locate, making it absorbing but not compelling....There is a muted, remote quality to the story's emotional core." David Denby of *New York* said much the same thing in different words: "Overall, *Billy Bathgate* can only be called tepid, and I came away unsure of why Benton had been drawn to the material....This is a gentlemanly film about an ungodly experience....The man who directed it is too civilized to make a great gangster movie."

The film begins in 1935, when Dutch Schultz is the top dog of New York City's underworld establishment. But such status does not mean the ugly incidents of his youth are now behind him. In the opening sequence, we watch as a suspected traitor, Bo Weinberg (Bruce Willis), recently Schultz's most trusted lieutenant, a deadly enforcer, is taken out on a tugboat, his hands firmly tied and his feet encased in cement. He's about to take a dive, but not before Schultz gloatingly torments his one-time protégé. Watching all this is a fifteen-year-old boy, Billy Bathgate (Loren Dean), a tough Irish kid who recently talked his way into the mob.

The book, narrated by Billy, shared his complex

Dutch Schultz is depicted as one more variation on the Gatsby myth, the gangster as tortured romantic, in this case obsessed with the elusive, unknowable Drew (Nicole Kidman) (photo by Myles Aronowitz, courtesy Touchstone Pictures).

prowess to draw Billy ever deeper in to her web.

Essentially, she is the character Jill Ireland played in *The Family,* part socialite and part slut, an ethereal seductress who has grown up with all the finer things of life but is magnetically drawn to the wild side. She may be nothing more than a self-interested opportunist, though the tough-guy hero is so melted by her mystique that he cannot bring himself to accept this. After bedding Drew, Billy knows he's violated the trust placed in him by the boss, who ordered Billy to make sure no one else seduces her, though Dutch certainly seems in no great hurry to pursue Drew himself. Indeed, Dutch's ambiguous attitudes toward her are a major weakness; the filmmakers do not seem to comprehend their own

Dustin Hoffman as Dutch Schultz: The gangster as sociopath (photo by Myles Aronowitz, courtesy Touchstone Pictures).

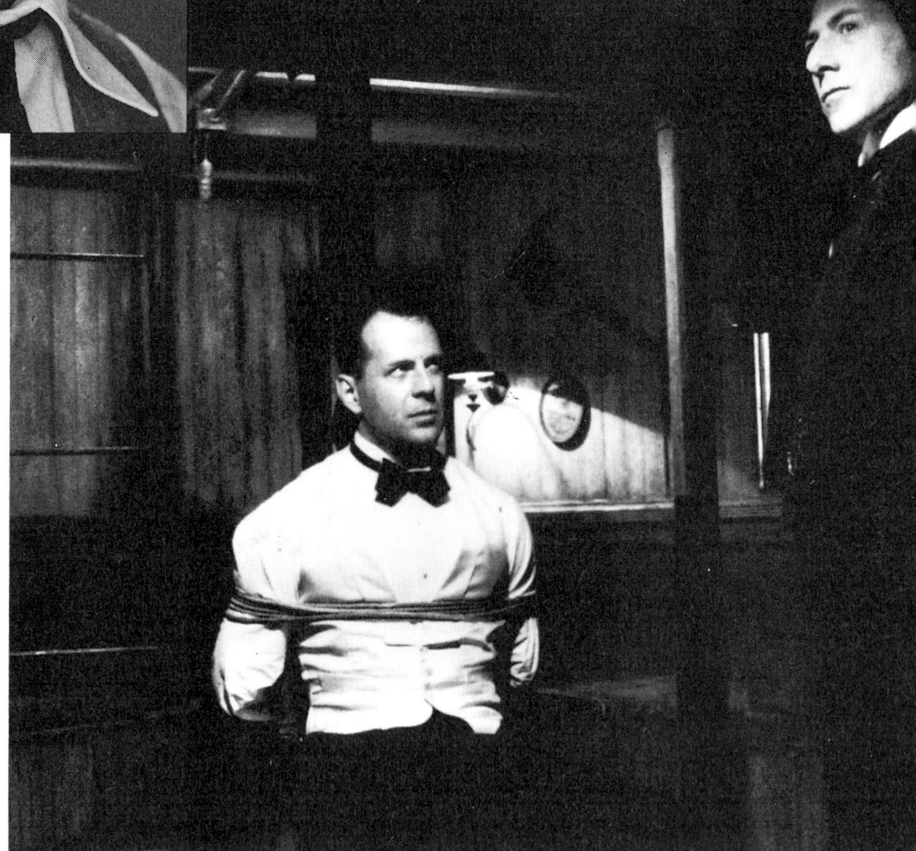

Bo Weinberg (Bruce Willis) waits for the moment when his onetime friend and boss will toss him over the side of the ship (photo by Myles Aronowitz, courtesy Touchstone Pictures).

thoughts and mixed emotions about all this, whereas the film only allows us to watch him squirm uncomfortably. Leaving Billy to watch over the doomed Weinberg, Dutch takes Weinberg's girlfriend, Drew Preston (Nicole Kidman), "down below," insisting she now belongs to him. Once Weinberg is out of the way, Billy is assigned by Schultz to watch over Drew. But like so many other modern crime-movie heroes, Billy is a closet romantic, his breath taken away by the gorgeous Drew, though he's unable to grasp what makes her tick. Her husband appears to be gay; she may or may not be deeply disturbed by the death of her gangster lover; her feelings for Schultz are difficult to understand. Whether she is attracted to her young "protector" Billy or just pretending to be in order to use him, as she apparently has everyone else, is unclear. Drew is fascinating, mysterious, unpredictable, perhaps unknowable; all those qualities conspire with her physical attractiveness and sexual character and so are unable to make us realize what's going on inside the mind of the Dutch Schultz of their imagination.

More problematic still, the title character doesn't really *do* anything. The best choice for the hero of a novel is an observer who watches other people in action and comments on what transpires. As readers, we *are* him and view what happens through his perspective. But when such a book is adapted to the screen—however handsomely—we're left with a character who basically just stands around, staring glumly. If books are based on thought and reflection, movies are motored by action. In being true to the novel, Benton and his co-adapters insured the film could not succeed, however well crafted.

Still, most of the key themes of modern gangster movies are present. The film's Dutch Schultz is an incarnation of the gangster as celebrity. With a quicksilver temper, Dutch is as apt to explode as he is likely, at unpredictable moments, to be charmed by something odd that catches his fancy. In flashback, we see the moment when Billy won his place in the gang. Dutch spots the kid absurdly juggling four balls on an el overpass and is, for reasons known only to him, touched and amused by Billy's reckless abandon. Billy will soon perceive Dutch as "the richest man in all of New York," though Dutch is in fact being hounded by the same IRS agents who earlier put Al Capone away.

Dutch's thoughtful lieutenant Otto Berman (Steven Hill) is a staid Jewish neurotic who quietly attempts to warn his boss that the wild, woolly days are all over. Throughout the late twenties and early thirties, the streets of New York (like those of Chicago) may have constituted an urban, eastern, twentieth-century replay of the Old West, but Berman grasps what Dutch misses: those days are already past. The gangsters who will survive are those who recognize this fact, turning to organized crime (by becoming "respectable") rather than clinging to an outworn notion of gangsterism as the crazed side of rugged individualism.

"Dutch's superego" is the way critic David Denby described Berman, and the film's triad of antiheroes might well be effectively analyzed in Freudian terms. Berman is the conscience of the group, the man who understands the codes and strategies of life. Billy, on the other hand, is unconscious enough to be the film's id figure, acting on his impulses without reflection. Dutch is the ego, absorbed by his notion of self, perpetuating the legend that has come to surround him. A man with two names—born Arthur Flegenheimer, he reigns as the King of the City under the pseudonym Dutch Schultz—he's one more Jekyll/Hyde gangster with a dual identity. He is always unpredictable—therefore always dangerous—because he is always two people inhabiting a single body, and no one knows for certain which will be encountered at any moment.

Where did this Jewish gangster get the name Dutch? From an earlier gangster (now forgotten) who bore that name. It's worth mentioning, too, that Billy—who idolizes Dutch as a father figure—is himself a budding Dutch, the son who would like to usurp the father's throne (he has already slept with the father's mistress) and who witnessed the gangland execution of his fore-

The gangster as upscale businessman: at a posh hotel, Dutch enjoys a quiet breakfast while reading the morning paper with his minions (courtesy Touchstone Pictures).

runner. This would be more effectively oedipal if only the Billy of the film looked fifteen, but he does not. When in the movie Drew seduces Billy, it appears a normal coupling between a slightly older woman and a strapping younger man. In the book, she was bedding a child—her master's unofficial adopted son at that—so the kinky, perverse quality that made this scene so effective in the novel is lost.

Billy also has a double identity, expressed by an assumed name; Bathgate is the avenue in the Bronx from which he hails. Like Dutch, he assumes a created personality and a corresponding new name as he becomes a gangster. Still, it was Hoffman as Dutch—though ostensibly a supporting role—that stirred the critics. David Denby observed, "Dutch can seem plausible and offhandedly benevolent, a noisy, self-serving businessman, blowing his own horn and ridiculing ene-

Like Bugsy Siegel and other gangster "heroes" in recent period-piece films, Dutch is portrayed as a social climber, wearing the finest clothes, hoping a classy mistress will elevate his status (courtesy Touchstone Pictures).

mies—and then suddenly he will fly into a rage and kill someone. Hoffman takes his time, letting us see Dutch's mental processes. But when Dutch feels that he's been betrayed, he destroys whatever is before him.... What's fascinating about the performance is that Hoffman exudes narcissism without sensuality. Compare him, for instance, with De Niro's creamy, pomaded Al Capone coming down the steps in De Palma's *Untouchables*. The Dutchman, for better or worse, is ruled by his chaotic mind."

Both Capone as re-created by De Niro and Dutch as defined by Dustin fit into Richard Schickel's concept of the gangster as "thug celebrity." Both revel in the knowledge that the media has turned them, and other killers like them, into dark antiheroes of the masses by romanticizing their unpleasant exploits. The outlaw as pop hero is of course nothing new; this notion can be traced back to Robin Hood. But in our century, the notion has been heightened and intensified, the cult of the mobster glamorizing those very characters most people would recoil from in real life.

The mythology of the early gangster films has become so embedded in our collective psyche that our filmmakers have a hard time putting those myths aside when they make contemporary movies; our actors draw on these shared film experiences in shaping their roles. The modern-made period gangster film, *Billy Bathgate* included, ends up being about the classic gangster film, however much Benton wanted to avoid the trappings of genre.

Three generations of crime: Otto (Steven Hill, *center*), the wise old man of the mob, stands halfway between middle-aged Dutch and youthful Billy Bathgate (photo by Brian Hamill, courtesy Touchstone Pictures).

THIRTY-EIGHT

New Jack City

(1991)

A Warner Bros. Film

CAST:

Wesley Snipes *(Nino Brown);* Ice-T *(Scotty Appleton);* Judd Nelson *(Peretti);* Chris Rock *(Pookie);* Allen Payne *(Gee Money);* Mario Van Peebles *(Detective Stone);* Vanessa Williams *(Keisha);* Tracy Camila Johns *(Uniqua);* also, Nick Ashford, Michael Michele, Russell Wong, and Thalmus Rasulala.

CREDITS:

Producers, Doug McHenry and George Jackson; director, Mario Van Peebles; Screenplay, Thomas Lee Wright and Barry Michael Cooper, from a story by Wright; cinematography, Francis Kenny; editor, Steven Kemper; music, Michel Colombier; production design, Charles C. Bennett; costume design, Bernard Johnson; running time, 97 minutes; rating, R.

The first film of the nineties to deal with the mobster scene in Harlem, as well as the roles played by African Americans both in the drug scene and police antidrug activities, was *New Jack City.* Thomas Lee Wright (who had previously penned the police thriller *Last of the Finest*) and *Village Voice* reporter Barry Michael Cooper collaborated on the script. The latter coined the phrase "new jack" to describe the emerging urban mind-set in the still-new decade. Playing a supporting role as a policeman, while also directing a feature for the first time, was Mario Van Peebles, who had previously worked only on television *(21 Jump Street, Wiseguy).* His father had won acclaim twenty years earlier with *Sweet Sweetback's Baadasssss Song,* now largely forgotten but in its time a controversial film, owing to graphic depiction of violence and unbridled reverse racism in telling the tale of a black man (played by the filmmaker) on the run from white authorities.

Back in 1972, there had been reports of race riots in cities where *Sweet Sweetback* played, as largely black audiences became so incensed by the film's vision that their outrage exploded on the streets. Just such a controversy would surround the release of *New Jack City,* as history repeated itself and a new generation of African-American viewers, too young to have even heard of *Sweet Sweetback,* likewise were more than entertained by watching. *New Jack City* seemed a call to arms, but one of the film's problems—which had been a problem with the earlier, elder Van Peebles's picture as well—was that the film stirred up righteous indignation without conveying a profound understanding of the issues it raised.

In other words, this was heady exploitation-entertainment, inciting the public in much the same manner that serious art often does, and for that reason it was in some circles mistaken for serious art. Wesley Snipes played the role of Nino Brown, the new breed of urban gangster; Brown makes all previous drug dealings seem innocent by comparison as he introduces crack to upper Manhattan. "Gone are the days of hustling on the street corner," Brown arrogantly announces to his gang, the Cash Money Brothers. "You change the product, you change the marketing strategy." He is, essentially, a brilliant businessman as much as he is a nouveau gangster; his "product" just happens to be the most dangerous drug yet.

Brown displays absolutely no respect at all, not for the people he works with and who constitute his gang; not for the women in his life, whom he uses and abuses; not for the old mob he intends to muscle out of the area; and not for the police who oppose him. He is the man without the code that had been so basic to earlier movie mobsters. As John Leland reported in *Newsweek,* "the central premise of Van Peebles's film is that the culture of greed that ran through Wall Street in the eighties also ran through American ghettos, only in grossly exaggerated form. It left intensified poverty on the one hand and, on the other, a new breed of superyuppie criminals. These are the new jacks: natty gangster Gekkos, with flashy sculpted hair, advanced computer systems, cellular phones, and high-tech weapons. Like Gekko in the

Wesley Snipes as Nino Brown *(center)* threatens henchman Gee Money (Allen Payne), while Kareem (Christopher Williams) looks on. The film was to the early 1990s what *Superfly* was to the early 1970s, offering mainstream audiences their first raw view of the evolving inner-city crime scene (courtesy Warner Bros.).

Detective Scotty Appleton (Ice-T) and his partner, Nick Peretti (Judd Nelson, *left*), make an arrest. The filmmakers were careful to balance the nihilistic black gangster with an idealistic African-American cop hero (courtesy Warner Bros.).

movie *Wall Street,* they believe that greed is good and that human life counts for little by comparison. Crack is their junk-bond capital, a new source of seemingly unlimited—and carelessly destructive—power. Their game is mergers and acquisitions."

Snipes offered a strong, riveting, attention-getting performance as Brown, who would just as soon be a white-collar wheeler-dealer on Wall Street but is ghetto-bound by birthright. What made the film so difficult thematically was Snipes's movie-star charisma. On the one hand, it was necessary for an actor with charisma as well as talent to play the part, this being the only way in which Brown's ability to dominate situations and people could be made viable. On the other hand, the same situation arose that had plagued the *Superfly* film some twenty years earlier. What was apparently intended as an honest, case-study portrait of an all-too-real character turned out, however inadvertently, to be a role model instead. Movie stars always romanticize the villains they play, even if they do not mean to.

That's precisely the problem Oliver Stone attempted to overcome in *Wall Street;* he was well aware that Michael Douglas's magnetism (as well as acting ability) might, if the writing and directing were not clear enough, transform a villain into an antihero. Just such a situation arose here. "We wanted audiences to be drawn to him but not identify with him," Van Peebles explained of Nino Brown. Whether or not he managed that difficult balance is debatable. Actor Snipes later admitted, "There is something that you unwillingly like about this guy. Your morals say, 'I'm not supposed to like this cat,' but he's got it going on."

Anticipating just such a situation, filmmaker Van Peebles tried to make the cops who oppose Brown at least equally as appealing, so the youthful, impressionable audience might turn to them as hero figures instead of Brown, especially when Brown becomes excessively violent, nasty, and out of control in the film's second half. That explains why rapper Ice-T was cast in the role of Scotty Appleton, a cop who goes undercover to get the goods on Brown and bring him down, while Judd Nelson (in dark glasses and goatee, looking like a misplaced 1950s beatnik) played the other half of their white-cop/black-cop team. As Nick Peretti, he was given

In addition to featuring rap music on the sound track, director Van Peebles cast popular rap star Ice-T as one of his streetwise cops. Warner Bros., the studio that had virtually created the socially oriented crime film some sixty years earlier, continued to adjust the genre for today's realities (courtesy Warner Bros.)

was at least directed at the audience in hopes of deterring young moviegoers from trying crack themselves. But whether the sentiment was sincere or not was debatable; some critics complained it was comparable to the "serious" statements regularly thrown in at the end of many X-rated films, a cynical attempt to offer a patina of art thanks to some obligatory message that would prevent the movie from being banned as worthless porno. It was generally felt that, such noble sentiments aside, *New Jack City* romanticized the Nino Brown character to the point where kids in the audience would see through the overt message to the subtext: Brown was the new antiheroic gangster, the Super Fly of the nineties.

Or, to reach back further, he would be in a class with the classic gangster roles of the thirties, which had elevated Irish and Italian mobsters to the level of tragic and romantic heroes. Like the most memorable of those films, *New Jack City* was a Warner Bros. release. As Ralph Novak said in *People* of Snipes's characterization, "pursuing money and pleasure with the unconcerned determination of a stalking crocodile...his performance

the key lines of dialogue intended to telegraph the movie's message: "It's not a black thing, and it's not a white thing," he says of crack cocaine. "It's a death thing."

As if this weren't enough, the filmmakers took an even more direct, sledgehammer approach in their epilogue, which reads: "If we in America don't confront the problem of crack cocaine and other drugs realistically—without empty slogans and promises but by examining what motors the human soul on the course of spiritual self-destruction—then the New Jack City (a society that's almost totally addicted to drugs) shall continue to thrive, and we shall forever be doomed to despair in the shadows of its demonic skyline."

The message, while hardly subtle,

Scotty and Peretti go undercover, where they meet Gee Money and Frankie Needles (Anthony De Sando) in order to infiltrate the newly formed mob. The plot is a virtual replay of Warner Bros. epics from the 1930s featuring James Cagney as the good guy and Humphrey Bogart as the bad guy, here updated for the contemporary crime scene (courtesy Warner Bros.).

Filmmaker Mario Van Peebles as Detective Stone *(second from left)*, flanked by Russell Wong as Detective Kim Park, as well as Peretti and Appleton; a multicultural crime force fighting the politically incorrect horrors of New Jack City (courtesy Warner Bros.).

ranks with Edward G. Robinson in *Little Caesar,* Paul Muni in *Scarface* or Marlon Brando in *The Godfather,* among film mob bosses." That is to say, he was the latest of the screen gangsters to strike audiences as a realistic depiction of a crime boss but was a romanticization of just such a person, however effectively the filmmakers hid their distortion to convince viewers they were seeing the real thing.

The newspapers covered, in detail, riots that broke out when teenagers were refused admission to the R-rated movie. There were incidents in New York City, suburban Boston, and in such far-flung cities as Chicago, Detroit, Houston, and Las Vegas; even Tukwila, Washington, was not spared. In Brooklyn, teenage boys from different housing projects, long locked in rivalry, fired more than one hundred bullets in and around a theater where *New Jack* was playing; a nineteen-year-old man was killed and a pregnant woman wounded. In L.A.'s Westwood, the Mann Theatre oversold an evening performance and several hundred frustrated would-be patrons went on a rampage throughout the upscale, college-oriented area.

Psychiatrist Thomas Radecki, research director for the National Coalition on Television Violence, insisted that "[*New Jack City* is] certainly playing a triggering role.... This film is like throwing gasoline on a fire." But such statements did not come only from outraged, threatened whites. The Reverend James Dixon of the Northwest Community Baptist Church in Houston attacked the film, insisting, "It plays on the minds of young blacks who are already in trouble." An alliance of black ministers in troubled Houston agreed that the film did indeed actively promote violence on the part of viewers.

Van Peebles defended his work, insisting that the message was precisely the reverse of what was being claimed: "The conclusion [of the film is that] anybody who takes crack dies, anybody who deals crack dies.... You see what drugs do to the people and how the drug king is put down. It's a piece of edu-tainment." That certainly was true; the bad guys get their just deserts in the end, just as Cagney lay in a pool of blood, moaning, "I ain't so tough," at the end of *Public Enemy,* or Edward G. Robinson—seeing the lifeblood drain out of him during the concluding moments of *Little Caesar*—wondered, "Is this the end of Ricco?" More important, however, is that audiences of the thirties thrilled to the gangster heroes' "Live fast, die young!" lifestyles, which dominated most of the movie, and coveted the beautiful molls who congregated around them. Was there any question at all that *New Jack City* presented Snipes as Brown in just such a light?

New Jack City, like Mario Van Peebles's later western, *Posse,* is strictly second-rate work, considerably flashier than anything Spike Lee or John Singleton have done so far, yet superficial in a way their films—even ambitious, admirable failures such as *Mo' Better Blues* and *Poetic Justice*—never are. Van Peebles, on the other hand, is all razzle-dazzle, turning out films that can overwhelm the unwary viewer with their glitzy surface and breakneck pace, but which lack the singular vision of the truly fine filmmakers, whatever their ethnicity.

No wonder, then, that in *Rolling Stone,* Peter Travers noted: "First-time feature director Mario Van Peebles puts a nineties twist on the blaxploitation pictures of the seventies, such as *Superfly*...in this slam-bang crime drama." Or, as Denby summed it up, "*New Jack City* is a violent and lurid work in which 'moral' messages (warnings against drugs) are part of the general clamor. It uses degradation and sadism both to horrify and excite us. Early on, the brutalities of a drug gang taking over Harlem are so flippantly presented (with rap music adding pulse to the shocks) that the audience might well think the director was urging on the brutality. In other words, the movie goes as far as possible in selling 'new jack' culture—the violent urban street life—and even further in punishing anyone who gets caught up in it. *New Jack City* is about as compromised as a movie can be."

THIRTY-NINE

Mobsters

(1991)

Universal Pictures

CAST:

Christian Slater *(Charles "Lucky" Luciano);* Patrick Dempsey *(Meyer Lansky);* Richard Grieco *(Ben "Bugsy" Siegel);* Costas Mandylor *(Frank Costello);* Lara Flynn Boyle *(Mara);* F. Murray Abraham *(Arnold Rothstein);* Anthony Quinn *(Masseria);* Michael Gambon *(Don Faranzano);* Nicholas Sadler *("Mad Dog" Coll);* Christopher Penn *(Tommy Reina).*

CREDITS:

Producer, Steve Roth; director, Michael Karbelnikoff; screenwriters, Mike Mahern and Nicholas Kazan; cinematography, Lajos Koltai; production design, Richard Sylbert; costume design, Ellen Mirojnick; running time, 104 minutes; rating, R.

Mobsters was inspired by the commercial success of 1988's *Young Guns,* which revived the then (seemingly) dead western genre by doing an old story over again, this time with popular Brat Pack stars, offering vast appeal for the youth market, as Billy the Kid and his gang. If such casting could effectively revitalize the cowboy film, producer Steve Roth wondered if it might not do the same for the gangster movie. So he hired Christian Slater, chief among the second wave of Brat Pack stars scoring big in the late eighties (Slater would costar with "aging" Emilio Estevez in the 1990 sequel *Young Guns II*), to play the top-billed lead in *Mobsters,* the film Leonard Maltin would jokingly refer to as *Young (Tommy) Guns.*

In fact, *Mobsters* shares the strong points of the first *Young Guns.* It boasts beautiful production values, which effectively bring the period to life, while never degenerating into an obvious rehash of earlier films on the subject, owing to the ultracontemporary cast and rough language, intense violence, and graphic sex. Unfortunately, *Mobsters* also shares the overriding flaws of the first *Young Guns:* an unfocused story line, marred by a sense that many key characters and their relationships were not fully developed, plus an aura of exploitation in the way violence and sex are presented in a superficial, smug manner, without the kind of overriding attitude toward such elements that might have placed the immoral acts within what is ultimately a moral narrative, the case with, say, *Godfather II.*

Producer Roth announced, "What we've done is taken the true ages of [the four characters] and portrayed them the way Warner Bros. did in the old days with the classic gangster movies." His comment implies a desire to create a modern period-gangster picture by aligning contemporary qualities with the old traditions. It is also incorrect, as Roth either did not know or did not care to admit, that the four men who formed New York's Syndicate weren't of the same general age, the oldest (Costello) being fifteen years removed from the youngest (Siegel). But this was Hollywood—the "new" Hollywood, perhaps, but still Hollywood—and what mattered was the rightness of the casting for audience appeal, not historical accuracy.

Still, the film didn't click at the box office, perhaps because its R rating kept it from being seen by the very kids it was intended for. So there was no sequel, though it's worth noting that only a few months later, Warren Beatty took Ben Siegel—here a dimly realized supporting character—and made him, at his next stage of life, the centerpiece of a truly epic film.

Mobsters starts strongly, with black-and-white images of New York's teeming streets in 1917, where we see horses mixing with cars, hanging laundry juxtaposed with expensively dressed street musketeers, and nasty toughs strolling the boulevards as serious-minded rabbis walk by in the opposite direction. Young boys gamble in the street, in front of a temple, until an elderly rabbi chases them away with the admonishment "What are you doing in the house of God?" While the buildings, costumes, and situations do ring true to the period,

Christian Slater as Charlie "Lucky" Luciano: the legendary gangster, reimagined as aspiring yuppie (courtesy Universal Pictures, photo credit Bruce McBroom).

there's also a sense that what we're seeing is a recollection of the past as it appears from the unique perspective of the Reagan-Bush era in American politics.

The notion of survival of the fittest is basic here. The rugged individualist chosen to tell the story is Charles Luciano (Slater), an Italian street kid who early on watches his weak father succumb to the cruelty of Don Faranzano (Michael Gambon). The elder Luciano pays the nasty man protection money even though the destitute immigrant family can ill afford it. Young Charlie, aware that Faranzano is locked in a turf battle with Don Masseria (Anthony Quinn), begins plotting eventual revenge for his father's degradation. Significantly, though, there is no sense of a viable relationship between Charlie and his father. So when, at the film's end, Charlie finally enjoys his revenge by hanging Faranzano out an apartment-building window and slowly cutting the rope to let the man drop, there is no sense that Charlie has at last settled the score for a slight against a man he dearly loved.

In that scene, Charlie—unlike other screen antiheroes before him—does not shed a tear for the wrong done years ago. Apart from the usual retribution story, *Mobsters* is not motored by an abiding sense that the hero has to rise to a position of power so as to achieve vengeance in the name of love and loyalty (Sergio Leone's *Once Upon a Time...in the West*). Instead, the film features a cold, clinical hero more interested in showing his adversary that he, unlike his weak father, is strong,

Gangster stories are easily adapted to the attitudes of any time frame. In the early nineties, the tough street punks of an earlier era (Costas Mandylor as Frank Costello, Patrick Dempsey as Meyer Lansky, Slater as Luciano, Richard Grieco as Benjamin "Bugsy" Siegel)...are naturally depicted as out-of-work kids who want only to become successful, and will do so illegally if there is no honest means at hand. Many of today's youth, unable to find jobs, had no trouble identifying despite the period costumes (courtesy Universal Pictures, photo credits Bruce McBroom).

has risen to the top of the heap, however much lying, cheating, and stealing it took. *Mobsters* is a movie about winning, American style. While the young heroes of the film may be called Luciano, Siegel, Lansky, and Costello, they—by the nature of the actors chosen to play them—resemble, perhaps represent, Reagan-era youth.

Though the film is a period piece, the sensibility is ultramodern. The boys have more in common with the character Charlie Sheen portrayed in *Wall Street* than they do with the gangsters played, in previous pictures, by Bogart, Cagney, and Robinson, despite Roth's statement. These mobsters have little if anything in common with Robert Warshow's gangster as tragic hero, rising only to eventually fall. At the end, they are on top of the world: they win, and win big. The mentor figure here, who counsels the boys much as Gekko (in *Wall Street*) did his own young charges, is Arnold Rothstein (F. Murray Abraham), who similarly tells this film's young heroes: "What's the secret of America? Money, Charlie—money is everything!"

The difference is, Stone's film took a highly moral, highly critical point of view on such thinking, making clear that Gekko the mentor was not only a villain but the devil incarnate, and that in listening to him, the young people of the eighties sold away their souls. No such thing in *Mobsters:* the young people here, Luciano included, are never inclined (as Sheen was in *Wall Street*) to turn their backs on such thinking and reject, even help imprison, their mentor. Though Rothstein is killed halfway through *Mobsters,* the young people continue to echo his words: "Money! Money! Money!" At the very end, when they have seized power from their elders (and are now in league with young Al Capone, planning the future of organized crime), they continue to think back on Rothstein as the only adult they ever liked and trusted.

That there's something downright Reaganesque about the way in which Abraham plays the part of Rothstein (the Oscar-winning actor from *Amadeus* certainly appears to have patterned his vocal inflections on the former president) only adds to the fascinating contemporization of this historical tale. But even in this world, money isn't everything. "This isn't about money," Meyer (Patrick Dempsey) tells Charlie at one point. "It's about friendship." That is the other overriding theme of *Mobsters.* From the beginning, there's a sense of otherness and apartness among the young people that casts them at odds with adults, which is at the core of this film's unique interpretation of the story.

The battle between upcoming youth and the reigning adults provides the film's dramatic conflict. The only

The old guard: Anthony Quinn as Don Masseria...and Oscar winner (from *Amadeus*) F. Murray Abraham as gambler Arnold Rothstein, who teaches the boys a rule that would be revived in the Reagan era: Money is everything! (courtesy Universal Pictures, photo credit Bruce McBroom).

young people Charlie is comfortable killing are Tommy Reina (Christopher Penn), who set Charlie up to "go for a ride" (Charlie was the only man ever to return alive after being dumped, earning him the nickname Lucky), and Coll (Nicholas Sadler), a maniacal hit man who

Generation gap, gangster-movie style: Don Faranzano (Michael Gambon, *center*) and his henchman Rocco (Robert Z'Dar) beat Luciano, who has tried to muscle in on their territory. Merely living through this ordeal earned Luciano the nickname Lucky (courtesy Universal Pictures, photo credit Bruce McBroom).

The old gangster Don Masseria (Anthony Quinn) stands in the way of the young criminal's achieving what he wants. A generation earlier, actor Quinn had himself played many young gangster antiheroes (courtesy Universal Pictures, photo credit Bruce McBroom).

hires out to adult gangsters for a price, but does not—like Charlie and his friends—understand that it's "okay" to double-cross adults to help other young people. Even after he has tried to kill them in a tommy-gun ambush of their car, Charlie and company are still willing to give youthful Coll a second chance.

The sense of loyalty to fellow youth is what ties the foursome together. "Two Jews and two Italians," Charlie sweetly says. He's aware that survival of the fittest can take on many shapes and guises. Near the beginning, Charlie rescues Meyer from some punks about to kill the seemingly weak and skinny Jew, when it might seem more appropriate for Charlie to let Meyer live or die on his own, however it turns out. The point is, Charlie does not save Meyer because he's one of those traditional liberal-minded movie heroes who can't stand to see the weak harmed. Charlie will allow many weak people to be harmed before the film is over. Though Meyer lacks physical strength, he's smart, and Charlie is smart enough to realize he needs Meyer, cannot build his crime empire without what Meyer has to offer, since Meyer is remarkably strong in the one place where Charlie often falters and knows it.

"Balls and brains," Rothstein confides to Charlie as the secret of success, gangster-wise. The film incarnates Charlie Luciano as a man who consciously realizes he has the balls while Meyer has the brains. There's also Siegel, just "bugsy" enough in the head to be the wild card they need for risky situations, and Frank Costello, the silent strong-arm who will supply muscle where it's needed. The adult gangsters are bigoted: "I don't talk business with Jews," the unpleasant Faranzano says, while Masseria rails about "niggers" in the streets causing violence, when in fact he's the cause. But the young heroes are without prejudice. At one point, the foursome is seen—while setting up a hit on one of their adult enemies—persuading a young black hotel employee to aid them, treating him with great respect, however fleetingly.

The film also attempts to turn Charlie into one more example of the gangster as romantic hero in Charlie's brief and underdeveloped scenes with Mara (Lara Flynn Boyle), the dance-hall girl with whom he becomes infatuated. These moments compare neatly with those in other contemporary gangster films and are a total reversal of the classic 1930s image of the gangsters as tough guys who like to push grapefruits into the faces of molls who talk back. Charlie is clearly infatuated with Mara the moment he passes her, by accident, backstage; he intervenes to rescue her from an ugly (and, significantly, older) gangster trying to put his hands on her. "Will you be my friend?" she asks when they're alone. He says he'd love to, and that he'll pick her up after the show. But, appearing vulnerable, she brings out the best—rather than the beast—in him by asking, "If you really want to be somebody's friend, it takes time, doesn't it?" Charlie—one more modern gangster who turns to putty at the sight of a beautiful woman—is touched by this and does not try to take her to bed. But when he meets her again, she surprises him by acting as the sexual aggressor, shocking Charlie by suddenly kissing him, making clear that she will define "friendship" for them, one more ambiguous woman.

Mara refuses to be possessed by Charlie as a replaceable moll (like those who hang around Bugsy), yet she refuses to let him speak of love. They are just what she says—trusted friends who share sex, money, and power—making clear that her character is not a period-piece reconstruction but a 1990s postfeminist woman wearing the outfits of a flapper.

Unfortunately, her character and their relationship is not sufficiently fleshed out. When Mad Dog Coll slips into their apartment to shoot Charlie and kills Mara by mistake, we can't really understand, much less share, his grief, so superficially was their relationship presented. Other elements are insufficiently developed. While the movie does an effective job of dramatizing the Luciano-Lansky relationship, Ben Siegel—such a remarkable character—quickly slips into the background, while Frank Costello appears to be silently following the others around, with no real personality of his own, not the case historically.

Even the casting seems off. Though Slater is fine, he might have been better cast as Bugsy, since Slater is highly proficient at playing off-the-wall characters. On the other hand, Richard Grieco—who might have been well cast as the slick, cool Charlie—is woefully wrong as Siegel, unable to suggest the character's Jewishness or his unpredictable nature. Simply put, as Pamela Young wrote in *Maclean's,* debuting director Michael Karbelnikoff (whose previous experience had been in TV commercials) created a film "that zooms along at the mindless, thoroughly contemporary clip of a video game."

FORTY

Bugsy

(1991)

A TriStar Picture

CAST:

Warren Beatty *(Benjamin Siegel);* Annette Bening *(Virginia Hill);* Harvey Keitel *(Mickey Cohen);* Ben Kingsley *(Meyer Lansky);* Joe Mantegna *(George Raft);* Elliott Gould *(Harry Greenberg);* Bill Graham *(Charles "Lucky" Luciano);* Wendy Phillips *(Esta).*

CREDITS:

Producer, Mark Johnson; coproducer, Warren Beatty; director, Barry Levinson; screenplay, James Toback; cinematography, Allen Daviau; music, Ennio Morricone; production design, Dennis Gassner; running time, 135 minutes; rating, R.

Arguably the most striking single gangster film of the past quarter century, *Bugsy* offers a sumptuous period biopic about the legendary Jewish gangster Ben "Bugsy" Siegel (1906–47). But the approach of coproducer/star Warren Beatty, writer James Toback, and director Barry Levinson reaches beyond the limitations of docudrama. Their vision of Siegel is as a romantic figure (an American Heathcliff whose Wuthering Heights is Las Vegas) and a tragic one (a man who, like Oedipus of old, eventually falls from a position of great power owing to a flaw in his character coupled with the workings of fate), combining in a single film the two great alternative possibilities for the modern gangster movie.

Bugsy not only portrays humanized mobsters in contrast to the old Hollywood clichés, but directly addresses that theme as part of its complex structure. As Richard Schickel put it in *Time,* "the film is a commentary on the conventions of the gangster genre, not a mindless repetition of them." In *New York,* David Denby added: "Like John Huston, whose *Prizzi's Honor* was deliberately absurd, the filmmakers realized it's no longer possible to do a Mafia movie straight. *Bugsy* isn't a put-on—it has a fine undertow of seriousness—but its portrait of a self-made hood is essentially comic. Everything in the movie is a little bit over the top—as if the whole giddy and exhilarating action were an emanation from Bugsy's speeding brain."

The moment of inspiration: while traveling through the desert with Virginia, Bugsy realizes that his own version of the American dream could easily unfold here (courtesy TriStar Pictures).

In fact, it emanates from Beatty's speeding brain. On the surface, Toback's screenplay retreads timeworn material. In 1942, Siegel, a compatriot in crime with New York mobsters Meyer Lansky (Ben Kingsley) and "Lucky" Luciano (played by the late rock impressario Bill Graham), travels to Los Angeles to extend their business dealings, becomes involved with actress/moll Virginia Hill (Annette Bening), and is eventually inspired to create the first Vegas supercasino, the Flamingo. But when that project fails financially, in part because Siegel's now trusted girlfriend has skimmed a third of the investment money, his old partners decide to whack Bugsy.

What makes the film so remarkable is the tone and themes the collaborators bring to, or discover in, their material. Immediately, they make clear that Bugsy is ambitious, not in the monetary sense but in terms of personal growth: he insists on finely tailored clothing and practices enunciation (to sound "classy"), even as he drives to a factory where he'll shoot a man who stole from Bugsy's partners. Making the opening even more powerful is that we first see Siegel kissing his wife, Esta (Wendy Phillips), and little girls goodbye, like any normal suburban businessman. The gangster-killer also lives a normal home life.

It's necessary that we watch Bugsy ruthlessly shoot a man early on, since the moviemakers will shortly portray him in a romanticized light. It would be dishonest if they didn't first provide a blunt, harsh portrait of his darker side. If we then choose to like, even admire Bugsy, it's our choice: the filmmakers have not withheld information to make him palatable. In California, he will humiliate one of his new partners, literally making the man get down on his hands and knees and crawl as punishment for a minor theft.

During this frightful and grotesque incident in Bugsy's L.A. home, his new mistress, Virginia, watches from an adjoining room; she becomes sexually excited by the mistreatment of Jack. While she has up to this point been sexually standoffish toward Bugsy (though a known slut, she likes to play hard to get with the criminal/killers she dates), Virginia goes out of control as a result of having witnessed the near-killing. When Bugsy tries to eat the dinner she earlier prepared for him, death, food, and sex all grotesquely meld together.

The film leads inevitably to the final confrontation between Bugsy and Virginia. His trusted ally Mickey Cohen (Harvey Keitel) makes Bugsy aware that Virginia has stolen $2 million from the organization's already overinflated $6-million investment. Bugsy cannot face this terrible truth. He was the first man ever to treat Virginia as anything other than a high-class whore, allowing her to supervise the building of the Flamingo while he was in an L.A. jail awaiting trial for homicide. Yet he fears Mickey may be right and confronts Virginia on his return to Vegas. She becomes so furious at the charges that he—and we—temporarily believe she must be innocent.

When she storms out of Vegas—and, presumably, Bugsy's life—we feel a great wrong has been done. When she returns for their final meeting, however, we learn she did indeed steal the money. Bugsy's greatness is that he is, at heart, an idealist. No wonder David Ansen's *Newsweek* story was titled "If Gatsby Had Been a Goodfella," though it's worth noting that in F. Scott Fitzgerald's novel, Gatsby is precisely that! Bugsy is a

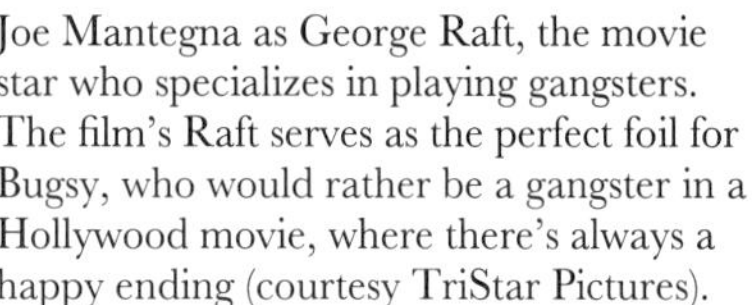

Joe Mantegna as George Raft, the movie star who specializes in playing gangsters. The film's Raft serves as the perfect foil for Bugsy, who would rather be a gangster in a Hollywood movie, where there's always a happy ending (courtesy TriStar Pictures).

Harvey Keitel as Mickey Cohen, the ultrarealist who stands in sharp contrast to Bugsy's Gatsby-like romantic (courtesy TriStar Pictures).

Ben Kingsley as Meyer Lansky, the gangster as soft-spoken businessman (courtesy TriStar Pictures).

Jewish Gatsby: a man who tries to rise above his humble origins, does so through a corruption of the American success dream, mistakenly thinking he can achieve respectability—class, even—through surface changes. Like Gatsby, Bugsy "sprang from a platonic conception of himself," not accepting his lot in life, reinventing himself as someone he would rather be. Like Gatsby, too, Bugsy has a dream, or, more correctly, two of them.

One is his vision of the woman he loves. The movie's conception of Virginia is not very different from Fitzgerald's Daisy Buchanan: a beautiful woman who is not quite what she seems. What makes Bugsy a romantic is that he believes in her image, even worships it. However naive he may seem, he is an admirably noble fool for clinging to such romantic illusions. Toback shares the moment when the hero first falls under his inamorata's spell. Bugsy is on a movie set, visiting his friend actor George Raft (Joe Mantegna), playing a scene in a gangster film. Watching take after take of a scene, Bugsy—sitting on the sidelines—soon knows all of George's lines and unconsciously begins mouthing them simultaneous with George's delivery.

Significantly, George—brandishing a club as he "fights" his actor enemies—jokingly asks Bugsy if he'd like to hop up and play the scene; Bugsy laughingly declines. In fact, though, that's precisely what, on some level, Bugsy wants: to be a gangster not in tawdry real life, but in the magical, mystical world of the 1930s Hollywood gangster movies, where everything is glamorized. In films, the gangster hero can be the kind of polished charmer Bugsy is desperately trying to be. Bugsy sees and falls in love with the extra Virginia when she plays her brief scene with George. What Bugsy desperately desires is to be George's character in that scene, and he will spend the rest of his life trying to turn grim reality into glamorous fantasy—to enjoy the moment of "incarnation" when the two finally blend.

His tragedy derives from the fact that in real life, things do not work out the way they do in the movies. But Bugsy won't learn that sad truth until the end. Meantime, he hops up, after the scene has been concluded, and approaches Virginia. He talks to her not the way he's been speaking to other people, but as George spoke in the movie within the movie (the brittle, tender-tough words of then-contemporary screen antiheroes) and she tosses back dialogue rather than simple speech. Together, they actually walk onto the abandoned movie set. For a transcendent moment, Bugsy is able to leave actuality behind, his life feeling, for a brief magical moment, like a movie. Together, Bugsy and Virginia walk down make-believe streets and into a sunset; we half expect *The End* to appear over this image.

Viva Las Vegas: American dreamer Bugsy oversees the creation of his ideal demimonde, the Flamingo Hotel (courtesy TriStar Pictures).

The degree to which Bugsy would like to be a reel, rather than real, gangster becomes clear in the scene depicting Virginia visiting his L.A. house to initiate their affair. As she arrives, Bugsy is on the phone with his wife, still desperately trying to balance a normal home life with his dark night-life, Dr.-Jekyll-and-Mr.-Hyde style. But the third element in the scene is the movie Bugsy watches while waiting: a screen test apparently made in which he reads (badly) the kind of lines George gets to say in movies. How significant, then, that when Bugsy is shot in that very same house at the film's end, he's once again watching the screen test. An assassin's bullet hits him, and he falls, dying. As he glances up, he watches as a bullet tears through the screen, allowing light to pour out of a hole—a hole that appears to be in the "body" of Bugsy himself, projected on the screen in black and white. The real Bugsy dies just as the screen Bugsy dies. Earlier, when Bugsy seduced Virginia that first night, we saw them slipping in and out from behind the blank white screen, as if slipping into reality and out of fantasy, then back again.

Bugsy represents all of us watching the film, in that he would like life to be more like the movies' idealization of life. It makes sense, then, that just before Bugsy boards a plane to fly from Vegas to L.A. for a supposed meeting with the organization (they have already ordered his elimination), Virginia comes rushing back to him at the last possible moment. Their airport scene together is staged as a precise replay of the famous *Casablanca* parting scene between Humphrey Bogart and Ingrid Bergman. For one brief, wonderful moment, the long-sought-after incarnation is complete: life feels just like a romantic movie. Yet at the same time that we see reel take precedence over real, Bugsy must face the ugliest of real facts: Virginia's confession that she stole from him and his friends. It is the one sin he could once never forgive; the sad look in his eyes suggests that, at this last possible moment, he has—like a true tragic character—at last learned something. He understands and appreciates that Virginia is only human, after all. If he cannot forget her wrong, he can clearly forgive it. Rather than fall into a rage, he accepts. The character has arced, grown as a person by accepting the fallibility of another rather than demanding that she live up to his ideal.

Hill and Siegel meet on a motion picture set. Throughout the film, Ben the idealist (at least, if James Toback's screenplay is to be believed) will attempt to make his life more like the glamorous make-believe existence he sees in the movies (courtesy TriStar Pictures).

So he can enjoy his *Casablanca*-like parting, feel like Bogart—indeed, for a brief moment, be Bogart. His other dream, however, proves more elusive: his vision of Vegas. It's worth noting that the two dreams should not be viewed separately, especially since the Flamingo is named for Virginia, after her nickname. They are two aspects of a single dream, and Bugsy is as much a doomed idealist with his casino as with the woman. It's abundantly clear that Vegas is to him much more than a moneymaking scheme. From the beginning, Bugsy—who ironically can't stand to have anyone steal from Meyer and Charlie—has, in Meyer's words, "no respect for money." It was the stealing, not the loss of the money, that outraged Bugsy.

"It's only dirty paper," Bugsy says of money, and he means it. So when he sees the untapped possibilities of the Nevada desert, he appears a kind of malevolent Walt Disney, envisioning an elaborate theme park for adults only, in which sex and gambling take the place of carousels and clowns. "An oasis with a casino," he sighs. Bugsy wants his world to be one where people can live out their nastiest movie-inspired dreams. Bugsy's favorite films are the Warner Bros. gangster epics: his Vegas will be a theme park in which people can slip into the forbidden fantasies that his pal George Raft portrayed. As Ansen wrote in *Newsweek*, "screenwriter Toback [found] in him a resonant American symbol of the thin line between crime and celebrity."

Sadly for Bugsy, his partners are realists rather than, like him, idealists. Incensed when Bugsy allowed their agreed-on $1-million investment to rise out of control, they are further incensed that his mistress was clearly stealing a third of their capital. Still, even Virginia could only steal so much. It was Bugsy who had gone out of control with the Flamingo; though it could have been built more economically, that would not have been the perfect place Bugsy envisions. When he must sell his most valuable commodity—his own shares in the Flamingo—to keep the workers going, he's told by a friend that he'll end up with nothing. Bugsy smiles and replies, "But the Flamingo will be there—and that's not nothing."

Bugsy clings to the desperate hope that somehow, some way, it will all work out. But his weakness for the woman he idealizes and his unwillingness to believe anything bad about her couples with destiny—forces beyond his control—to destroy him. "He has a fatal

In the film's opening, Bugsy makes clear that, despite his dapper appearance, he has not forgotten how to use a gun, and use it ruthlessly (courtesy TriStar Pictures).

flaw," Annette Bening said at the time of the film's release, "he has hubris. And fate is unkind." Bugsy does believe, incorrectly it turns out, that he can conquer anything. On Christmas Eve, movie stars are scheduled to fly to Vegas for the opening of the Flamingo, which will attract national attention and help bring in the tourists needed to make it pay off. But it rains, the planes cannot safely leave L.A., and the casino is a huge, empty neon cavern on opening night. Uncontrollable elements—the weather—allow Bugsy to finally see he cannot exert the kind of control he believes he's capable of. Still, it's his insistence on trying—and his coming so very close—that gives him great dimension. As Richard Schickel wrote in *Time:* "To the list of tragic American dreamers, people who martyred themselves for visions that stubbornly refused realization while they lived—one thinks of rocket scientist Robert Goddard and car manufacturer Preston Tucker—it seems we must now add the name of Benjamin Siegel," at least if we are convinced that Toback's portrait is more truth than fancy.

Toward the end, even old friend Meyer Lansky concurs with the other partners that whether or not Ben was in on the siphoning off of funds, according to gangster morality, Siegel must be held responsible for the financial disaster and therefore whacked. "He's not interested in money," Meyer says. "He's interested in an idea." Bugsy is like Beatty, whose most personal film projects—*Bonnie and Clyde, Shampoo, Reds, Dick Tracy, Bugsy*—are clearly highly ambitious idea-projects he believes in. How neat to note, in this context, that the woman playing Virginia became his leading lady offscreen as well as on. As writer Toback put it, "[Warren] combines an elegant and well-cultivated charm with a tensely impacted psychosis. The role gave him a historical person through whom he could express his wild extremes."

Some critics complained that the film was part of a growing, dangerous trend (Oliver Stone's *JFK* was another example cited) toward exalting unworthy people into movie heroes. Daniel Seligman of *Fortune* complained that *Bugsy* conveniently left out Siegel's rape arrest, as well as his known blackmailing of Hollywood stars, doubting that Siegel ever patriotically offered to fly to Italy and assassinate Mussolini. Let's recall, though, that such aggrandizing of questionable people into epic, romantic, and/or tragic figures is nothing new. Sophocles did it, Shakespeare did it, and in our own century John Ford did it. There is no historical proof whatever to suggest that Oedipus, Henry V, or Wyatt Earp were the great men those artists transformed them into. Art has to do with allegory, and *Bugsy* is a fitting allegory for the American dream, employing—as Robert Warshow put it in his classic essay so many decades ago—the gangster as tragic hero.

Director Barry Levinson shot *Bugsy* in the grand style of old movies, an approach that visually informs us that what we're watching is myth rather than reality. Understandably, Meyer orders Ben's execution with great reluctance. To paraphrase Shakespeare, Meyer might well say of Ben what Mark Antony said of Brutus, whose mistaken decisions nonetheless began (in the play, if not necessarily in real life) with the most admirable of motives: he was the noblest mobster of them all.

Kevin Costner as Jim Garrison: a controversial real-life D. A., transformed into a modernized Frank Capra crusader (courtesy Warner Bros).

FORTY-ONE

JFK

(1991)

A Warner Bros. Release

CAST:

Kevin Costner *(Jim Garrison)*; Sissy Spacek *(Liz Garrison)*; Joe Pesci *(David Ferrie)*; Tommy Lee Jones *(Clay Shaw)*; Gary Oldman *(Lee Harvey Oswald)*; Jay O. Sanders *(Lou Ivon)*; Michael Rooker *(Bill Broussard)*; Jack Lemmon *(Jack Martin)*; Walter Matthau *(Sen. Russell Long)*; Donald Sutherland *("X")*; Kevin Bacon *(Willie O'Keefe)*; Ed Asner *(Guy Bannister)*; Brian Doyle-Murray *(Jack Ruby)*; Jim Garrison *(Earl Warren)*; also, Laurie Metcalf, John Candy, Vincent D'Onofrio, Sally Kirkland, Wayne Knight, Tony Plana, Tomas Milian, Sean Stone, Lolita Davidovich, and Frank Whaley.

CREDITS:

Producers, A. Kitman Ho and Oliver Stone; director, Stone; screenplay, Stone and Zachary Sklar, based on the books *On the Trail of the Assassins* by Jim Garrison and *Crossfire: The Plot That Killed Kennedy* by Jim Marrs; cinematography, Robert Richardson; editors, Joe Hutshing and Pietro Scalia; music, John Williams; production design, Victor Kempster; running time, 188 minutes (theatrical release); rating, R.

The November 22, 1963, assassination of President John Fitzgerald Kennedy was the crime of the century. Initially, the public perceived it as the act of a single man, a maniac with communist leanings who, in a sincere but misguided act, changed the course of history. Then, conspiracy theories came into play: Oswald had been part of some incredible plot—perhaps engineered by the Russians and/or Cubans—to kill the president. He might even be what he claimed moments after being arrested, "a patsy." But patsy by and for whom? Numerous conspiracies blamed everyone from the CIA to the Mafia, possibly even a coalition of the two.

Three decades having passed, coupled with the "new" Hollywood's openly embracing what was once considered too controversial for inclusion in a commercial movie, allowed Oliver Stone to openly accuse actual people of having been involved in the plot. In fact, the new freedom of the screen might have allowed Stone to go too far; however aesthetically crafted, *JFK* reeked with a *National Enquirer* reckless attitude toward the facts. No one would ever claim that Stone's film seemed timid, though the old adage about fools rushing in where wise men feared to tread was raised. Numerous critics insisted that the filmmaker hit below the belt, presenting wild conjecture as if it were proven fact, doing so with such superlative cinematic technique that the public accepted his virtual fiction as docudrama. Most viewers sat spellbound, believing everything they saw, yet Stone eventually admitted he'd embellished, interpreted, simplified, even invented characters (such as the key "witness" portrayed by Kevin Bacon, who in fact never existed) to heighten dramatic impact.

Like so many self-referential modern crime films, *JFK* is as much about the media and its impact (the movie we are watching is, importantly, part of that media) as it is about the crime itself. The opening image features news footage of retiring president Dwight David Eisenhower delivering one of his last speeches, which we see on television. Throughout the movie, key characters watch TV: people in a bar observe the murder of Jack Ruby on the tube. Later, New Orleans DA Jim Garrison (Kevin Costner) and his wife (Sissy Spacek) are viewed in their bedroom, watching a highly negative televised report on Garrison's one-man crusade to catch the Kennedy conspirators. There's nothing Stone's Garrison can do to alter a perception that the cynically powerful media creates. However, during the course of *JFK*, Stone—who defends Garrison down the line—takes just such an approach to David Ferrie and Clay Shaw, both portrayed as instrumental in the horrific conspiracy, though in fact neither was proven guilty of having done anything wrong.

That opening image of Eisenhower is significant beyond the introduction of the media theme. The outgoing president warns the American public against what he tagged "the military-industrial complex." At first, it might seem this famous pronouncement was included only to place the story in its proper historical context. But as the Garrison of Oliver Stone's imagination—a

In his methodical search for the truth, Garrison goes through all the motions of the assassination (courtesy Warner Bros.).

white knight who, like Eliot Ness in old Chicago (a role also played by Kevin Costner), goes out to apprehend all-powerful bad guys—pursues the case, he and we realize Kennedy was killed (at least in this film's intriguing if less than convincing view) because of his desire to end the war in Vietnam. A Washington-based mystery man (Donald Sutherland), meeting with Garrison in front of the Lincoln Memorial, informs the DA that American industrialists needed the millions they'd make selling war machines to the military, eager to justify its existence through combat. Stone never entertains the possibility that X (presumably based on L. Fletcher Prouty, former aide to the Joint Chiefs of Staff and, as such, one more man with an ax to grind) was nothing more than a whacko who sold the DA a bill of goods.

The movie implies that Lyndon Johnson promised the powerful influences he'd continue the war if they whacked the man who had won the Democratic presidential nomination away from him. The old Texan, according to Stone, is the ultimate mobster. Then, Mafia and anti-Castro Cuban elements, equally angry for opposing but complementary reasons (profits and politics) that Kennedy might be soft on Havana's communist leaders, were manipulated into performing the actual execution, with the cooperation of the FBI, CIA, and the Secret Service, among others. When Bobby Kennedy attempted to pick up the fallen banner five years later, the same forces quickly eliminated him. Terrence Rafferty noted in *The New Yorker:* "Since our direst suspicions about the way the government operates frequently turn out to be justified, Stone knows that in 1992 few members of the audience are likely to reject his conspiracy scenario out of hand. The assassination could have happened the way *JFK* says it did, and for this filmmaker 'could have' is good enough. Platoon leader Stone carries out his mission here with his characteristic indifference to intellectual niceties. *JFK* is a guerrilla raid on our sensibilities. Stone, with his overheated temperament and his propulsive, cut-to-the-chase filmmaking style, doesn't bother to try to win the hearts and minds of the audience with coherent, rational argument; he simply takes them prisoner. For all its apparent meticulousness, *JFK* finally seems as muddled as the Warren Commission report. It's a thick gumbo of truths, half-truths, unverifiable hypotheses, and pure rant, and Stone ladles it out indiscriminately. In essence, the conspiracy case that Stone makes amounts to a series of inferential leaps proceeding from a speculation. It's all bombast and has the fevered tone of tabloid television; it plays like an endless episode of *America's Most Wanted.*"

Clay Shaw (Tommy Lee Jones) listens patiently as Garrison mounts his case against the businessman (courtesy Warner Bros.).

David Denby of *New York* noted the same flaws, but took a far more charitable approach: "The movie is appalling and fascinating—unreliable, no doubt, but an amazing visual experience nonetheless. *JFK* is an amalgam of facts and speculations, but at its core—a core that no amount of ridicule can convince me is less than great—Stone re-creates, from many points of view, what might have happened. *JFK* is a monomaniac's treasure trove. Saying that *JFK* isn't always convincing is hardly to dismiss it, as many overly literal types, blind to the powers of film, have already done. Stone has established a dense web of contingency, 'coincidence,' and design. He has made, if you insist, a fiction of the assassination, a countermyth" to the official myth of the Warren Commission report. Still, Stone fails to mention that, even among ardent Kennedy-conspiracy enthusiasts, Garrison was considered something of a black sheep. When the briefly glimpsed network news documentary insists that Garrison blackmailed, bribed, and threatened potential witnesses, we see Costner's Garrison reacting as if his unimpeachable personage has been unfairly smeared; in fact, there is proof aplenty that Garrison did precisely what he was accused of.

In court, near the film's end, the credibility of Garrison's "witnesses" against businessman Clay Shaw are destroyed, supposedly by clever lawyer's tricks. The record makes clear they were indeed whackos, compulsive liars, career criminals, and other assorted unreliables. It's also obvious that Garrison, whose authority did not extend beyond New Orleans, convinced himself that people living in his town were the criminal masterminds; the idea that the alleged conspiracy might well have begun elsewhere never occurred to him. At movie's end, when Shaw (Garrison suspects the right-winger wanted Kennedy dead because he was soft on communism) is found not guilty by a jury, we're supposed to accept that a great injustice has been done. In fact, any fair-minded moviegoer who sat on that jury would have arrived at the same conclusion.

Stone combined elements of two separate books, one written by Garrison, the other containing information by other (and, in the eyes of many close observers, more reliable) conspiracy theorists. Though most viewers simply assumed Stone was telling them the truth, Stone compressed and collated facts. He later admitted that the Garrison of his film was "actually a composite of several real-life conspiracy theorists," and that as director and cowriter, Stone had transformed Garrison (by most accounts, an abrasive and less than pleasant fellow) into "a Frank Capra character," one of those soft-spoken, decent heartland American populists played by Gary Cooper and Jimmy Stewart, simple guys who discover some ugly truth and attempt to bring it to the people, despite the efforts of self-important bureaucrats and all-powerful government officials who would keep it from ever reaching the masses. Like John Doe, Mr. Smith, and a dozen other Capra heroes, the film's Jim Garrison wants only to perform a selfless act for the good of society at large, his ironic reward being public disgrace and ridicule when the wickedly powerful make him appear to be an enemy of the people. The viable possibility that Garrison was in fact an ambitious, irresponsible, obsessed man, who eventually got the comeuppance he deserved, apparently never occurred to Stone or, if it did, was dismissed as irrelevant to the muckraking drama he planned to fashion, and in fact expertly fashioned.

Garrison (Kevin Costner) becomes convinced of a conspiracy (courtesy Warner Bros.).

JFK was, in fact, not the first crime film to re-create the Kennedy assassination and insist that a conspiracy eliminated the president; 1973's *Executive Action,* released a decade after the event, likewise argued this point…

Edward James Olmos as Santana: the Hispanic godfather (courtesy Universal Pictures, photo credit Tony Friedkin).

FORTY-TWO

American Me

(1992)

A Universal Release

CAST:

Edward James Olmos *(Santana);* William Forsythe *(J.D.);* Pepe Serna *(Mundo);* Evelina Fernandez *(Julie);* Daniel A. Haro *(Huero);* Domingo Ambriz *(Pie Face);* Vic Trevino *(Cheetah);* Daniel Villarreal *(Little Puppet);* Danny De La Paz *(Puppet);* Vira Montes *(Esperanza, Santana's Mother);* Sal Lopez *(Pedro, Santana's Father);* Panchito Gomez *(Young Santana).*

CREDITS:

Producers, Sean Daniel, Robert M. Young, and Edward James Olmos; director, Olmos; writers, Floyd Mutrux and Desmond Nakano (and Olmos, uncredited); cinematography, Reynaldo Villalobos; editors, Arthur R. Coburn and Richard Candib; music, Dennis Lambert and Claude Gaudette; production design, Joe Aubel; costume design, Sylvia Vega-Vasquez; running time, 126 minutes; rating, R.

What *The Godfather* was to American gangsters of Italian descent, *American Me* was intended to be for the Hispanic gangster. This epic spans the varied experiences of three generations of a single L.A. Latino family, as their initial hopes for achieving a piece of the pie are dashed by the harsh realities of prejudice. The film, cowritten, coproduced, and directed by star Edward James Olmos, attempted to bring the sad lot of Hispanic life to the mainstream audience, making his dark, nihilistic vision palatable by presenting it within a modern gangster film.

Olmos plays Santana, who in the opening sequence is seen entering prison. Most of the film takes place there (the scene were actually shot in Folsom, featuring actual inmates and guards), making *American Me* the nineties' equivalent of *The Last Mile, Each Dawn I Die,* and *The Big House,* those Warner Bros. 1930s films that followed their gangster antiheroes behind bars. However, prison life as presented here is considerably bleaker than anything in those earlier social melodramas. According to Olmos and his collaborators, the Hispanic Mafia of the West Coast was created in prison when Latinos like Santana banded together to survive. The racist-white Aryan League and the black-power organizations were already powerful, and equally hostile to men of Mexican ancestry. Out of an organization formed to insure survival, a network grew, through which Santana and his key followers were able to control a vast criminal organization that extended far outside the prison walls, and deep into the barrios.

But after the initial glimpse of Santana as a mature man in prison, the film quickly follows his thoughts back to the beginning. We see his parents on the night when he was conceived, in June 1943. They are easygoing, likable young people out on a date. But they are mobbed by unruly servicemen, all fired up by the Hearst newspapers and Walter Winchell radio show, both of which have suggested that white American culture is being diluted by Hispanic "thugs" wearing zoot suits. The young lovers are viciously attacked, Santana's father beaten while the mother is held down and raped by sailors. When the police finally arrive, they walk past the white sailors and arrest the Latinos for starting a riot.

From this harsh, unsparing sequence, it's immediately clear that the film is social protest. A reconsideration of the zoot-suit riots (Olmos had earlier appeared in the 1981 film *Zoot Suit,* which likewise addressed this ugly incident), *American Me* shows that the gangs supposedly hassling white passersby may themselves have been the victims. In addition, the film—in showing the crushed idealism and destroyed innocence of the couple—makes clear that Hispanics were forced by such violent abuse into a ghetto mentality. Dramatically, the scene also plays a key role in the story to follow: Santana's personal problems will stem from his poor relationship with his father, who we later learn could not look the boy in the eyes, unsure as to which of the rapist sailors might be his biological father.

Santana's own story is not much prettier. To avoid his abusive father, as a teenager he stays away from

In 1943, Esperanza (Vira Montes) and Pedro (Sal Lopez) ready themselves for a night on the town…(courtesy Universal Pictures)

…little realizing they will stumble onto the infamous zoot-suit riots and become victims. Filmmaker Olmos hoped for a sociological tract as well as a crime film (courtesy Universal Pictures, photo credit Tony Friedkin).

home as much as possible. Santana and a pair of buddies, pursued by white racists as they walk home one night, break into a bar to hide out and are arrested for illegal entry. While in juvenile prison, Santana is raped by another teenage inmate and, refusing to accept that he can be rendered powerless by anyone else, kills the boy. His brief sentence is turned into a longer one, and the moment he grows too old for juvenile, he's transferred to Folsom. The film's hardly subtle but nonetheless effective message is that simply by trying to survive with a sense of dignity and self-respect, the Hispanic male is forced into criminal activity. Absurdly enough, the American system transforms going to jail into his only viable career opportunity.

In or out of jail, Santana wants respect more than anything else. After killing his rapist, he is ushered from the general juvenile prison area to that reserved specifically for hard cases; on the voice-over, we hear him explain that "the respect I earned made it worthwhile." Decades later, when Santana is (briefly) on the outside and awkwardly attempting to romance a sweet young woman, he takes her out to help him buy a pair of boots. When the salesman unconsciously slights him by casually telling Santana to wait a moment, Santana demands the man look him in the eye and take a more respectful tone when he speaks. Eventually, Santana is killed by his own people when he makes the mistake of appearing weak (thereby losing respect) after requesting that a fellow Hispanic gangster, blamed for a bad situation he may or may not have been responsible for, be spared.

However difficult Santana's life (and death) may be, the film paints an even bleaker picture for the future. The children seen in Santana's home, including his little brother and his girlfriend's son, are in the last frame of the film seen joyriding around East L.A., performing drive-by shootings. Santana's story is sandwiched between the upbeat image of his parents just before the rape and the downbeat shot of a little boy firing a gun randomly at people sitting on their front steps. This disheartening view of Hispanic life in our cities lacks the slightest shred of hope.

Olmos views the gangster as a Jekyll/Hyde character, much as Coppola did in the first installment of the *Godfather* saga, in which Michael tried to balance his nor-

The boys in the yard: Huero (Daniel A. Haro), Mundo (Pepe Serna), El Japo (Cary Hiroyuki Tagawa), Santana (Olmos), Cheetah (Vic Trevino), Pie-Face (Domingo Ambriz), and J.D. (William Forsythe) form the Hispanic Mafia as a means of surviving while behind bars (courtesy Universal Pictures, photo credit Tony Friedkin).

mal home life with his underworld activities. In *American Me,* this Jekyll/Hyde dichotomy—the man maintains his self-image as a decent human being by keeping his gangster activities separate, at least in his own mind, from everything else he does—is expressed in an exchange between Santana and the young woman that appears, in its entirety, twice in the film. First, we hear it at the very beginning, as a kind of prologue to what follows, then again toward the end, in its dramatic context, when their relationship fails and he needs some explanation as to why.

"You're like two people," Julie (Evelina Fernandez) cries. "One is like a kid—doesn't know how to drive a car, or make love. That's the one I cared about. The other one—the other one I hate. The one who knows...knows how to run drugs...the one who kills people."

"Until now, I would have considered it a sign of weakness to even consider what you said. Now, I realize you were right," Santana concludes.

In our eyes, Santana has transformed at long last into a human being, for he has at least realized that his drug dealing was not an act of "revolution" with the ultimate good of the Hispanic people as his aim (the great lie he kept telling himself), but simply an illegal activity, performed for power, control, and money. Yet in the eyes of his gang members, this realization makes him weak and expendable.

No question about it, *American Me* was made with integrity; it is a work of serious ambitions, containing numerous intense and effective sequences. And, yes, the message does come through, if with a sledgehammer approach. Still, the film is something less than successful. As Brian D. Johnson noted in *Maclean's,* "despite its gritty realism and noble intentions, *American Me* fails to rehabilitate the tried formula of the prison movie. The violence, which is both visceral and frequent, verges on exploitation. And the movie becomes a vicarious excursion into underworld exotica...the director, like his character, loses sight of the perspective that informs the violence, and the movie congeals into lurid tragedy." That last word seems too lofty for what we see; "lurid melodrama" might have been a more fitting phrase. But Johnson was right on the mark when he wrote that "*American Me* is imprisoned by its own dire realism."

David Denby of *New York* complained that while the film "may be authentic in such details as tattoos, lingo, the rituals of greeting and death...*American Me* is a mess, incoherent in many details, large and small....Olmos wants to attack violence and macho bullheadedness in a movie that for much of its length celebrates, precisely, violence and macho bullheadedness." One sequence in

Santana is arrested by police officers as the woman he loves, Julie (Evelina Fernandez), looks on hopelessly...

...later, imprisoned Santana is visited by Esperanza (Vira Montes) and six-year-old Paulito (Abraham Verduzco). The film insists that the system is stacked against a Santana, who will forever find himself behind bars no matter how hard he tries to go straight (courtesy Universal Pictures, photo credits Tony Friedkin).

particular stands as proof of what Denby says: Olmos chose to intercut Santana's first attempt at heterosexual lovemaking (having spent most of his life in a prison, he's never known a woman until well into his mature years) with a parallel sequence in prison, in which the son of a competing Mafia don is gang-raped and then killed by having a knife shoved up his rectum, on specific order from Santana. The former material is touching; there's something special about the idea of a grown man, and a particularly rugged-looking one at that, fumbling as he attempts to romance a more experienced and delicate-looking lady.

The film fumbles even on the level of drama. Santana, J.D. (William Forsythe), and Mundo (Pepe Serna) are never effectively individualized the way Michael, Sonny, and Fredo were in the *Godfather* films. We never understand what makes each tick as an individual, so there's a cold, distanced quality when we watch them form the Mexican Mafia. A few critics, however, took the film as Olmos intended it. "*American Me* is a fiercely impressive film," Jack Kroll and Lynda Wright reported in *Newsweek*. It "shows the fearsome logic that makes ethnic gangs the inevitable social structures that arise with the breakdown of values and opportunity. The movie takes you inside this alternative society, making you feel its perverted pride in the macho codes of bravado, tribal loyalty, and vengeance."

FORTY-THREE

Reservoir Dogs

(1992)

A Miramax Release of a Live America Film

CAST:

Harvey Keitel *(Mr. White);* Tim Roth *(Mr. Orange);* Michael Madsen *(Mr. Blonde);* Chris Penn *(Nice Guy Eddie);* Steve Buscemi *(Mr. Pink);* Lawrence Tierney *(Joe Cabot);* Randy Brooks *(Holdaway);* Kirk Baltz *(Marvin Nash);* Eddie Bunker *(Mr. Blue);* Quentin Tarantino *(Mr. Brown).*

CREDITS:

Producer, Lawrence Bender; coproducer, Harvey Keitel; writer/director, Quentin Tarantino; cinematography, Andrzej Sekula; editor, Sally Menke; music supervisor, Karyn Rachtman; production design, David Wasco; costume design, Betsy Heimann; running time, 90 minutes; rating, R.

The story is now legendary, at least among film buffs. In 1991, Quentin Tarantino was working in a middle-of-nowhere video store by day, at night knocking off stories he hoped to someday turn into movies. A year later, he was a formidable "player" in Hollywood, after selling his script *Reservoir Dogs,* even talking his way into the job of director, then winning accolades—as well as controversy—at film festivals like Sundance, where this minor gangster yarn earned a controversial reputation as the most brutally nasty film in years. *Reservoir Dogs* was lauded for its economy of storytelling and intricacy of narrative line; at the same time, it was loudly condemned for overt, oppressive violence at a time when politicians, as well as the public, were beginning to question whether the ever more intense brutality in popular entertainment was a reflection of our society or in fact a key cause of violence in our streets.

The movie is a fascinating example of low-budget, high-energy independent filmmaking; however, the violence does finally go over the top, ceasing to service the narrative, becoming nonsexual pornography, a wallow in blood and guts. "Aggressively brutal," said Vincent Canby in his *New York Times* review, clearly put off by this quality even as he admitted to being impressed by the film's "dazzling cinematic pyrotechnics." In those comments, Canby described the Jekyll/Hyde aspects of a work that introduced a young, undeniably talented filmmaker while also raising fundamental questions about how far a director can and should go when addressing issues of crime and violence in mainstream entertainment.

The film is one more of those homages to film noir, mounted by a moviemaker who, like the Scorsese of *Mean Streets,* devoured gangster films of the late forties and fifties, making their moral, emotional, and intellectual essences the chief substance of his own work. In particular, the sad, sleazy little stories of bands of outsiders, brought together for a big heist that goes all wrong, were at the heart of Tarantino's script; he freely admitted to being inspired by John Huston's *The Asphalt Jungle* and Stanley Kubrick's *The Killing.* To immediately establish a comparison between his film and those, director Tarantino insisted that the first character we see onscreen, Joe Cabot, be played by an actor closely associated with movies of that era. It turned out to be Lawrence Tierney, veteran of 1945's *Dillinger* and other hoary, sordid little gangster sagas, though on the eve of the film's release, Tarantino confided that if Sterling Hayden (star of both the Huston and Kubrick films) had still been alive, he'd have been the perfect actor to play the part.

Cabot is an old mobster, a character who in the opening lunchroom sequence meets with younger men for a jewelry store robbery that he's masterminding. During this sequence, Tarantino reveals his talents as a director as well as writer. The dialogue is as real and pungent as anything written by David Mamet; the characters become so involved in their discussion of hidden meanings in the lyrics from Madonna's songs, interwoven with a discussion about the art of tipping, that it would be easy to believe this is an actual conversation,

Harvey Keitel as Mr. White: The gangster as contemporary cowboy (photo by Linda R. Chen, courtesy Miramax Films).

overheard accidentally. Meanwhile, Tarantino's cinematographer, Polish-born Andrzéj Sekula (here making his American debut), was instructed to move his purposefully unsteady camera in and out of the scene, cutting from close shots on individual faces to images of the men as a group, allowing us a sense that we are not observers but cast members.

Then, Tarantino does something surprising, refreshing, even brilliant: he cuts to the chase by police that follows the disastrous robbery attempt. In doing this, he purposefully violates the expected structure of all grungy-little-heist films: a growing sense of suspense as the characters move closer to the planned robbery, which in the past we've always been allowed to see carried out on-screen. By not allowing us to see the robbery—not even in the constant flashbacks—Tarantino essentially plays mind games with his audience, effectively frustrating us by breaking all the rules of the subgenre he's working within.

Whereas gangster films about organized crime are most often concerned with the theme of respect, gangster films about small-time heists invariably deal with betrayal. That's certainly the case here. The post (unseen) robbery sequence allows us to watch Mr. White (Harvey Keitel) driving the getaway car,

The not-so-magnificent seven: Quentin Tarantino's unlovable losers leave the diner and begin their trek toward destiny (photo by Linda R. Chen, courtesy Miramax Films).

while Mr. Orange (Tim Roth) is stretched out in the backseat, bleeding profusely, his guts seemingly about to spill out as he desperately holds himself together. Mr. White heads for an immense, empty warehouse where the anonymous men (they refer to one another as various colors owing to Joe Cabot's insistence this is the best way to avoid betrayal) have agreed to meet. There, the drama proper takes place, as the burly son of Cabot, Nice Guy Eddie (Chris Penn), withdrawn Mr. Pink (Steve Buscemi), and the quietly menacing sociopath Mr. Blonde (Michael Madsen) all arrive, even as Mr. Orange lies in a corner, bleeding while writhing in pain and, at moments of consciousness, screaming for help, as the others ignore him.

What they are most insistent on is discovering which member of their group betrayed the holdup to the police. Midway through the film, the flashbacks of each man in turn eventually make clear it is Mr. Orange, actually an undercover cop. We know this, though the other characters do not. However, the nastiest gang member, Mr. Blonde (who mindlessly cuts off the ear of a policeman they've captured while dancing to the Stealer's Wheel rock-'n'-roll standard "Stuck in the Middle With You") and their equally unpleasant confederate, the ironically named Nice Guy Eddie, deduce it must be Mr. Orange. That creates the film's most fascinating moral dilemna: Mr. White defends the vulnerable, wounded Mr. Orange (he insists on his innocence throughout) from the others, an act of courage that is given a bizarre edge by our knowledge that he's guilty of the very betrayal he's been accused of.

Tim Roth as Mr. Orange, the police detective who infiltrates the gang, then is wounded during the robbery (courtesy Miramax Films).

Michael Madsen as Mr.Blonde: The kinda guy who'd cut off a cop's ear and dance around to "Stuck in the Middle With You" as he does it (photo credit Linda R. Chen, courtesy Miramax Films).

"Ninety minutes of stylized mayhem and playground machismo" is what Terrence Rafferty tagged the film in *The New Yorker,* noting "a spare, hermetic, deliberately stagy quality that suggests a theatre-of-cruelty exercise.... Tarantino's compositions, which rely heavily on long shots and low angles, emphasize the characters' absurdity. Tarantino, abstracting wildly, wants us to feel

The moment of truth: Mr. Pink and Mr. White face off in the kind of confrontation that has become a ritualistic moment in contemporary gangster films (courtesy Miramax Films).

as if we had crash-landed in an alternate universe: the Planet of the Goons." According to Jonathan Romney of *The New Statesman,* the problem as well as fascination of this film both derive from its being "about the glamour of violence, but [Tarantino is] not quite sure whether [he wants] to analyze it or relish it."

This sense of ambivalence that runs through the film—and many responses to the movie—derives in large part from *Reservoir Dogs*'s being open to deconstruction interpretation. When Mr. White loudly threatens the crazed Mr. Blonde, this cold-eyed character responds with a movie reference: "Wow, that was really exciting. I'll bet you're a big Lee Marvin fan." In fact, Tarantino had directed Keitel to deliver his previous speech as Lee Marvinish as possible, so that Madsen's comments ring comically true. It is the same response that the audience might well have just had, or at least a film buff (in particular, gangster-movie buff). Critic Jonathan Romney went so far as to argue that "the film's point is that the life of crime is entirely about acting...gang members (assigned roles to play by Joe Cabot, the 'director' of their 'performance') quibble over their parts, then get into them like Method trainees, erasing their own identities (as they assume the color-coded names Cabot has provided). Play a part well enough, the film seems to say, and action becomes an act, and morality simply what's beyond the proscenium arch." Thus, the failed robbery could be interpreted as a carefully rehearsed stage performance that unaccountably goes all wrong, the befuddled and confused actors desperately turning to wild improvisation. It's significant that Joe Cabot does not appear again; like a good director of a stage play (which is essentially what transpires in the warehouse), he retires from the scene after offering his final "notes."

FORTY-FOUR

The Firm

(1993)

A Paramount Picture

CAST:

Tom Cruise *(Mitch McDeere);* Jeanne Tripplehorn *(Abby McDeere);* Gene Hackman *(Avery Tolar);* Hal Holbrook *(Oliver Lambert);* Terry Kinney *(Lamar Quinn);* Wilford Brimley *(William Devasher);* Ed Harris *(Wayne Tarrance);* Holly Hunter *(Tammy Hemphill);* Gary Busey *(Gumshoe);* David Strathairn *(Ray);* Paul Sorvino, unbilled *(Mafioso).*

CREDITS:

Producers, Scott Rudin and John Davis; director, Sydney Pollack; screenplay, David Rabe, Robert Towne, and David Rayfiel, from the novel by John Grisham; cinematography, John Seale; editors, William and Frederic Steinkamp; music, Dave Grusin; production designer, Richard MacDonald; running time, 154 minutes; rating, R.

Though John Grisham's novel *The Firm* was published in 1991, it might best be considered the last important novel of the eighties. That is the decade during which, at least by implication, the book (and subsequent film version) is not only set but also about. The hero, Mitch McDeere, is a representative figure for the Reagan era: an overeager, opportunistic, self-serving young man, the virtual apotheosis of yuppie mentality. Mitch is the Horatio Alger of the Greed Decade, a smart, superficial climber who uncritically lives out the traditional American dream in a uniquely 1980s manner. Overcoming his humble origins, first by marrying up (he hitches his star to a bright, classy young woman, Abby), then by graduating from Harvard Law School on a scholarship, he at last parlays top-of-his-class status to a coveted position at Bendini, Lambert & Locke, a small, prestigious, conservative law firm based in Memphis, Tennessee.

Up to this point, *The Firm* appears to be shaping up as a strong social melodrama with a legal backdrop, though hardly a crime film. That, however, is precisely what the movie becomes. The modern gangster-movie theme of organized crime invading previously sacrosanct areas of business and culture is nowhere else so strikingly rendered as in Grisham's work. No area of the business or legal world could seem as far from the mob as this firm; it is the bastion of traditional WASP thinking. Even their hiring of someone like Mitch, anything but a blue blood, seems a belated egalitarian approach by a firm that only a few years earlier would have demanded a pedigree. The firm is less than comfortable about Mitch's modestly liberated wife wanting a career, even one as conventional as teaching. Though they initially tolerate her "whim," it isn't long before they induce her to become something of a Stepford wife, a beautiful zombie who has lunch with other firm members' trophy wives, then goes home to dutifully prepare dinner for her husband.

Despite this surface show of ultraconservatism, something about the firm is unspeakably modern. Shortly after joining, Mitch is approached by a pair of menacing-looking characters. One of them, Wayne Tarrance (Ed Harris), reveals he's an FBI agent who wants Mitch to work as a mole. The firm's activities as tax attorneys led Mitch's partners to a Chicago mob family. Before long, the firm was involved in a complex money-laundering venture for the Mafia. This reality is driven home to Mitch when he notes a mob boss (Paul Sorvino) arriving for meetings with the apparently solid WASP members of the firm.

Whereas the mob and the WASP Establishment may at one time have been perceived as standing at opposing ends of American lifestyles, they have in our time become all but indistinguishable. Organized crime is now part of the Establishment, whereas the old order has gradually allowed itself to become thoroughly corrupted, now nothing more than a posh front for the underworld. The underworld has surfaced, while Main Street, USA, has sunk into the mire. That is a theme of the contemporary, not the classic, gangster film. Before

Mitch realizes that his "mentor" is in fact drawing him ever deeper into a seemingly wholesome world that is actually owned by organized crime (courtesy Paramount Pictures).

1950, there were the good guys and the bad guys, and the dividing line was clear. During the postwar era, however, such distinctions became blurred. Films like *The Phenix City Story* implied that organized crime was making inroads, weaseling its way into the solid, upstanding American communities. Yet the films of that era managed to remain positive. While exposing such situations, the films were crusading documents, optimistically implying that this infusion could be halted if only the public was made aware, through movies such as the one they were watching, of the problem. That is not the case with modern crime movies, as typified by *The Firm.* Here, the attitude is that the corruption has long since been completed, is an undeniable fact of life. These movies are not warnings, merely statements of the obvious.

When the FBI insists Mitch make his choice, either help them get the firm or accept that he himself is a part of the corruption, Mitch decides on realistic, rather than idealistic, grounds. He is not moved to do the right thing; his only concern is that he make the choice that, in the long run, will be best for him. The firm has purposefully been hiring poor but brilliant boys like him, believing their hunger will induce them into gradually accepting the corruption. The thousand-dollar suits, the tony cars, the first-class flights to the Cayman Islands appear the proper perks for having made it, a deserved reward for the hard work and undeniable excellence. They turn out to be baubles dangled

Oliver Lambert (Hal Holbrook) introduces some "fresh blood" into the conservative tax-specialist firm of Bendini, Lambert & Locke. Like John Grisham's novel, the film insists that even such onetime WASP sanctuaries of old-fashioned elegance are no longer sacrosanct (courtesy Paramount Pictures, photo credit François Duhamel).

in front of wide-eyed climbers to induce them to surrender to ever greater corruption. Mitch also senses that those rare youthful additions to the firm who, upon realizing this, did attempt to maintain morality have "accidentally" died in boating accidents and the like. Though the government offers to cover for him via the Witness Relocation Program, Mitch knows this is not a 100-percent-foolproof solution, as the firm's mob contacts have long memories and endless means to track down informers. A true Machievellian prince, Mitch plays the FBI against the firm. In the film's ironic ending (quite different from that of the book), Mitch actually cuts a deal with the mob boss, who at least still pledges allegiance to the Mafia's credo, rather than trust the feds (who have proven to be a sleazy lot, wishing to use Mitch for their own ends) or the hypocritical firm.

As with Sorvino, the casting of Wilford Brimley as the deadliest of all hit men for the firm/the mob was based not only on acting ability but our collective moviegoing memory of previous roles. In this case, though, filmmaker Pollack self-consciously played off the power of reverse typecasting. In previous pictures like *Country* and *Cocoon,* as well as the TV show *Our House,* Brimley had become a contemporary symbol for the charming curmudgeon, the nation's favorite grandfather. Moreover, he'd appeared in a long-standing series of Quaker Oats commercials that likewise projected a squeaky-clean image. When his character, Devasher, is then assigned to knock off Mitch, the effect borders on the grotesque, as the beloved old man menacingly stalks the youthful hero. Brimley was smart enough to realize he'd taken the grandfatherly bit as far as it could go; the wisest career move was to purposefully undermine it, which he did here with malicious relish.

Jeanne Tripplehorn as Abby, Mitch's upper-crust wife, who immediately sees through what is taking place (courtesy Paramount Pictures).

Mitch, who fulfilled his ambitions and graduated law school with honors, comforts his upscale wife, Abby (Jeanne Tripplehorn), when she fears that they are, for all intents and purposes, living in Stepford (courtesy Paramount Pictures, photo credit François Duhamel).

Cruise, who had emerged as the most popular young star of the 1980s, was perfectly cast as a representative figure for his times. His role made no major acting demands on him (as, say, *The Color of Money* and *Rain Man* had), instead allowing him to play off his

Mitch on the run: the shot recalls Cary Grant being pursued by the crop duster in Hitchcock's *North by Northwest,* another example of the "referencing" in contemporary films (courtesy Paramount Pictures, photo credit François Duhamel).

natural charisma. The notable performances are the supporting ones, including Gary Busey as the hipster detective Mitch turns to in his early stages of panic, and the gumshoe's spunky, funky secretary (Holly Hunter) who carries on (and, indeed, all but solves the case) after her boss's untimely demise. The finest acting is delivered by Gene Hackman as Avery Tolar, Mitch's "mentor." A once idealistic lawyer who long ago sold his soul for things material, Tolar is now the firm's agent for corrupting young inductees, turning them into carbon copies of himself. Hackman's performance perfectly crystallized the film's essential theme. His Tolar is a unique and believable person, cynical and bitter but not without touches of remorse, even self-loathing, for the corruption he has wallowed in, now using lawyerly skills to corrupt the young. Tolar views the world as a cesspool: this is the way life works, and to refuse to succumb would be naive idealism. Yet every time he corrupts a kid like Mitch, he relives his own loss of innocence. Tolar is caught in a hell of his own making.

In *The National Review,* John Simon defined the film as an example of a new, emerging type of crime thriller, in which the gangster not only appeared to be a bastion of the old established order but also knows how to use state-of-the-art communications equipment: "the kind of film whose excitement depends largely on computers, fax machines, surveillance devices, and other technological wonders suited to make action mechanistic, characters robotic, dialogue jargon, and villainy thrive. This is neither the old film noir nor the old-fashioned melodrama in which people were still people, however corrupt, and not mere adjuncts to diabolically cunning machines that rule the world." Though Simon made clear this did not appeal to his traditionalist taste in thrillers, he nonetheless defined a new subgenre that spoke for its era as effectively as the noir had for the late forties. *The Firm* revitalized the crime thriller by bringing it into the era of cynicism and computers.

FORTY-FIVE

The Fugitive

(1993)

A Warner Bros. Release

CAST:

Harrison Ford *(Dr. Richard Kimble);* Tommy Lee Jones *(Sam Gerard);* Jeroen Krabbe *(Dr. Charles Nichols);* Julianne Moore *(Dr. Anne Eastman);* Joe Pantoliano *(Renfro);* L. Scott Caldwell *(Poole);* Sela Ward *(Helen Kimble);* Andreas Katsulas *(Sykes);* Daniel Roebuck *(Biggs);* Tom Wood *(Newman).*

CREDITS:

Producer, Arnold Kopelson; director, Andrew Davis; screenplay, Jeb Stuart and David Twohy, based on characters created by Roy Huggins; cinematography, Michael Chapman; editors, Dennis Virkler and David Finfer; music, James Newton Howard; production design, Dennis Washington; running time, 128 minutes; rating, PG-13.

One unique subgenre of the crime film is the "wrong man" movie, perfected by Alfred Hitchcock during his long and distinguished career, both in England *(The 39 Steps)* and America *(The Saboteur).* Television took on the wrong-man concept between 1963 and 1967 with *The Fugitive,* Roy Huggins's classic continuing drama about Dr. Richard Kimble (David Janssen). Wrongly convicted of murdering his wife, Kimble went on the run after escaping from prison, always searching for the one-armed man (Bill Raisch) he'd seen leaving his home on the night of the killing, likewise pursued by an obsessive police detective (Barry Morse). A combination of a Road Runner/Wile E. Coyote chase cartoon and *Les Misérables,* the series set a disguised Kimble down in a different situation each week, wherein he impacted on the lives of characters played by guest stars, only to have his cover blown just as Lieutenant Gerard closed in, once again slipping away in the nick of time.

The only disappointment about the old show was the ending. In a much-anticipated, widely watched two-parter, Kimble finally proved his innocence by returning to his hometown and unmasking the culprit as a childhood friend (J. D. Cannon). But this man's supposed motivations seemed desperate and contrived. After four years of devoted watching, during which time most viewers assumed that if not the one-armed man himself, the killer must be the overly dedicated Gerard, the ending played as a facile deus ex machina, dramatically and emotionally unsatisfying.

Like so many other baby-boomer favorites from thirty years earlier, ranging in style and subject from *Twilight Zone* and *The Untouchables* to *The Beverly Hillbillies* and *The Addams Family, The Fugitive* was ripe for a major-motion-picture remake. Such shows had never slipped out of the public's consciousness, all of them constantly exposed to new generations of couch potatoes via regular reruns. But whereas most TV-inspired projects resulted in overblown and synthetic packagings that failed to convey the simple, basic charms of the originals, *The Fugitive* proved to be the true gem. By taking only the essential premise from the show, then mounting a totally original interpretation, the filmmakers came up with a fresh variation on a time-honored, rather than time-worn, theme.

One key element of the success was the choice of Andrew Davis as director. One year earlier, he had proven his talent at mounting contemporary crime films with a strong action-adventure orientation via *Under Siege,* essentially *Die Hard* on a ship and the best of the Steven Seagal martial arts vehicles. Back in 1985, Davis had directed another martial arts expert, Chuck Norris, in *Code of Silence,* pitting the star against both the Mafia and corrupt police, likewise providing that nonactor with his finest hour on-screen. Wisely forsaking the purposefully claustrophobic scope and emotionally intimate style of the hour-long TV episodes, Davis expanded the *Fugitive* concept for a wide-screen, state-of-the-art spectacle, emphasizing big-scale stunts and intense edge-of-your-seat suspense, finally providing a grandstanding

Kimble's escape (courtesy Warner Bros.).

final confrontation between the film's Kimble and Gerard rather than their underplayed interchanges of the original.

Davis made the very kind of film audiences of today want to see, one that just happened to be based on a beloved old idea. In soft-spoken, wholesome-looking Harrison Ford and darkly charismatic Tommy Lee Jones, he found popular actors of our time who in no way resembled the stars (surly and tight-lipped, respectively) of the show, or in any way imitated their approach to the roles, thereby dismissing all unflattering comparisons. Finally, scriptwriters Jeb Stuart and David Twohy came up with a resolution in which a fellow physician (Jeroen Krabbe) turns out to be the true culprit, resulting in a far more believable and therefore satisfying conclusion than had been the case with the old show.

They did, however, understand that one key element of the show's success came in Kimble's willingness to expose himself to arrest (and certain death) for the sake of strangers around him. Here, Kimble, while hiding out at a Chicago hospital, notes that a doctor has misdiagnosed an accident victim, then wins great viewer sympathy by risking his neck to make certain that the patient is sent to the proper ward. Tired of amoral 1990s antiheroes, moviegoers found an acceptably old-fashioned hero here, one willing to consider the good of others as well as his own fate. A modern equivalent of Gary Cooper, Harrison Ford was able to convey such heroics with total conviction. As a movie, then, *The Fugitive* had it both ways, being a successful variation on the series while standing firmly on its own cinematic feet, playing as a singular piece for that rare person who never heard of the show and therefore approached this work without any tinge of nostalgia.

Kimble is constrained (courtesy Warner Bros.).

inspiring sequences, crawling about on Lincoln's nose at Mt. Rushmore.

Today, we can note the seams in that classic; owing to the modern audience's visual sophistication, Hitchcock's intercutting between studio mock-ups and the actual Mt. Rushmore locations is obvious in a way that it was not back in 1959. We can tolerate such discrepancies in older films owing to our appreciation of the limitations of moviemaking in those times, but would not sit still for them now. *The Fugitive* is completely state-of-the-art, making Kimble's leaps and escapes appear totally plausible.

It hardly seems fortuitous that the old show ran between 1963 and 1967, those awkward, uneasy years between the death of Jack Kennedy with his optimistic dream of a New Frontier and the subsequent assassinations of Robert Kennedy and Dr. Martin Luther King,

Kimble at his moment of truth, when the good doctor must choose between serving mankind and helping himself (courtesy Warner Bros.).

Chief among the spectacular sequences were the brilliantly staged train/bus wreck in which Kimble is accidentally freed while on his way to a penitentiary for execution, and an unforgettable dive from a dam and down into a waterfall that ranks with the most memorable stunt sequences ever put on film. Janet Maslin of the *New York Times* admitted to having reservations about yet another remake of an old crime tale, but was happily thrilled to discover "a cliché-free story told at a breakneck pace. In appreciating *The Fugitive*, it's worthwhile to mention what the film is missing. It has no gratuitous bloodshed, no noxious posturing, and no sadism. There are no schoolyard insults or four-letter witticisms, of the sort so often used when nothing better comes to the screenwriters' minds." In this respect, the film appeared less a remake of TV's *The Fugitive* than a contemporary variation on such Hitchcock crime-thriller/fit-for-the-entire-family entertainments as *North by Northwest,* with its own wrong-man hero involved in big-scale vertigo-

Tommy Lee Jones in his Oscar-winning role as deputy U.S. marshal Sam Gerard, accompanied by his assistants (Joe Pantoliano and Daniel Roebuck). *The Fugitive* is that rare case of a beloved old TV series being effectively transformed into a modern motion picture (photo by Stephen Vaughan, courtesy Warner Bros.).

events that immediately lead to the radicalization of mainstream America during the final years of that troubled and remarkable decade. With his constant assuming of new poses, as well as endless anxiousness without having done anything to feel guilty about, the show's Kimble served as a fitting metaphor for the American people of that time, trying on new pop-culture roles in a manner that Alvin Toffler described with the term *future shock*—changes coming so rapidly that the public could not adjust to them, until the pressure finally resulted in a kind of inner explosion. The motion picture instead transformed the fugitive story into an equally fitting allegory for our own times. As Philip French wrote in *The London Observer,* "the central populist thrust, like that of *The Firm,* is an indictment of corporate greed and professional corruption." Though based on a 1960s series, this movie was for, and about, the nineties.

The kind of spectacular, expensive set-pieces so impossible on weekly television were now fully realized in this expansive retelling of the tale (photo by Stephen Vaughan, courtesy Warner Bros.).

FORTY-SIX

True Romance

(1993)

A Warner Bros. Release

CAST:

Christian Slater *(Clarence Worley);* Patricia Arquette *(Alabama Whitman);* Dennis Hopper *(Clifford Worley);* Val Kilmer *(Mentor/Elvis);* Gary Oldman *(Drexl Spivey);* Brad Pitt *(Floyd);* Christopher Walken *(Vincenzo Coccotti);* Saul Rubinek *(Lee Donowitz);* Bronson Pinchot *(Elliot Blitzer);* Michael Rapaport *(Dick Ritchie);* Chris Penn *(Nicky Dimes).*

CREDITS:

Producers, Samuel Hadida, Steve Perry, and Bill Unger; director, Tony Scott; screenwriter, Quentin Tarantino; cinematography, Jeffrey L. Kimball; editors, Michael Tronick and Christian Wagner; music, Hans Zimmer; production design, Benjamin Fernandez; running time, 118 minutes; rating, R.

In a much-discussed 1994 *New York* magazine essay, Tad Friend argued that white trash had already emerged as the overriding pop-culture iconography for the developing decade. The very lifestyle that, during the first half of the century, our upwardly mobile mainstream had attempted to escape from had, owing to a pendulum swing in manners and morals, ironically transformed into an ideal at a time when people were downscaling expectations. This reversal in values had germinated during the late 1950s with the advent of Elvis, when teenagers adopted the greaser attitude in open rebellion against the suburban-conventional sensibility of their parents. Though those parents believed that in time the kids would grow up, it didn't happen. As the baby boomers aged, they continued wearing blue jeans and listening to rock 'n' roll.

As the century moved inexorably toward its conclusion, what had once been considered déclassé behavior became exalted as the nouveau norm. Case in point: the ascent of trashy Roseanne Arnold as TV's wife/mother superstar, in sharp contrast to wholesome Donna Reed of a bygone era. *Married With Children*'s blue-collar urban redneck family of slackers had supplanted the ever-aspiring couple on *I Love Lucy*. Ultimately, there was the presidency of Bill Clinton, whose nickname among Secret Service agents is, not coincidentally; Elvis, Clinton, who grew up worshiping Elvis; was the inevitable head of state for such an era.

By *white trash,* Friend referred to "the galloping sleaze that has overrun both rural and urban America." The *National Enquirer* in print and *A Current Affair* on TV had usurped the positions once held by the *New York Times* and *60 Minutes* as key news organs for a public that no longer wanted the media to lift them ever upward, but was rather looking for a wallow. "It's also the phrase that best gives voice to the stifled longing of the well-to-do, who covet what they perceive as the spontaneous authenticity of the poor," Friend continued. Which explains why well-to-do teenagers bought pretorn jeans or affected the fishnet stockings, rhinestone earrings, cherry-red nail polish, and dime-store barrettes of the urban underclass. Madonna was the natural cultural icon for this age in which once-vulgar tattoos were now a status symbol.

Naturally, movies had to adjust to the phenomenon if they were to remain relevant. "Now screenwriters are obsessed with the idea of the road-tripping, spontaneous, and often murderous poor," Friend wrote. "It is ever tempting to Hollywood to impute authenticity to the ignorant—and to give them bodacious bods." Such movies included *Guncrazy* with Drew Barrymore, *Kalifornia* with Brad Pitt, and most notably *True Romance,* written by Quentin Tarantino, whose *Reservoir Dogs* had established the budding filmmaker as the voice for an entire generation. Though brilliant, he was a slacker: despite an estimated IQ of 160, Tarantino had dropped out of school, scorning traditional education to instead immerse himself in pop culture, becoming a walking-

Christian Slater as Clarence Worley, who, like his creator/counterpart Quentin Tarantino, is a comic book freak and video store junkie (courtesy Warner Bros./Morgan Creek Productions).

talking encyclopedia of information about rock 'n' roll and such cinematic subgenres as the women's prison pictures produced in the Philippines and Asian-made martial arts epics. In his scripts, Tarantino created an apotheosis of junk culture, filtered through his striking imagination, absorbing everything that was irresistibly tacky from the past, perfectly presenting this punk package as the natural drama for the last decade of the twentieth century, an era in which the American mainstream loudly hooted down any and all previous ambitions to better itself, gleefully taking as many giant steps backward as possible. This was an age in which the kind of geek shows (Joey Buttafuoco, Lorena Bobbitt, et al.) that had once been relegated to the worst areas of the rural South were now on view everywhere, everyday, via Phil Donahue, Oprah Winfrey, and their endless imitators. It was impossible for people to continuously watch such stuff without inadvertently absorbing the antivalues therein suggested.

William Faulkner had, long ago, satirized the Snopes clan of Mississippi degenerate lowlifes as everything that an upwardly aspiring person would want to avoid. If he were writing today, he would more likely aggrandize them, as contemporary novelist Dorothy Allison did when, proudly proclaiming herself to be white trash, she admitted, "We're dangerous. We don't necessarily care for your life." This attitude was expressed by the title character Ashley Judd played in the 1993 movie *Ruby in Paradise* when she asked, "Why slave your life out when you can just take? Are there any real reasons for living right anyway?" Which explains why, if Quentin Tarantino had not come along when he did, Hollywood would have had to invent him; Tarantino provided the perfect artistic voice to express what was just then happening.

"Movies give us an airbrushed dream of white trash," Friend concluded, "alluring and deadly." That certainly describes to a tee Clarence Worley (Christian Slater) and Alabama Whitman (Patricia Arquette), a Bonnie and Clyde for the nineties who mindlessly journey across America in a fuchsia Cadillac (the automotive equivalent of pink lawn flamingos) on a murderous spree. The film is a fantasy projection of Tarantino's personality, a vision of what might have happened to him had circumstances propelled the writer into just such an unexpected excursion along America's seamier side. A Detroit comic-book salesman and pop-culture aficionado, Clarence idolizes Elvis, even consults the ghost (Val Kilmer) of the King—that great germinator of the now dominant white-trash culture—at moments of doubt. On his birthday, Clarence always treats himself to a kung fu triple feature, precisely how Tarantino indulged himself before hitting the big time.

His boss decides to send over a hooker; though Alabama is bubbleheaded, Clarence falls madly in love. When he heads to her pimp's residence, confronting the "Wigger" (played by Gary Oldman in dreadlocks, visually suggesting this white character's conscious assimilation into black street culture), Clarence kills the man. Upon learning this, Alabama initially looks shocked. "You are so-oo-oo...," she muses, and the audience waits for her next word: *horrible? violent? out of control?* "Romantic!" she sighs, throwing herself into Clarence's arms and kissing him wildly. In the white-trash sensibility, a whore views the killing of her pimp as the ultimate tribute by a new beau. Clarence is the lowbrow conception of a romantic hero, the amoral idealist who eliminates the unpleasant elements in his idiot inamorata's life.

He also steals a cache of cocaine, which they plan to sell. Unfortunately, it belonged to the mob, the villainous adult/established organized criminals always (in the contemporary crime film) at odds with the punk rebel youths. This sets up the film's best single scene: a slick mafioso (Christopher Walken) confronts Clarence's father (Dennis Hopper) in his dilapidated downscale apartment, planning on torturing the man to discern Clarence's whereabouts. Realizing this, Clarence's father manipulates the mobster into killing him quickly (so he won't be tempted to talk) by elucidating, in the most racist language imaginable, a theory. Centuries ago, the Moors entered Sicily and impregnated the women, making this mob kingpin part black. "Tarantino's specialty is hyperarticulate viciousness and 'playful' sadism," a shocked David Denby noted in *New York*. True, the scene serves as a virtual attack on the concept of political correctness. Anyone subscribing to the notion that our language (in life and films) ought to be rendered inoffensively sterile was shocked beyond belief. Yet this sequence remains one of the classic moments in modern movies, dealing honestly and artfully with the reality of racist thinking, as well as with words as they are truly employed by the immense American underclass.

Eventually, *True Romance* arrives where all modern crime films end, one way or another: in Hollywood. Just as Tarantino was the blue-collar boy who somehow found himself awash in corporate boardrooms of the contemporary movie business, so does his alter ego, Clarence, wind up in essentially the same place. The final shoot-out (cops, criminals, upscale Hollywood sleaze types plus the alluring low-life hero and heroine) occurs in a producer's office-suite. This is clearly a symbol as well as a clever setting. "A movie-mad fairy tale with a body count for modern times," Janet Maslin tagged *True Romance,* indicating that movies—particularly old crime movies—form the true subject of Tarantino's work. All roads lead to Hollywood; here, the place where crime films are conceived and then created serves as the logical spot for this contemporary crime film to reach its violent resolution.

Tony Scott seemed an unlikely choice to direct, considering his previous work: competent, conventional, soul-less exercises in slick, superficial action-adventure *(Top Gun, Beverly Hills Cop II)*. As it turned out, though,

Christopher Walken as the film's cold-blooded mafioso, Vincenzo Coccotti (courtesy Warner Bros./Morgan Creek Productions).

The modern man of a thousand faces, Gary Oldman, as Drexl Spivey (courtesy Warner Bros./Morgan Creek Productions).

Young love, true love: when Clarence informs Alabama that he's just killed her pimp, she's absolutely charmed, considering this a truly "romantic" gesture (photo by Ron Phillips, courtesy Warner Bros./Morgan Creek).

Alabama finds herself, like so many other crime film characters before her, under the gun (courtesy August Entertainment).

Scott's commerciality did not bury Tarantino's grunge sensibility, instead servicing it, allowing Tarantino an avenue into mainstream theaters that his earlier auteur piece as writer-director, *Reservoir Dogs* (a favorite of critics and cultists, though hardly a commercial success), had not achieved. "It's Tarantino's gutter poetry that detonates *True Romance*," Peter Travers remarked in *Rolling Stone*. Indeed, *True Romance* served as a second helping of the Tarantino vision that would continually electrify audiences throughout the 1990s.

Alabama Whitman and Clarence Worley, Quentin Tarantino's first stab at creating a Bonnie and Clyde couple for the nineties (photo by Ron Phillips, courtesy Warner Bros./Morgan Creek Productions).

FORTY-SEVEN

Carlito's Way

(1993)

A Universal Film

CAST:

Al Pacino *(Carlito);* Sean Penn *(David Kleinfeld);* Penelope Ann Miller *(Gail);* John Leguizamo *(Benny Blanco);* Ingrid Rogers *(Steffie);* Luis Guzman *(Pachanga);* James Rebhorn *(Norwalk);* Joseph Siravo *(Vinnie Taglialucci);* Paul Mazursky *(Judge Feinstein).*

CREDITS:

Producers, Martin Bregman, Willi Baer, and Michael S. Bregman; director, Brian De Palma; screenplay, David Koepp from the novels *Carlito's Way* and *After Hours* by Judge Edwin Torres; cinematography, Stephen H. Burum; editors, Bill Pankow and Kristina Boden; music, Patrick Doyle; production design, Richard Sylbert; running time, 141 minutes; rating, R.

Carlito Brigante is, like Tony Montana in *Scarface* and Michael Corleone in *Godfather III,* a gangster. That superficial similarity aside, this was an entirely original part, offering Al Pacino a unique challenge. If the gangster is our modern equivalent of the Shakespearean tragic hero, then Pacino's role in *Scarface* was his Richard III, the cold, calculating killing machine, a ruthless Machiavelli who cares for nothing but ascending to the top, pursuing power for the sheer sake of power. Pacino's role in *Godfather III* was his King Lear, the grand old man who attempts to pass on his dubiously achieved kingdom to the proper successor but is destroyed by the loss of his deeply loved daughter. Pacino's role as Carlito, the Puerto Rican gangster who returns to East Harlem after a five-year stint in prison and is soon deeply involved in a moral, philosophical assessment of his criminal past, is, in the words of Richard Alleva of *Commonweal,* "the gangster as Hamlet."

Carlito resembles many gangster heroes of classic Warner Bros. films from the 1930s, including Eddie Bartlett, James Cagney's character in Raoul Walsh's *The Roaring Twenties,* as well as a dozen other similar heroes of lesser films who also hoped to go straight but were forced back into a life of crime owing to their "codes": loyalty to a former cohort who begs the hero to help on one last heist and cannot be turned down. Filmmaker Brian De Palma effectively updated these familiar formulas for the realities of our time. Carlito is a "businessman" who tried to carve out his American dream via the drug trade instead of bootleg beer. "The J. P. Morgan of smack," one mobster tellingly calls him. His cohort is David Kleinfeld, upscale Jewish lawyer who began flirting with life on the wild side (representing wiseguys in court, proving adept at getting them off) and now balances the two sides of his existence, displaying fine old British paintings in his mahogany-lined office, then slipping off for a night of whoring and coke-snorting in glitzy/sleazy clubs: "Dershowitz on drugs," as a number of critics labeled him.

It was Kleinfeld who, in 1975, secured Carlito's release from prison after only five years (he'd been sent to Sing Sing for a thirty-year stretch) owing to irregularities (wiretapping) Kleinfeld uncovered in DA Norwalk's case against Carlito. Before walking onto the street as a free man, Carlito lectures Judge Feinstein (played by film director Paul Mazursky): "I ain't saying my 'way' would've been different had my mother not died when I was a kid. I was already a mean little bastard when my mother was alive." That speech, dazzlingly delivered by Pacino in his self-consciously grandstanding style, expresses the film's attitude toward criminal behavior: people are not criminals because they were neglected, abused, or disenfranchised by an insensitive society, but because it is their nature, and because they chose to be criminals.

We are what we make of ourselves, qualifying

Al Pacino as Carlito Brigante: the gangster as anachronism (courtesy Universal Pictures, photo credit Louis Goldman).

Carlito celebrates his early release from prison with lawyer David Kleinfeld (Sean Penn). One critic described Penn's performance as "Dershowitz on drugs" (courtesy Universal Pictures, photo credit Louis Goldman).

Carlito's Way as the thematic polar opposite of Edward James Olmos's *American Me*, which placed the blame squarely at the feet of society. Carlito now wants to make of himself an honest businessman, running a disco until he amasses enough money to head for the Bahamas and buy into a car rental business. He is sucked back into the mire not by the workings of fate (the vision of Coppola in *Godfather III*) but by his character. Carlito's "way" is to follow his code religiously. Kleinfeld has played fast and loose with mafiosi; if he is to avoid being hit, he must use his yacht to spring mobster Tony T. from Riker's Island. Kleinfeld asks Carlito to help, and though Carlito's girlfriend begs him not to go along, Carlito's choice is predetermined by his adherence to his code. He cannot let a friend down.

That is what separates him from the new breed of codeless gangsters now inhabiting the streets. As Carlito observes shortly after his return: "Ain't no more rackets out here. Just a bunch of cowboys, ripping each other off." That idea of cowboys is a key element, for Carlito has much in common with Gregory Peck as Ringo in *The Gunfighter*. Carlito here will eventually be gunned down not by Tony T.'s family of mafiosi, pursuing him as he tries to meet his woman and run away to Florida, but by Benny Blanco, the punk kid who earlier tried to befriend Carlito, then challenged him, all but disappearing from sight until he appears and pulls the trigger.

That moment concludes the film's third act, a long and involved chase sequence that more than makes up for the oftentimes long-winded, occasionally obvious drama preceding it. "In the climactic shoot-out," David Denby wrote in *New York*, "the camera seems to disregard the laws of gravity and mechanics and simply floats through the air from one perfect vantage point to another." In *The New Yorker*, Terrence Rafferty noted that Carlito was "a conventional genre piece embellished by a thrillingly imaginative visual style. Like much of De Palma's work, *[Carlito]* has a handful of brilliant, unnervingly powerful sequences that seem to detach themselves from the whole—to float up from the mundane narrative and take us, for a while, into some freer, higher air. When he brings off one of his daredevil set pieces, you can forgive him almost anything, even his clunky storytelling, because it's evident that his real interest lies in expanding the possibilities of visual expression. And, although his stylistic flourishes sometimes seem to come out of nowhere, they're never mere-

As is so often the case in American crime movies, the man's woman is also his conscience: Gail warns Carlito against associating with the arrogant Kleinfeld (courtesy Universal Pictures, photo credit Louis Goldman).

ly decorative; he's always trying to make the audience see more, and more clearly." Owen Gleiberman of *Entertainment Weekly* added: "As a director, Brian De Palma is never happier than when he can stop the show for one of his intricately executed, have-camera-will-travel suspense scenes, the kind that allow him to imagine, for a few heady moments, that he really is Alfred Hitchcock. Carlito and his pursuers play cat and mouse amid the corridors of Grand Central and end up firing at one another while riding up and down a pair of escalators. You can feel De Palma's joy at devising this ingeniously kinetic showdown—at liberating himself from the pesky burden of plot, dialogue, character."

One example of De Palma and screenwriter David Koepp (*Jurassic Park*) choosing to translate Edwin Torres's richly detailed accounts of contemporary criminals into visual language stands out. In the books, Gail is a teacher and social activist, whereas in the film, she becomes a ballet dancer who falls on hard times and turns stripper. Though some overly sensitive feminist critics interpreted this as a male moviemaker's superficial desire to have the female lead take off her clothes, De Palma's decision was aesthetic, not exploitative. Whereas in a novel it is possible to tell us in words about a subtle shift taking place inside a character's mind, in a movie we have to see that shift. This is achieved by having us glance over the shoulder of our voyeuristic hero as Carlito watches Gail dance for the first time, appearing elegant, pristine, virginal; to the film's Carlito, she is a classy goddess. When he then comes across her in a seedy joint, performing her bump-and-grind routine, he's devastated. We don't need any explanation: we see her current decadence, as opposed to her dashed dreams, in her reaction to him, as well as his disappointment in her, right there in Pacino's eyes.

Carlito is one more modern gangster as romantic hero, in love not so much with his woman as with his romanticized dream of her. It's to Carlito credit that, unlike many fellow modern gangsters, he will overcome his limiting romanticism, learning to accept Gail for the extremely good (if flawed) character she is. Some romantic dreams will not die, however, including Carlito's image of the paradise he would like to share with Gail. The movie begins at the end, when Carlito is shot; as he falls, De Palma's jarring camera angles, slow-motion effects, and striking black-and-white photography imply that Carlito is near the end of his life. The story that unfolds in flashback form is a colorful kaleidoscope of memories that pass through his mind as he lies dying. The first and last thing he spots is a billboard, advertising a sunny island resort. It is, of course, an overly idealized image, but Carlito—romantic that he is—believes if

His back against the wall, Carlito realizes he can still kill the old way (courtesy Universal Pictures, photo credit Louis Goldman).

he and Gail are ever able to make it there, then their lives will be perfect. It is this dream that sustains him through all that follows; it is this dream that he is contemplating when death overcomes him.

This adds an element of fatalism to the film or, as Rafferty put it, "tragic inevitability.…De Palma's direction in this opening sequence is so gravely beautiful that you start preparing yourself for the exhausting, cathartic emotional experience of genuine tragedy." Rafferty argued that De Palma was not able to sustain this level of involvement, owing to an ordinary story and a character who was never as engaging as he might have been. Other critics agreed; Gleiberman of *EW* argued that as "a deeply honorable man, Pacino is trying for something quieter and more emotional (than his selfish, amoral Tony Montana in *Scarface*). Yet the character as written is so morosely well-intentioned that he's a bit dull. Watching *Carlito's Way*, I never really believed that a heroin dealer and coolly pragmatic killer could be such a simple, romantic guy." Certainly, a major problem throughout Pacino's career (and one key reason why he

The gangster as romantic hero: Carlito is reunited with his one-time dream girl and attempts to accept her far seedier reality (photo credit Louis Goldman, courtesy Universal Pictures).

acter who has no relationship whatsoever to any other role Penn previously played.

Carlito's Way was to have been filmed in the midseventies, as a comment on the then-contemporary street scene. Pacino agreed to do Carlito with several different directors, though for various reasons the film failed to get made. Interestingly enough, then, what was originally to have been a "now" movie had instead to be rethought as a period piece, a movie about drugs in the age of disco and pre-AIDS sexual liberation. Janet Maslin wrote in the *New York Times:* "The film's real heart is in the very places Carlito speaks of escaping [from]: the seedy social clubs and slick dance palaces where the story's main action unfolds. In these settings, letting his camera swoop and soar in countless unexpected ways, De Palma captures the grandiose romanticism" of an anachronistic hero who recoils in horror at the new breed of gangster who was just then muscling his way onto New York's mean streets.

dropped out of films for more than five years) is that he has never quite defined his position in films. Someone like Robert De Niro is more an actor than a star, so completely losing himself in a character that within minutes we totally forget who is playing the part. On the other hand, Clint Eastwood is always the same, transforming any number of tough cops, war heroes, and western gunslingers into differently costumed versions of his own basic star personality. Pacino offers a bit of both; though he is mesmerizing (as always) as Carlito, he is mesmerizing in the same way that he was mesmerizing in *Scent of a Woman* or *Serpico;* we always remain aware that it is indeed Pacino playing the part. In contrast, there is Sean Penn; within seconds, we have forgotten who is playing the role of Kleinfeld, so completely does he immerse himself in this specific character, a char-

Carlito finds himself drawn into Kleinfeld's latest scheme, and he is too loyal a friend to let the man down (photo credit Louis Goldman, courtesy Universal Pictures).

FORTY-EIGHT

Romeo Is Bleeding

(1994)

A Gramercy/Polygram/Working Title Production

CAST:

Gary Oldman *(Jack);* Lena Olin *(Mona);* Roy Scheider *(Don Falcone);* Annabella Sciorra *(Natalie);* Dennis Farina *(Nick);* Juliette Lewis *(Sheri);* Michael Wincott *(Sal).*

CREDITS:

Producers, Hilary Henkin and Paul Webster; director, Peter Medak; screenplay, Henkin; cinematography, Dariusz Wolski; editor, Walter Murch; music, Mark Isham; production design, Stewart Wertzel; running time, 110 minutes; rating, R.

In the late 1980s, Americans wallowed in the first wave of delirious relief following Gorbachev's announcement that glasnost would herald the end of the Cold War. That happy euphoria proved short-lived; with communism crumbling, Russia embraced the worst aspects of decadent capitalism. A drug culture soon flourished; with it came organized crime in the form of a Soviet Mafia. *Romeo Is Bleeding* was the first major film to acknowledge that alliance, dramatizing the way in which the American and Russian Mafias symbolically began sleeping together by introducing two representative characters who do precisely that: Roy Scheider as Don Falcone, an aging American mobster, involved with Lena Olin as Mona Demarkov, deadly Soviet hit lady who immigrates and, like so many previous immigrant criminals from diverse countries, buys her American dream of success with a gun.

Near the end, a bound-and-gagged Falcone stands in a field, watching as another man digs the grave into which he will shortly be placed, still alive, then covered. Mona observed all this coolly.

> FALCONE: *(nervously)* We could have shared it all.
>
> MONA: *(cynically)* We did.

It's impossible to feel much for Falcone, however, since he brought about his fate by soliciting the second man, Jack Grimaldi (Gary Oldman), to kill Mona before she could do precisely what she's doing: seize power. Like Falcone, gravedigger Jack fell under Mona's hypnotic spell. So it is Falcone who will be killed, though Jack eventually turns his gun on the delectable dame. *Romeo* offers a modernization of film noirs from the 1940s, here endowed with a postperestroika spin. Screenwriter/coproducer Hilary Henkin effectively retained essential elements of the past (seedy hero, sordid settings, duplicitous women, uncontrollable greed, endless plot reversals, clever twists of fate) while neatly updating those elements for political and social realities of the nineties.

Likewise, director Peter Medak employed an arch, shadowy visual sensibility, augmented by a mood-drenched musical score recalling the bygone aesthetic of a big-city saloon. The result is a film that, like Lawrence Kasdan's erotic thriller *Body Heat,* clearly takes place today, yet allows us the impression of characters who live in a netherworld, their early-1990s reality drenched in a nostalgia for the enduring film style of the late 1940s.

The focal character is Jack, second cousin to Harvey Keitel's on-the-take cop from *Bad Lieutenant.* A member of the Organized Crime Task Force, Jack assists in the Witness Protection Program, holding mobsters like Nick Cessare (Dennis Farina) in safe limbo till they can be relocated to some obscure spot in the Southwest, in appreciation for information about organized crime bosses. But Jack is playing both sides of the fence; he supplies information to Falcone, who then assigns hit lady Mona to eliminate a betraying criminal before he can sing. In the case of Nick, Mona goes too

far for Jack, killing not only the gangster but also the cops guarding him. When authorities then grab Mona, Jack—true to form—reports the location to Falcone through their contact man, Sal. But Mona has already been moved, then escaped her captors. Falcone gives Jack an ultimatum: find Mona and eliminate her in three days or suffer the consequences.

Having enjoyed the rush from living his dangerous double life, Jack realizes it's now careening completely out of control. Likewise, his personal life falls apart. Jack has been carefully balancing a sordid affair with Sheri (Juliette Lewis), a cocktail waitress, and a seemingly normal home life with Natalie (Annabella Sciorra), his conventional wife. Sheri greets him in a dingy room, wearing garish red lingerie; Natalie patiently waits for him at their suburban tract house, humbly offering a dinner she's prepared from her new happy homemaker's recipe book even as Jack, sounding like a TV sitcom cliché, announces, "Honey, I'm home." But Jack is stressed as the two women appear to switch identities, Sheri ever more traditional, Natalie doing inexplicably kinky things. Then again, this may merely be Jack's perception. *Romeo* is accompanied by his voice-over narration, suggesting that we share Jack's subjective vision of the events.

Jack finds himself in an even wilder place when the very woman he has been contracted to hit, Mona, suggests he double-cross Falcone, convincing the mobster that some other body is Mona's. In so deep that he can't get out, the by now fatalistic Jack agrees, little realizing his own mistress will provide the necessary corpse. Before long, the film's plot is as complicated (and nearly incomprehensible) as that of Howard Hawks's *The Big Sleep*. Whether that statement is perceived as a compliment or a criticism depends entirely on whether one can accept the unique rules of the noir subgenre.

Importantly, "Romeo" is a nickname for Jack, who, in the tradition of other heroes of modern gangster movies, remains a true romantic throughout. When we first encounter Jack, he is living under the name Jim Doherty, having himself been relocated to the ironically named Holiday Diner, a greasy spoon out on the desert near Phoenix, Arizona. Jack glances through an album of old photos, each page lovingly displaying one of the women he has loved and lost. He keeps glancing at the calendar, hoping desperately that the last of those women still alive (wife Natalie) will walk through the door, carrying the suitcase with $350,000 in dirty money

Gary Oldman as Jack: the crooked cop as romantic existentialist (courtesy Gramercy Pictures).

Jack, who has been living a double life as a middle-class suburbanite and career criminal, is unmasked and apprehended much as Jekyll and Hyde are in the old Robert Louis Stevenson story. He is likewise a symbolic second cousin to the character played by Harvey Keitel in *Bad Lieutenant* (courtesy Gramercy Pictures).

he handed her, instructing her to meet him at this place on May 1, this year or next or…

"Jack," he says of his former self, "was a romantic guy." We see that romanticism in every aspect of his life, beginning with his job, which entails keeping an eye on gangsters through binoculars. Like the voyeuristic heroes of Hitchcock films, Jack is entranced by what he sees: particularly, an old gangster who enjoys three young women simultaneously. The other cops get a kick out of watching, but Jack wants it all for himself: "What's he got that Jack don't have?" What the man has is, simply, the gangster lifestyle. Jack wants to possess what he sees, without giving up the conventional. He wants to have it both ways, and that will set into motion his tragedy. Understandably, then, he makes his sad little cocktail waitress play out scenes that are pallid imitations of the spied-upon gangster's exotic escapades.

When Jack is with Natalie, he tells her that he loves her and sounds completely sincere. When he's with Sheri, he says precisely the same thing, again appearing to mean it. One might interpret Jack as the consummate actor, and to a degree that's true. However, the key to understanding Jack is that he's split right down the middle, meaning everything that he says to his wife yet also meaning what he says to his mistress. He makes elaborate plans to run away with each, in emotional denial of the encroaching truth: the two schemes are mutually exclusive.

When Jack is with Sheri, he's unable to make love unless she first plays out a scenario in which she's Marilyn Monroe; ultimately, Jack wants to make love to a dream, a movie-inspired dream at that. If we feel for Jack, it's for the same reason we were able to feel for James Cain's heroes; despite a hard-boiled surface cynicism, he is a softy at heart.

Jack cannot go to bed with a woman without falling

Mona (Lena Olin) makes love to Jack after handcuffing him to the brass bed: the film noir woman, revised and redesigned for the post-perestroika age (courtesy Gramercy Pictures).

in love with her; when he does that, he turns over the reins of power to the woman, who then drives the one-time driver. Noir has always dealt with the vulnerability of tough guys for seemingly delicate women, and Jack is just such an unkempt romantic. "Can I tell you what makes love so frightening?" Jack asks his sympathetic listener. "It's that you don't own it. It owns you." For a proper sense of closure, *Romeo* ends with a return to the framing device: the Holiday Diner, which echoes the isolated roadside station in what many now consider the greatest of all forties noirs, *Out of the Past,* that equally pathetic little place where Robert Mitchum waited hopefully, endlessly, romantically, for double-crossing Jane Greer to see the error of her ways and someday return.

Lena Olin as Mona, the modern liberated woman as cold-blooded hit lady (courtesy Gramercy Pictures).

Likewise, Jack thinks he sees Natalie showing up on the annual anniversary of the agreed-upon date and rushes to meet her. But Natalie's image dissolves into thin air, because what he (and we) have seen is the way things ought to be in Jack's still-romantic mind, not the way they really are. "She could come walking through that door any minute," Jack/Jim insists. "I bet she still loves me." That's what we hear him say; what we see is the endless desert surrounding him, a desert that represents what his life has become. His desperate desire for more ultimately left him with nothing except those romantic dreams, which, though shattered, he still clings to. Jack has to; he possesses nothing else.

Even Mona is something of a romantic, at one point growing sentimental when she weepily describes her "first time" to Jack; then we realize she's talking about the first time she ever hit a man, not the first time she made love. As in so many modern gangster movies, sex and violence quickly become intertwined here. Mona likes to kill her previous lovers, preferring to do that while the man is handcuffed to a bed. When she straps Jack down in precisely that position, and dons an S&M black leather costume before joining him, it's impossible for Jack (or the audience) to tell whether she plans to kiss him, kill him, or first do one and then the other.

"Very modern," someone says about Mona after she coldly kills the cops along with her target Nick, "doesn't care about nothing." Another says, "It's not her talking that Falcone's afraid of. She wants it all." Falcone himself notes that this is true, telling Jack, "Eventually, I'll be destroyed. The next generation of barbarians is waiting to take over. People like Mona. I don't have to throw open the doors for them." He is the film's Michael Corleone, the once-barbaric gangster who has become elegant (thousand-dollar suits, mansionlike home, haute cuisine on the table) in his sunset years and is now offended by the harsh nouveau styles of today's contemporary mobsters.

Mona is merely the representative of the future. "It's the fall of Rome out there," one of Jack's fellow cops sighs. That is the vision of not only *Romeo Is Bleeding,* but of the modern crime movie: a world beyond repair, in which violence has become widespread and the once-dominant codes (even for criminals) have been tossed aside, into the gutter. It is not a pretty picture, yet it is one that the grim gangster films of the nineties insist upon.

Jack (Gary Oldman) finds himself under (or, in this case, above) the gun (courtesy Gramercy Pictures).

UC SANTA
PLATO
SLUG
SANTA CRUZ
BANANA

FORTY-NINE

Pulp Fiction

(1994)

A Miramax Films Release

CAST:

John Travolta *(Vincent Vega);* Samuel L. Jackson *(Jules);* Uma Thurman *(Mia);* Harvey Keitel *(the Wolf);* Tim Roth *(Pumpkin);* Amanda Plummer *(Honey Bunny);* Maria de Madeiros *(Fabienne);* Bruce Willis *(Butch);* Christopher Walken *(Koons);* Eric Stoltz *(Lance);* Rosanna Arquette *(Jody);* Ving Rhames *(Marsellus Wallace);* Frank Whaley *(Thug).*

CREDITS:

Producer, Lawrence Bender; director and screenwriter, Quentin Tarantino, from stories by Roger Avary and Tarantino; cinematography, Andrzej Sekula; editor, Sally Menke; music, Karyn Rachtman; production design, David Wasco; costumes, Betsy Heimann; running time, 153 minutes; rating, R.

Following *Reservoir Dogs*—a critical if not commercial smash—Quentin Tarantino clearly had no competition as the most significant auteur to emerge in the crime-film genre since Martin Scorsese unleashed *Mean Streets* more than twenty years earlier. Tall, lanky, and awkward looking, Tarantino was a twenty-year-old high school dropout in 1983 when he accepted a $4-an-hour job as a clerk at Video Archives, a small specialty shop in California's Manhattan Beach area. The meager pay meant little to him, considering that he was allowed unlimited free rentals. Shortly, he was the customers' favorite employee, enthusiastically recommending esoteric items and seemingly possessed of an encyclopedic knowledge of junk movies. Tarantino freely admits to having been a "film geek," one of those social misfits who have nothing in life to sustain them (good job, girlfriend, etc.) other than an abiding love of the films "polite" people would never consider watching: Three Stooges comedy shorts, ultraviolent Sonny Chiba martial arts mini-epics, and women-in-prison flicks—exploitation items shot in faraway places, boasting such titles as *Caged Heat* or *The Big Bird Cage.*

Endless hours were spent sitting around a table in some shabby diner that hadn't been updated since the 1950s, in discussions of the Madonna phenomenon or various other aspects of pop culture. For the great majority of film geeks, that's where it all begins and all ends. Tarantino, though, went a step further. Returning to his apartment, he would set to work writing down those long-winded, labyrinthian, bizarre discussions word for word in screenplay form, turning life into art or at least a reasonable facsimile thereof. Eventually, Tarantino giddily yanked noir into the nineties by remaining faithful to the essence of old crime films and the irresistibly seedy pulp novels that inspired them, while at the same time revealing his vivid ear for the way people really do talk today.

Jules, Vincent, and the Wolf (Harvey Keitel) study a bloody mess and decide how to handle the situation (photo credit Linda R. Chen, courtesy Miramax Films).

The commercial opening of *Pulp Fiction* was preceded by ecstatic word of mouth from the previous spring's Cannes Film Festival, where Tarantino had been hailed as the new boy genius of the American cinema, and an equally strong reaction several months later when *Pulp Fiction* opened the New York Film Festival. The script had been strong (if grotesque) enough to lure A-list actors to the ensemble project. At a time when people of liberal values and middlebrow tastes were attempting to create a healthier environment through a more sensitive approach to minority issues in the media and a corresponding de-emphasis on sex and violence in film and TV, Tarantino gleefully thumbed his nose at all such do-gooders, unleashing a movie composed almost exclusively of racial epithets and random violence: a virtual attack, through art, of the notion of political correctness.

Pulp Fiction is constructed of three interlocking stories, all taking place in L.A. during a twenty-four-hour period. Like *Reservoir Dogs,* it begins (and, unlike the earli-

Honey Bunny (Amanda Plummer) and Pumpkin (Tim Roth) discuss the possibility of robbing the diner they're sitting in. The couple represent yet another Quentin Tarantino update of *Bonnie and Clyde*, bridging the gap between the young lovers in *True Romance* and *Natural Born Killers* (photo by Linda R. Chen, courtesy Miramax Films).

er film, also ends) in a diner, where Pumpkin (Tim Roth) and Honey Bunny (Amanda Plummer), second cousins of the characters played by Christian Slater and Patricia Arquette in *True Romance*, engage in one of those characteristically elliptical Tarantino conversations. The two small-time criminals discuss at length the curious fact that no one ever robs diners, an oversight they hope to correct with the guns concealed under their shirts. Tarantino then cuts away (we will not see these two again until the very end) to a pair of misanthropic hit men. Scraggly, long-haired heroin addict Vincent (John Travolta) is partnered with Jules (Samuel L. Jackson), who sports a wildly anachronistic 1970s Afro lifted right out of one of those black-exploitation films Tarantino adores. The two casually discuss such mundane matters as the strange names assigned in Paris to familiar items on the McDonald's menu, while sauntering over to an apartment in which they will brutally execute several young men. The mundane casually leading into the grotesque is essential to Tarantino's strategy. The third plot involves prizefighter Butch (Bruce Willis), ordered by the mob to throw a bout, who instead beats his opponent to death, then attempts an escape with his well-intentioned but none too bright girlfriend (Maria de Medeiros).

The three plots constantly rub up against one another. Vincent will be assigned to whack Butch for his transgression, though not before he has a near-transgression of his own. Assigned to entertain the seductive wife, Mia (Uma Thurman), of brutal mobster Marsellus (Ving Rhames) while this ganef godfather is out of town, Vincent takes her dancing in a trendy retro-fifties diner (waiters are doubles for Marilyn Monroe, Buddy Holly, and other 1950s icons) in hopes of avoiding a situation in which they'll end up in bed. This allows Tarantino to have Travolta twist to a Chuck Berry standard, a happy homage to the actor's early hit *Saturday Night Fever*. Fate then intervenes in the form of Mia's drug overdose, which sets the two tearing off to Vincent's dealer (Eric Stoltz) and his flaky girlfriend (Rosanna Arquette), who offer bemused advice and a slight amount of help.

At the movie's end, Vincent and Jules have breakfast in that diner glimpsed in the opening (epitomizing the shabby reality of a 1950s diner, in comparison to the sleek, sprawling idealization of such a place that Vincent and Mia visit in midmovie). While the two are engaged in another of those extended absurdist conversations (this time, their subject is the relative cleanliness of pigs and dogs), would-be criminals Pumpkin and Honey Bunny attempt their robbery. The film, elliptical in structure, has at last come full-circle, ending where it began. The couple is stopped in its tracks by the cold-blooded team of professionals who, coincidentally or owing to the workings of fate, happen to be there.

Earlier, however, Tarantino leaped forward in time to show Vincent being killed by Butch. Vincent's fatal flaw is that he spends too much time reading in the bathroom (another characteristic Tarantino touch), so was unfortunately in the can at that moment when Butch

A nervous suburbanite (Quentin Tarantino) looks on as the Wolf calls his gangland bosses. Tarantino does not merely perform cameos, but in fact plays key (if small) roles in his movies (photo credit Linda R, Chen, courtesy Miramax Films).

Bruce Willis as Butch: a brilliant variation on the traditional pulp-fiction boxer paid to take a fall, who then just can't go through with it (photo credit Linda R. Chen, courtesy Miramax Films).

(whom Vincent was assigned to whack) returned to his apartment to retrieve a beloved relic before fleeing L.A. Such a daring plot gamble would prove disastrous in most films, yet it's another wild narrative ride that Tarantino, in his endearingly goofy way, somehow manages to pull off. He purposefully breaks every rule of story structure or tonal consistency only to prove that rules really do exist to be broken, if the filmmaker can but dazzle and delight us with his transgressions.

The reviews were ecstatic. In *Entertainment Weekly,* Owen Gleiberman wrote: "Watching *Pulp Fiction,* you don't just get engrossed in what's happening on-screen. You get intoxicated by it. We're caught up in dialogue of such fiendishly elaborate wit it suggests a Martin Scorsese film written by Preston Sturges with its densely propulsive fervor, its peppery comic blend of literacy and funk. *Pulp Fiction* is the work of a new-style punk virtuoso. Tarantino creates a dizzying spectacle of life at its darkest, only to release us, with a wink, into the light." *Variety* hailed the film as "the *American Graffiti* of crime pictures."

Tarantino himself (who did a cameo in *Reservoir Dogs*) plays a key role at precisely that moment when the film's jaundiced, off-kilter vision of reality insists the real world is always on the verge of spilling over into a grotesquerie quite beyond anything we can generally agree upon as ordinary. In the heightened ugliness of our era, reality has become surreal. What was once considered a dramatist's distortion of actuality has, in an America that's long since left any vestige of normalcy behind, emerged as nothing more than a passing comment on the way things are. While Jules drives away from a hit, Vincent—still holding his pistol—turns to speak with a friend in the backseat, accidentally blowing the young man's head off. The car is literally awash in blood, as are Vincent and Jules, so they stop by the home of a friend (Tarantino), a pathetic henpecked husband who lives in an *Ozzie and Harriet* suburban house that the hit men, drenched in gore, invade.

Enter Winston Wolf (Harvey Keitel), a criminal genius paid huge sums by top mobsters to repair just such impossible situations. Wolf arrives on the scene, exuding the professorial aura of a brain surgeon who never operates himself, calmly overseeing the most delicate work. His final diagnosis is classic: Jules and Vincent ought to wash away the blood from the car, then dispose of their dirtied clothes. Wolf's exalted reputation resides in his ability to maintain a sense of quietude, applying the dictates of simplicity in situations so over-the-top that a lesser man would have insisted dire steps needed to be taken. Similarly, Tarantino's talent rests in his ability to make us see the existential absurdity of all this and accept it as not only a part of the contemporary crime genre, but also—more frightening still—as a commentary on the world we live in.

Uma Thurman as Mia, a bizarre combination of sex kitten, gangster's moll, and vulnerable child-woman. She feels at home in a retro-fifties diner, since Mia was drawn from the portraits of just such shady ladies presented in paperback novels of that era (photo by Linda R. Chen, courtesy Miramax Films).

FIFTY

Natural Born Killers

(1994)

A Warner Bros. Release

CAST:

Woody Harrelson *(Mickey);* Juliette Lewis *(Mallory);* Robert Downey Jr. *(Wayne Gale);* Tommy Lee Jones *(McClusky);* Tom Sizemore *(Jack Scagnetti);* Rodney Dangerfield *(Mallory's Dad);* Russell Means *(Old Indian);* Edie McClurg *(Mallory's Mom);* Balthazar Getty *(Gas Station Attendant);* Joe Grifasi *(Duncan Homolka);* O-Lan Jones *(Mabel).*

CREDITS:

Producers, Jane Hamsher, Don Murphy, and Clayton Townsend; director, Oliver Stone; screenplay, Stone, David Veloz, Richard Rutowski, from a story by Quentin Tarantino; cinematography, Robert Richardson; editors, Hank Corwin and Brian Berdan; music, Budd Carr; production design, Victor Kempster; costumes, Richard Hornung; running time, 119 minutes; rating, R.

If *Bonnie and Clyde* served as the archetype for the modern crime movie, the germination point for all the emerging themes and stylistic techniques that would follow, then *Natural Born Killers* rates as the apotheosis of that contemporary genre, taking the very same subject matter to its logical if frightening conclusion. Like *Bonnie and Clyde,* this is the story of two young outlaw lovers, on the lam from the Establishment, transformed into pop celebrities by the media.

Yet *Natural Born Killers* is as much a film of the mid-1990s as *Bonnie and Clyde* was of the late 1960s, so as much has changed as has remained the same. Now, the tone of romantic lyricism has disappeared, along with the period-piece trappings, replaced by an MTV phantasmagoria of grunge and gore. Oliver Stone's self-consciously cruel, unrelentingly nasty, seductively hallucinatory cinematic nightmare is as perfectly in tune with our times as Arthur Penn's appealingly balladic road movie was for the beginning of the hippie era. The film's first hour concerns the wild killing spree of Mickey (Woody Harrelson) and Mallory (Juliette Lewis) as they travel around the Southwest, punk/grunge variants of the characters played by Martin Sheen and Sissy Spacek in *Badlands.* Mickey and Mallory kill a total of fifty-two people (the murders graphically portrayed on-screen), including an elderly Indian (Russell Means), whose death is the only one they regret. He had apparently achieved a Native American equivalent of Eastern nirvana that the twosome truly admired. Other people, mainly hapless rednecks, are slaughtered like cattle, though Mickey and Mallory always leave one witness alive to tell the tale, thereby contributing to their growing cult status.

Juliette Lewis and Woody Harrelson as Mickey and Mallory. The contemporary crime film, set into motion with 1967's archetype *Bonnie and Clyde,* reaches its frightening apotheosis with *Natural Born Killers* (photo by Sidney Baldwin, courtesy Warner Bros.).

During the second hour, the captured couple are interviewed by a brash, arrogant TV reporter named Wayne Gale (Robert Downey Jr.). He combines the worst qualities of Robin Leach, with his overarch British accent accentuating the forced ebullience, and Geraldo Rivera, with his stomach-wrenching sanctimoniousness and pretentions to serious journalism. The newspaper columns and folk ballads about Bonnie and Clyde have given way to the full-blown media circus that surrounds such contemporary incidents, a point driven home at the end when Stone cuts away from his characters to images of their real-life counterparts, including Amy Fisher, the Menendez brothers, Tonya Harding, and—a late entry edited in days before the film's release—O. J. Simpson.

Like all films that derive from the pen of Quentin Tarantino, *Natural Born Killers* (a cross between his earlier *True Romance* and David Lynch's *Wild at Heart*) is played halfway between heightened drama and outright parody. It is an outlandish joke that Stone—better known for such relatively realistic films as *Born on the Fourth of July* and *Platoon*—vividly brought to the screen as an extended rock video, with most individual shots held no longer than a few seconds. Purposefully bizarre camera angles, garish neon lighting effects, and wildly cartoonish acting all conspire to transform *Natural Born Killers* into the screen equivalent of a bad drug experience. Stone went so far as to alternate between black-and-white imagery and full color shots, so surrealistic and stylized that they looked less real than the black and white.

Ordinarily a realist, stylistically speaking, Oliver Stone flirted with full-blown phantasmagoria for this over-the-top dream film about violence, American style (courtesy Warner Bros.).

The movie is as much about television, and the impact it has on contemporary culture, as it is about crime. The ultimate crime, *Natural Born Killers* seems to be saying, is the exploitation of the garish and the gory for the great American middle class, who watch their tabloid shows and revel in the nightly doses of white-trash losers cutting and killing people resembling those watching at home. The opening image of the movie is a TV screen. The camera pulls back to reveal it is located in a back-roads diner, where a waitress's search for something "exciting" to watch will shortly be interrupted by the first batch of brutal murders by Mickey and Mallory, who, at film's end, are the subject of the very show this waitress likes best, though this time she will be listed among the victims.

Most striking of all is the flashback sequence in which Mallory's troubled childhood is presented in the style of an old-fashioned TV sitcom, complete with phony laugh track. The conventional format exists in ironic contrast to the incendiary material, including abuse and incest. Near the end, Gale makes a wild play in hopes of capturing the highest ratings ever by broadcasting his TV show *(American Maniacs)* from the prison where Mickey and Mallory are held, doing so on Super Bowl Sunday. However outrageous the concept may sound, it isn't far from Phil Donahue's oft-discussed idea of telecasting an execution live on his show and, presumably, interviewing the person just before. In our ever more exaggerated times, it's difficult to mount a parody, since life is itself so grotesquely exaggerated. When everyday life becomes surreal, a film has to stretch ever further to appear distorted; *Natural Born Killers* does just that.

In *Newsweek,* David Ansen wrote that Stone "wants to deconstruct the way the media present murder for our delectation. From shot to shot, the style changes: from black and white to color, slow-mo to normal speed, 16 mm to 35, while the background music leaps from rock to opera. Disorienting us, Stone wants us to note how the medium alters the message—he wants to force us to watch ourselves watching a movie." Jack Kroll added: "A creature of the media himself, he's assaulting the media for its crucial role in a process of dehumanization that seems to be an inescapable feature of mass society."

Earlier films would have attempted to psychoanalyze Mickey and Mallory, explaining why they do the terrible things they do. This modernist movie makes fun of any desire to try to "understand" them: they are precisely what the title tells us they are, killers without consciences, incapable of rehabilitation and uninterested in the process. The warden (Tommy Lee Jones, in an uncharacteristically cartoonish performance) goes so far as to hire a supercop named Scagnetti (Tom Sizemore), himself something of a pop celebrity owing to self-aggrandizing books he's penned. Scagnetti visits the

Wayne Gale (Robert Downey Jr.) exploits Mickey for the purpose of high ratings (courtesy Warner Bros.).

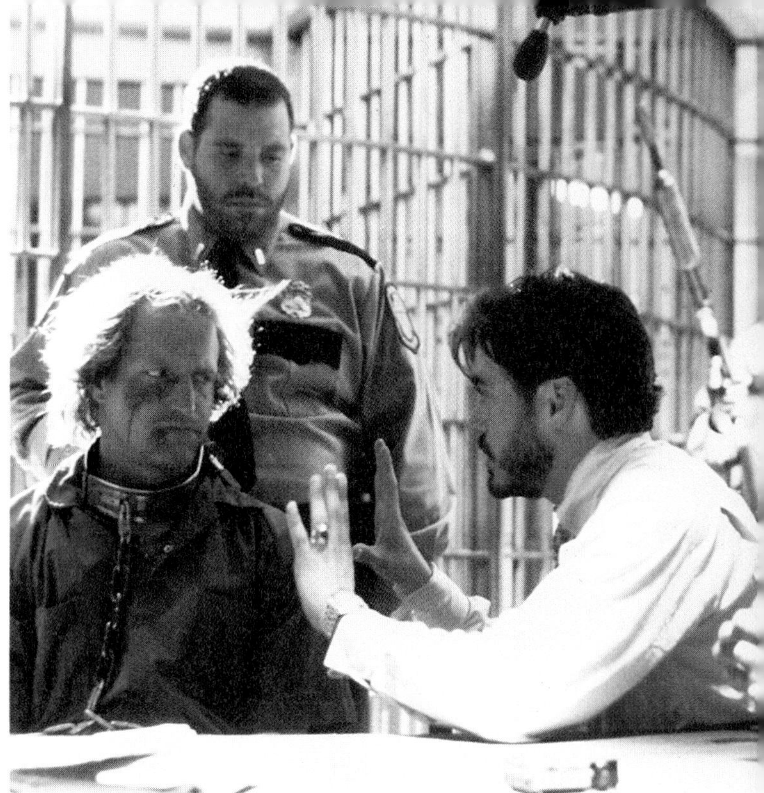

prison to "eliminate" the couple, who have continued their killing behind bars. Scagnetti is, in his own way, as exploitative as Gale. He fancies himself a modern Pat Garrett (who in fact wrote a book called *I Shot Billy the Kid*), increasing the dimensions of his legend by exploiting his role in the Mickey and Mallory case. But Gale's big broadcast inadvertently allows for a prison break, and here *Natural Born Killers* takes a different approach from its predecessor *Bonnie and Clyde*. There, the loving couple went out in a hail of bullets, victims of the Great Depression and their own inadequacies. Here, Mickey and Mallory escape and prosper, last glimpsed several years later driving in a trailer, surrounded by their children, an off-kilter caricature of normalcy.

Twenty-seven years earlier, Penn was accused of romanticizing his young killers by casting glamorous movie stars and showing the criminals' tender sides, which endeared Bonnie and Clyde (or, more correctly, the film's incarnations of them) to the then-emerging youth audience. Stone similarly shows Mickey and Mallory enjoying tender moments together; however wild and crazy their costumes and hairdos, Harrelson and Lewis radiate movie-star charisma. In the film, a contemporary youth is interviewed by the media, and though he claims not to be in favor of serial killing, he nonetheless insists that "if I were going to be a serial killer, I'd be Mickey and Mallory." He doubtless speaks not only for himself, but for all the young people his age sitting in the theater, watching the film. He is one and the same with those young people, identical in appearance to him, who really did stand by the side of the road one night in June 1994, to get a glimpse of O. J. Simpson in the white Bronco—holding a gun to his head and threatening to blow his brains out—rapturously, unconscionably cheering on a man who had just been accused by the police of killing his wife and her friend.

Owing to moments like this, *Natural Born Killers* offended the sensibilities of many middle-class, middle-aged Americans, who considered these to be frightful characters, dangerous as potential role models for impressionable kids, also complaining that the film's violence was flamboyantly overstated. Ironically, most of those people had themselves, as giddy teenagers a generation earlier, slipped off to watch *Bonnie and Clyde*, despite the warnings of their own parents. Today, *Bonnie and Clyde* seems mild; it's difficult to believe it created the fervor that it did. Yet in 1967 it stood in sharp contrast to the rural Romeo and Juliet films the parents of those sixties teenagers had seen in their own youth, films like Nicholas Ray's *They Live by Night* with Farley Granger and Cathy O'Donnell, which had been considered a bit

Woody Harrelson as Mickey, set against the most vivid pop-art backdrop since Lee Marvin in *Point Blank* (courtesy Warner Bros.).

too violent by their parents, who, in the 1930s, had enjoyed *You Only Live Once* with Henry Fonda and Sylvia Sidney. Simply, each generation accepts its era's unique variation on the universal theme, then rails against the next one.

The teenagers who consider their parents so many fuddy-duddies and can't understand why this "neat" film creates an uproar will doubtless react in horror when, at some point toward the end of the first decade of the next century, their own teenage children discover and respond to their own outlaw road film. In the meantime, *Natural Born Killers* exists as the reverse bookend to *Bonnie and Clyde*, providing a sense of closure by taking all of that earlier movie's onetime excesses to the limit. It offers an extreme (for now, at least) example of the genre, thereby temporarily closing the book on the modern crime movie.

Oliver Stone, best known for his ultrarealistic movies like *Born on the Fourth of July*, here took Quentin Tarantino's eccentric screenplay to its logical extreme (photo by Sidney Baldwin, courtesy Warner Bros.).

Mickey discovers he's become a contemporary icon and pop celebrity to the youth of America, as real life begins to appear absolutely surreal in the crazed 1990s. As one teen puts it, "I don't condone serial killers, but if I were going to be one, I'd want to be Mickey and Mallory!" (photo by Sidney Baldwin, courtesy Warner Bros.).

About the Author

Douglas Brode is a film historian who lives in central New York. Professor Brode teaches the Film Directors course at Syracuse University's Newhouse School of Public Communications and serves as coordinator of the Cinema Studies Program at Onondaga College in Syracuse. His previous books include the college text *Crossroads to the Cinema* and, for Citadel Press, *Films of the Fifties, Films of the Sixties, The Films of Dustin Hoffman, Woody Allen: His Films and Career, The Films of Jack Nicholson, Lost Films of the Fifties, Films of the Eighties, The Films of Robert De Niro, The Films of Woody Allen,* and *The Films of Steven Spielberg*. His next book, *One Shot Wonders,* will chronicle the many celebrities from the worlds of music, politics, sports, and letters who have starred in a single motion picture. Brode's articles have appeared in such popular magazines as *Rolling Stone* and *T.V. Guide,* as well as more esoteric journals, including *Cinéaste* and *Television Quarterly*. His original play, *Heartbreaker,* has been professionally produced.